Flight Accidents
in the 21st Century
U.S. Air Force

Flight Accidents in the 21st Century U.S. Air Force

The Facts of 40 Non-Combat Events

HENRY BOND

McFarland & Company, Inc., Publishers
Jefferson, North Carolina

All images have been publicly released by USAF and carry the credit USAF/Public domain.

Library of Congress Cataloguing-in-Publication Data

Names: Bond, Henry, 1966– author.
Title: Flight accidents in the 21st century U.S. Air Force : the facts of 40 non-combat events / Henry Bond.
Description: Jefferson, North Carolina : McFarland & Company, Inc., Publishers, 2019 | Includes bibliographical references and index.
Identifiers: LCCN 2018053974 | ISBN 9781476674025 (softcover : acid free paper) ♾
Subjects: LCSH: Airplanes, Military—Accidents—United States—History—21st century. | United States. Air Force—History—21st century.
Classification: LCC UG1243 .B66 2019 | DDC 363.12/493—dc23
LC record available at https://lccn.loc.gov/2018053974

British Library cataloguing data are available

ISBN (print) 978-1-4766-7402-5
ISBN (ebook) 978-1-4766-3350-3

© 2019 Henry Bond. All rights reserved

No part of this book may be reproduced or transmitted in any form or by any means, electronic or mechanical, including photocopying or recording, or by any information storage and retrieval system, without permission in writing from the publisher.

Front cover: Emergency responders at the scene of a C-5 Galaxy crash, April 3, 2006, at Dover Air Force Base, Delaware (U.S. Air Force photo/Doug Curran)

Printed in the United States of America

*McFarland & Company, Inc., Publishers
  Box 611, Jefferson, North Carolina 28640
    www.mcfarlandpub.com*

Acknowledgments

Thanks to Robert Ingram—Air Force Installation and Mission Support Center JBSA–Lackland, Nicolas Bourriaud, Andrew Brown, John Armitage, Tariq Goddard, Hannah Knowles, Anthony Lam, Ingrid Pollard, Julian Rodriguez, Emily Tsingou, Chris Turner, and Sean Wyatt.

Table of Contents

Acknowledgments   v
Preface   1

The Accidents

1. Pitch up   9
2. Number 3 engine idle   13
3. Landing strut   18
4. Caught a tailwind   21
5. Fly-by   25
6. Zero-G parabolas   29
7. Arctic Thunder   32
8. C-Bleed hot   36
9. Ground-rush in Germany   41
10. Flameout Volk   45
11. Mist-up AirVenture   48
12. Warthog seizure   52
13. Walan Rabat   57
14. Overshoot Shank   61
15. Paddy field   65
16. Communications mast   69
17. Titanium fire   73
18. Belly flop   76

19	Cut-up wake	80
20	Fuel-line shutoff	83
21	Flaps gone	87
22	Roll off the top	92
23	Spatial D	96
24	Dutch roll	100
25	Stockton impromptu	104
26	Okinawa corkscrew	108
27	Birdstrike Luke	112
28	Lights-out intercept	116
29	Racetrack gun pattern	120
30	Fuel-line leak	124
31	Cley goose strike	128
32	Domestic object	132
33	Down to Louisiana	136
34	Ghostrider	139
35	Fire by the microwave	143
36	Unseen traffic	147
37	Goggles case	151
38	Three-out takeoff	156
39	Inadvertent shutoff	160
40	Eject, dude	165

Conclusions   169
Sources   183
Index   191

Preface

The supposition that the U.S. military, or the U.S. "military-industrial complex," exists as an astounding overlord of the Earth, the absolute imperial power of the age, or "the world's policeman," is not really controversial. The concept, the philosophy, or simply, the *reality* of American postwar militarism or at least militarization—the foundation of any successful state should be a strong military that assimilates advances in technology as vital to retaining a fighting advantage—has been set out and theorized frequently since the 1950s (see for example: Barnet, 1969; Fulbright, 1970; Hooks, 1991).

Within the scene of contemporary critical theory, thinkers as diverse as Jean Baudrillard (2008; 2014), Paul Virilio (2007; 2008) and Noam Chomsky and Edward Herman (1995) have discussed U.S. military power at length.

The U.S. military mega-machine exists: that has been firmly established, it seems, but as a machine it remains remote from scrutiny by the curious—if not exactly hidden, then at least *disguised*; and certainly not accessible to the ordinary person. We might catch the occasional glimpse of a U.S. warplane coming or going, but we know little about the nature and purpose of its *mission*.

The U.S. military often seems to exist in the mode of a "parallel universe" as set out by French theorist Jean Baudrillard in his essay "In Praise of a Virtual Crash," published in a collection of essays, *Screened Out* (2014).

For Baudrillard, certain aspects of modern life have begun to function quite independently of life as it is lived and experienced by the ordinary person—they have become instead *orbitalized* and *virtualized*. Baudrillard's examples include developing world debt, activity on the major stock markets, and nuclear weapons. Under the phenomenon of virtualized-orbitalized activity, these technologies and activities seem to bear no relationship to the real world or are expressly excluded from it. Wars continue *but not using nuclear weapons.* Developing world debt and some national sovereign debt has become virtualized—the amounts are no more than figures on a page as the repayment of such vast amounts is unrealistic and implausible. Or a precipitous stock-market decline seems to leave the ordinary person unaffected, so very different from the Great Crash of '29 when the effects of a drastic stock market decline were immediate social catastrophe.

The activities of the U.S. military, it may be argued, have also come to function as *orbitalized* and *virtualized* as set out by Baudrillard: U.S. military activity is ongoing daily (all over the world), but this activity has no overt or clear-cut impact at the level of ordinary life. The activities carry on *autonomously*, definitely separated from the realm of ordinary experience.

The U.S. military machine is, by tradition and by culture, rife with a tendency to secrecy and propaganda—"propagation of particular doctrine." There is a strategic and combat advantage gained from surprise, and since in modern warfare a hostile operator may emerge stealthily from anywhere on Earth at any moment, it is prudent and valid to pursue a readiness to not disclose operational details.

The U.S. military today is, it might be argued, comparable to capitalist big business as theorized by Brecht, and discussed by Walter Benjamin (2009) in the early twentieth century. For Brecht, the investigative journalist-photographer interested in an exposé on, say, workers' conditions at a large company is usually confronted with a monolithic, imposing and *impenetrable* architectural facade: the corporation allows no public access to its operations.

If the journalist does finally gain access to the factory behind the façade, this will often be as part of public relations exercise and will be a sanitized and idealized tour.

And following Brecht (ninety years later), an unchanged characterization is still basically valid when thinking about the U.S. military today: we may see very well the outside perimeter walls of the U.S. base, but we know very little about what is going on inside it. Or we may attend, say, a USAF airshow event and in that case actually see some of the military hardware, but such an event is, of course, a public relations exercise and little is learned about training priorities.

The first-person accounts of life in the U.S. Army including Owen (2012) or O'Neill (2017) may seem initially to be a possible source of insights, but as recent revelations have shown, such books are typically heavily pre-censored and agreed and signed off by military command before publication. They are, in fact, a format of propaganda.

My research question here below emerges from a consideration of this lack of access. And my basic research question might be formulated thus: by what mechanism and by what means may an external civilian gain some detailed insights into the U.S. military machine as it functions today?

In seeking to begin to answer this question, and confronted with the different components of the U.S. military, I was drawn towards the USAF: if the U.S. military has a stunning global reach, it must be, I boldly determined, primarily because of its Air Force capability—the U.S. can and will *sail* into battle around the world, but its military power is defined really by creation and maintenance of a global network of air bases.

Gaining detailed intimate knowledge of the USAF is a challenge. What I was looking for was some way in, some slight tear in the fabric of the circus tent, so to speak, by which I might look on at the events happening inside the big top—something like a chink in the armor which would enable me to catch sight of the daily operational activities.

At this moment in my research process I turned to the work of French critical theorist Paul Virilio. Virilio's life in critical writing has concentrated on theorizing technology and its social impacts. One of Virilio's basic premises is that we, in the liberal West at least, tend to designate air disasters and other such incidents as bizarre and unfortunate tragedies rather than, more realistically, an inevitable consequence of the technology: "When you invent the ship, you also invent the shipwreck; when you invent the plane you also invent the plane crash; and when you invent electricity, you invent electrocution ... every technology carries its own negativity, which is invented at the same time as technical progress" (Virilio, 1999).

For Virilio the negative and unwelcome side effects of technology are not generally confronted. The public tends to deny or forget about the negatives, so enamored are they by the supposed positive and seductive benefits.

In order to counter this trend, one of Virilio's suggestions—an urgent exhortation would characterize it better—is a proposal that we build a "Museum of the Accident." In Virilio's museum, each technology would be considered principally in terms of the damage done—so the room on nuclear-based electricity generation would focus on, say, the Chernobyl disaster of 1986. In Freudian psychoanalytic terms these negative effects are the *repressed* of each technology: the things we would rather not think too much about because they are disturbing, horrifying and even unbearable.

My reaction to Virilio's call to action was to ponder on what contribution I—as a confirmed acolyte—might make to any such museum.

To begin, I simply strung together the two most cogent keywords defining and framing my research interest: "accident+USAF." And so began a number of initial Internet searches. I soon became aware of the numerous USAF accidents and blunders that happen quite often.

One of the document types which showed up frequently in these searches was an official USAF document type, the United States Air Force Aircraft Accident Investigation Board Report. Each one is the record of an official investigation into a USAF disaster, or in Air Force terminology, a "mishap."

These USAF accident reports were compelling and perplexing: the complete detailed information on the each disaster was not hidden—or classified—but was instead *freely available* in the .pdf format shared and hosted on certain Internet sites, e.g., Airforcemag.com.

The reports were written up in non-user-friendly prose, but were nevertheless enthralling: beyond the astonishing details of the events of each air disaster, the reports perhaps more importantly allowed an insight into the types of mission being flown and the substance of the daily comings and goings at U.S. air bases around the world.

I began to build an archive of these reports, and as I worked, I sought to cross-reference the accident report with news items from reliable news sources.

In some instances a copy of the official report was impossible to find on the Internet, and in such cases I wrote directly to the home base of the USAF squadron concerned and activated a Freedom of Information request for a copy of the report required—the crash of a B-2 Spirit worth around $2.2 billion at Andersen Air Force Base on the Island of Guam, 23 February 2008, is an example a report that was not freely available and which I therefore requested.

The process of the FOI request was professionally handled from beginning to end. A written acknowledgment of the initial request was sent, and later, I received an email containing a passcode enabling me to retrieve—once only—the relevant document from a USAF secure server.

The status of these report documents was—and remains—fascinating: on one hand they contain copious *publicly released* information; on the other hand, the information is near-impenetrable to the lay reader, given that the house style is replete with an astonishing number of USAF-specific acronyms and USAF-specific jargon. The documents had been written in *de facto* code: ostensibly in ordinary English, but in fact largely incomprehensible to anyone but the most committed reader.

It was then that I began to recognize a unique opportunity to contribute to the Virilian Museum of the Accident: visitors to such a museum would likely benefit from knowledge of USAF accidents, and so it would be worthwhile, I decided, to prepare plain-English versions of some of the these official accident reports—versions that would be comprehensible to *any museum visitor*.

Forty such texts on forty of the most indicative and unsettling USAF non-combat accidents in the twenty-first century are included below and comprise the substantive majority of this volume. The original reports are actually coded—obfuscated—using two definite techniques: extensive use of obscure acronyms and the extensive use of arcane and USAF-specific jargon. A hundred, sometimes up to two hundred acronyms are used in each report—a list of acronyms used appears in the front matter of each report and often runs over several pages.

In the USAF style guide (I am unclear if such a volume exists), anything—a place, a person, an object, an action—which is subject to being referred to more than once will usually be given an acronym: keystroke economy must always be prioritized over readability in the USAF. Take the following sentence, for example: "The Squadron's Director of Operations was present when the crew went through their pre-flight briefing." Under the USAF house style this becomes: "The 20 EBS's Director of Operations was present at the end of the MC's PTOB."

No reader, not even long-serving military personnel, would recognize all the acronyms used in any given report, as new mission- or case-specific ones are always introduced. In other words, the document is not immediately comprehensible to any reader—civilian or serviceman. The extreme use of acronyms is offered as a style as if it were perfectly ordinary and unremarkable and not at all obtuse—the supposition being that a "formal" document demands copious acronyms.

The second mode of coding present in the original texts was the extensive and unnecessary use of jargon and USAF-specific style conventions. A simple sentence such as, "The crew made their way to their allocated aircraft late due to having only arrived at the Base at 7:42 p.m." might appear in a report as, "The flight stepped later than expected as the crew had only been in country since 1942."

Jargon use often shades into the use of unhelpful and unnecessary euphemism: the jet "contacted terrain" rather than crashed; the "ejection sequence was interrupted" rather than, "the pilot was blasted into a radio mast." In common usage a "mishap" describes a minor incident—like, say, a seven-year-old child grazing an elbow while out playing. For the USAF, "mishap" is the required term for referring to an air disaster causing perhaps loss of life and the destruction of jet a often worth hundreds of millions of dollars.

As I read avidly, I slowly became an adept as an interpreter of USAF report-writing style—slowly, rather painfully, I became conversant with the language used. I also became military-aviation savvy. I became familiar with the culture of the USAF airman, his aircraft, his sorties, his daily life on base.

And using this broad comprehension I was able to write up my plain-English texts. In each instance my target was a 1,500-word "translation" from an initial document of around thirty or so typed pages.

Notwithstanding my efforts to write up a plain English précis of the events of each air accident under consideration below, there is one aspect of aviation terminology that requires a special technical pre-primer: the stall.

Taking the auto as a reference point, a stall—e.g., "Annoyingly, I stalled the Prius just as the lights changed"—refers to a sudden loss of power to an automobile's engine. This type of stall closely parallels the USAF aviation "compressor stall." A jet engine sucks in and compresses fresh air, mixes this compressed air with highly flammable jet fuel, and then ignites the mixture to create the engine "thrust." A compressor stall is a sudden loss of aircraft power that results when the engine stops producing thrust.

A compressor stall is something fairly common to the USAF airman. A plane's jet engine (or one of them) may lose power for any one of myriad reasons. In many instances a compressor stall is recoverable or at least troubleshootable, since most military aircraft will continue to glide without power for some time before an emergency need be called.

On the other hand, and very importantly, there is another designation of a stall: a mid-air stall, or an *aerodynamic* stall. In this sense, a stalled plane is no longer moving through the air fast enough to successfully outrun the effects of gravity. That is, an aerodynamic stall is any situation—with or without power loss—in which a plane is moving *too slowly to sustain flight*.

For each USAF plane, the aerodynamic stall speed is generally memorized by pilots, and during moments when a plane is slowing down, such as when it is coming in to land or turning around through a tight angle, air-speed will be under near continuous scrutiny by the crew. Numerous automatic systems are configured to alert the pilot if he is approaching stall speed by providing visual, audible, and physical signals. In the seconds before a stall, the control column in many jets will literally begin to vibrate (the "stick shaker").

Slowing to a speed below a plane's stall speed will quickly cause a loss of "lift," at which point the plane will begin to fall from the sky with a trajectory and behavior similar to any object weighing many tons falling through air.

A second technical-operational point worth stating at the outset is the significance of an emergency ejection from an aircraft. Emergency ejection is a big deal: it is an event that a pilot can undergo once or at most twice in his entire career. This is not for punitive reasons, but for health and safety requirements: the stress on the human body (particularly the spine) during ejection is intense (often measured or estimated in units known as g-force: multiples of the down-force of gravity). It is determined by USAF physicians that after a first-ever ejection, a pilot may return to flying duties, but after a second one he will be thereafter limited to "duties which do not include flying" for the remainder of his career.

The net outcome of the process of preparing a plain-English text of the below air accidents is, in each a case, a slight loss of *nuance*. My hope is that the overall picture of the events remains accurate in its essence: the below material was not written up in the manner of, say, the scriptwriters of *Zero Dark Thirty*, in which inconvenient but accurate detail is often replaced by a finessed Hollywood version of events. In my texts I have added nothing besides some key background information. It is not, and has not been, my intention to revisit or reconsider the sequences of events contained therein in any instance. Any deviation from the facts as published is not intentional or desirable.

The texts below are solely an exercise in précis and decoding (e.g., many acronyms, etc.), or translation, and are not concerned with reevaluation. If my description appears to differ from the published timeline of events on any point or detail, it is the original report which remains primary and sovereign.

I neither endorse nor reject the published accident reports: the below is a writing exercise in which the precision of the original report has sometimes given way to the pressure of readability. For example, if a report notes that "the 3-ship of F-22s departed Andersen at 1617," I might well have written that up as, "Three Raptors took off from Andersen Air Base on Guam shortly after 4:15 p.m." Meaning that if a reader requires the exquisite detail, my versions are essentially less precise: that is the price paid for readability.

In very few instances do USAF Accident Reports mention those involved by name. In many cases the names of the airmen involved in the incident were, however, released to the press, and wherever the names of the airmen involved were published in a press article from a reliable news source, I have personalized the events by importing the names of the airmen involved.

Although I have learned a lot of Air Force jargon and many technical terms in preparing this volume, in the end I am a critical theorist and writer by trade, not an airman. There may be on occasion unfortunate gaps in my knowledge leading to a misapprehension (although hopefully very rarely). However, if any reader notes an inaccuracy, I would welcome the opportunity to correct it for a future printing, and kindly request the reader contact the author c/o the publisher.

The photographs herein reproduced are extracted in each case from the official USAF Accident Report, dated as per the accident reviewed. These images form part of a document which is, in accordance with AFI 51-503, Aerospace and Ground Accident Investigations, "a publicly releasable report." Hence all photos, unless otherwise stated, carry the following credit: USAF/Public Domain.

The Accidents

1 Pitch up

Location: Andersen Air Force Base
Date: 23 February 2008
Aircraft type: B-2 Spirit
Fatalities: none
Cost of damage: $2.2 billion

The Pacific island of Guam is an unincorporated U.S. territory—the Island is officially self-governing, but those born there are American citizens by birth. Guam was invaded by the Japanese during World War II and was recaptured by U.S. forces during July–August 1944.

The island consists of approximately twenty-two square miles of land,

The burned-out wreckage of the B-2 *Spirit of Kansas* close to the runway at Andersen Air Force Base on the island of Guam. A catastrophic crash and post-crash fire caused the destruction of the plane valued at $2.2 billion.

around one-third of which is given over to U.S. military bases and sites—a presence that angers locals, who liken the U.S. military buildup to a form of imperialist colonization.

The island has a definite strategic significance for the USAF: keeping air bases on Guam allows the U.S. to offer a continuous strike-ready bomber capability in the Asia-Pacific region. Guam is six thousand miles west of the coast of California and the bases are *strategic* primarily insofar as time saved: an airborne attack mission taking off from a base on Guam could reach and bomb targets in, say, North Korea, China, Indonesia, or Japan, within two hours.

Andersen Air Force Base is one of several key U.S. military sites on the island of Guam. One of the types of aircraft stationed at Andersen is the B-2 Spirit—a heavy bomber. The B-2 is a "flying wing" clad with a super-high-tech light-absorbing material. It appears as an object beyond the ordinary aesthetic realm of military aircraft design.

The *flying wing* shape can strike the uninitiated as implausible—its appearance is that of a prop a Hollywood art director might commission with an aesthetic that is reminiscent of, say, the transportation devices owned by Bruce Wayne in Christopher Nolan's *Dark Knight* series. At the level of the visual-photographic, the jet's cladding renders the plane mercurial, capricious and inconstant. In different photos, the fuselage appears to take on dissimilar hues depending on the light: now burnt umber, now emerald green, now slate gray, now cobalt blue, now charcoal black.

Due to its design and on-board technologies, the B-2 has a radar cross-section which is not proportional to its size. It appears on hostile radar screens—if it appears at all—as a plane only a few percent of its actual size: a quality known in military aviation as "stealth."

Each B-2 jet has cost $2.2 billion to produce (only twenty-one have ever been built). The B-2 is the most expensive per-unit combat aircraft ever purchased by the USAF.

B-2s are often deployed to Andersen from their main home base, Whiteman Air Force Base, in Missouri. Whiteman is about seventy miles east of Kansas City.

A typical B-2 deployment tour to Guam is four months. In late February 2008, one such tour was coming to an end for *Spirit of Kansas* one of the B-2s in the fleet.

The last mission of any such deployment is the return flight back to Whiteman from Guam: seven thousand miles nonstop with the B-2 getting mid-air refueled at least twice en route and an airborne flight time of around sixteen hours.

1 Pitch up

On the morning of 23 February 2008, following a day's delay due to poor weather, the order came for *Spirit of Kansas* to commence one such return flight back to Whiteman Air Base. The two pilots that day were Major Ryan Link and Captain Justin Grieve. The two had never flown together before.

The B-2 jet has two seats. The left seat is for the pilot actually flying the plane, the "aircraft commander." The pilot in the right seat on an active service mission is responsible for weapons and tactics, and is designated the "mission commander."

The pilot in the right seat is generally analyzing air-data (scrutinizing the copious information on the visual display screens) and also feeding the airman-at-the-controls information—such as calling out speed in knots during takeoff.

It was Link who was flying in the left seat in *Spirit of Kansas* on the morning of the 23rd. He first made his way out to the B-2 around 9 o'clock in the morning and did a "walk around" visual inspection of his plane to assess any potential issues.

Then, continuing ground checks, Link started up his avionics—on-board computer systems—and noticed on his terminal display a message: "AIR DATA CAL." The system was requesting recalibration for the external air-pressure sensors.

A number of air-data sensors are mounted at certain points over the exterior of the B-2, and via these the plane's on-board computers can determine accurately altitude, air-speed, speed of ascent, angle of attack, etc. These sensors are the main real-time data-input feeds on which the computer relies to make many in-flight calculations.

Link placed a call to the ground staff at Andersen and at around ten-fifteen a technical engineer arrived to carry out the recalibration.

One thing that can affect the readings from the data sensors is moisture. Particularly when airborne, sensor readings can be affected by ice. And this being the case, the B-2—as is typical also throughout Air Force and commercial aviation—has a heating system built in to the sensors: the "pitot heat," which can be turned on or off manually at any time to burn off moisture and/or ice.

Guam is a very humid part of the world with a tropical climate, and it was known by some (but not all) ground-crew engineers that in order to recalibrate the B-2's sensors, turning on pitot heat first was good practice.

However, on that particular morning the engineer did not consider putting on pitot heat before the air-data recalibration. To be fair, it was not a mandatory or even a standard aspect of the procedure.

What the technician did on that day was manually input the barometric atmospheric reading as per the military weather pages that he had jotted down from the intranet before heading out to fix the problem.

The technician soon completed his task and handed back over to the pilots. The B-2 was now all set and was soon underway on its taxi out to the allocated runway.

The initial stages of takeoff commenced unremarkably up to the point that takeoff engine thrust was set and the brakes were released.

Once the brakes were released, the aircraft moved forward, gaining speed to at least 100 knots (115 mph). At nineteen seconds after brake release, a message on the jet's visual display flashed up: "CAUTION FLIGHT CONTROL SYSTEMS," together with a yellow warning light.

As Grieve looked to his screen to investigate further, the light went out again—the message "rescinded."

This prompted the following dialogue:

LINK: Master Caution, what is it?
GRIEVE: It is AOA [Angle of Attack].
LINK: Continue or abort?
GRIEVE: It's gone. Continue.

A few seconds later Link "rotated," that is, he pulled back on his control stick to take off. The control did not respond as expected. Link's precise thought as he was rotating back: "This is spongy."

Link looked at his visual display. He later remembered having only one thought about what he observed: "Huh, that's weird." What the display showed was his jet 15 degrees nose-high—an unexpected, unusual, and hazardous angle, too abrupt for a B-2 takeoff.

Rather than a smooth angle of ascent, the jet had pitched up violently and immediately stalled only eighty feet in the air. The jet began to "porpoise"—bouncing around unpredictably as it descended.

Grieve's initial reaction, unspoken: "What is he doing?" Then he looked over and saw Link "pulling back hard on the stick." Grieve, alarmed, spoke over the intercom, and told Link to hit TRT—full takeoff thrust.

Grieve was watching on helplessly as Link tried to recover the jet: "It seemed like several seconds passed as I was watching him and looking outside and going, 'Holy cow. What's going on?'"

At this point Grieve spoke for a second time to Link on the intercom: "Dude, I think we're going to have to get out of this aircraft." To which Grieve heard no response.

Link was focused only on keeping the jet airborne: "I've put the stick full forward and the throttles up full forward." He also used the flight control surfaces in an attempt to level the jet: "The only thought I recall at that time is trying to fly."

Even with full take off throttles on, the bomber was unstable, drifting—and not more than twenty feet off the ground.

As the recovery attempt continued, at one moment the bomber's left wingtip began to dip down towards the runway. Seconds later it scraped, dragged and "grabbed" the runway.

At the moment that Grieve saw the wing dipping, just before it made contact with the ground, the situation became obviously critical.

Grieve: "I distinctly remember looking at my hands and looking at the ejection seat [lever] and going, 'Holy cow. You gotta be kidding me.'"

Grieve pulled on his ejection lever.

The setup with the emergency ejection system was that it was on auto mode, meaning that if either one of the two pilots were to commence ejection, the system would eject both. And this is what happened: the two pilots launched to safety.

Link was taken by surprise, as he was not even thinking about ejecting as far as he could later remember, and Grieve had no time to call a "bail out" warning.

Three seconds after ejection, the pilotless B-2 crashed on the runway at Andersen and burst into flames. A ferocious post-crash fireball of burning jet fuel engulfed the aircraft, destroying it beyond repair within minutes, causing the single most costly loss in U.S. aviation history.

The Accident Investigation Board ascertained that three of the plane's twenty-six spatial sensors were capturing corrupted or incorrect data. These were being affected by excess moisture.

Entirely due to the moisture issue, key spatial-altitude data was erroneous, and inaccurate information was being fed through to the digital displays in the cockpit.

2 Number 3 engine idle

Location: Dover Air Force Base, Delaware
Date: 3 April 2006
Aircraft type: C-5 Galaxy
Fatalities: none
Cost of damage: $180 million

The wreckage of the C-5 that crashed on its approach to Dover Air Force Base on 3 April 2006. The nose section broke cleanly away from the main fuselage upon impact with the ground, turning through 90 degrees as it skidded through dry scrubland almost one mile short of the runway. The $179 million jet was declared unrepairable soon afterwards.

The Lockheed C-5 Galaxy is a large and heavy aircraft used by the U.S. military for airlifting goods, vehicles, and soldiers. The largest of the airlift planes in the inventory, the Galaxy is a $180 million flying semi-trailer big-rig, a "gigantic plane" that "looms above the flightline at the height of a six-story building."

A C-5 is loaded up much like a sea ferry: vehicles including tanks just roll on up into the cargo hold via the large aft door. Or forklifts can load on up to 135 tons of equipment and supplies, often packed into seven-foot-high, eight-foot-deep reusable "Tricon" steel containers. There are also seats for up to seventy-five personnel above the cargo deck.

In 2006, at least twenty-six C-5s were based at Dover Air Force Base, the home of several USAF Airlift Wings.

On Sunday, 2 April 2006, one of the active C-5 crews at Dover—the group of airmen included three pilots, three engineers, and five loaders—was handed an airlift mission to be flown on the 3rd as callsign REACH4059. They were to on-load 50 tons of palletized Army "sustainment supplies," fly the cargo to Kuwait International Airport, south of Kuwait City, and

2 *Number 3 engine idle*

offload it. The mission was straightforward and workaday for the crew. As was usual, the flight would not be direct, but would be broken into two legs with a typical layover at Ramstein Air Base, in southeast Germany.

The only notable and perhaps unwelcome aspect of the mission was a rather early call time: 1 a.m. on Monday morning. The crew were not a dedicated night crew (and so habitually rising in the small hours) and none of them got off to bed before 9 p.m. on Sunday night. When the brutal early-morning alert came at 1 a.m., nobody had had more than four hours' sleep. (While many aircrews habitually use amphetamines for long flights, sedatives such as Ambien—as favored by special ops—are forbidden.) The flight was scheduled for takeoff at 5 a.m., with crew "show" time—reporting ready for work—of 2 a.m.

As the pallets were going in, one of the spinning rails on the cargo floor got damaged and there was a delay while the bent rail was swapped over and replaced. With repairs completed, and with the copilot Lt. Col. Harland Nelson at the controls, the heavily laden jet took off one hour and twenty minutes behind schedule at 6:20. The sun was up, dawn had just broken; it was a clear morning with excellent visibility.

Around ten minutes into the flight, as Nelson was still climbing towards his initial altitude of 7,000 feet, he and the aircraft commander—the pilot, Capt. Brian Lafreda—observed a hazard light flashing on the cockpit dashboard with a warning message: ENGINE 2 TR NOT LOCKED.

The message was alerting the pilots to the fact that the thrust-reverser of one of the four jet engines was not correctly in its off position. The thrust-reverser is deployed immediately upon touchdown, forcing the jet of super-compressed hot air into a stream against direction of travel, helping the plane to quickly decelerate.

One of the engineers onboard made his way into the cargo hold and did a visual check: he looked out of a left-side window and gazed at the engines. When deployed, the thrust reversers on a General Electric TF-39, as fitted on the C-5B model, are clearly observable as hinged sections of engine casing that lift up and away from the main engine cover. There was nothing out of place as far as could be seen with the naked eye.

The engineer returned to the flight deck, and at that point there was a discussion among four of the crew—two engineers and the two pilots—as to the best course of action. Soon it was decided for safety's sake to shut down number-two engine completely and just return to base.

This was not any big emergency; the C-5 has four jets and can fly "one out" with no problem. It was only for reasons of correct procedure that Lafreda called an in-flight emergency to the tower at Dover and took over the controls.

In gaining control of the jet, Lafreda shut down the questionable engine completely—the number-two engine—and began to maneuver the jet for the short return flight (they had been airborne for only around eight minutes when the decision to return was made).

The engine throttles on a C-5 are positioned in the cockpit in a row. The pilot at the controls can move any one of them individually or move them forward and back in concert, as needs be. As Lafreda began to get set for landing, the pilot momentarily placed all four engine throttles to idle (around 20 percent thrust), as is usual. He then set the wing-flaps to 100 percent—max lift, but high drag (with the reduced power situation in mind). Then he increased engine thrust, as he began his descent towards the runway.

At this moment, for some reason—perhaps the very early start was a factor—the pilot got it into his head that his "out" engine was his number-three engine, and this throttle he placed into the idle position, believing it to be redundant. He also continued to increase power on the number two throttle, as if that engine were still running.

With the plane now turned around and on its way in to Dover, this somewhat surprising confusion remained unrecognized by anyone on the flight deck: unbeknown to those aboard, the jet was returning to base "two out."

A C-5 can still fly on only two engines as long as all the flight calculations are made on that basis—flying "two out" fully laden would require extreme caution and unique approach calculations.

As the descent in to Dover continued—about three miles out and one minute to landing—the plane was a little slower than expected and was getting perilously close to its air-stall speed (the minimum required speed in order to remain airborne).

Observing the airspeed, copilot Nelson called first, "Little slow," and then encouraged the pilot at the controls to "[Give it a] lot of power."

The jet was passing through 300 feet altitude but coming in 10 mph too slowly, causing a number of in-cockpit audible warnings to sound: "Don't sink.... Don't sink.... Too low: terrain.... Too low: terrain." As the C-5 neared its minimum speed the pilot's control column began to physically vibrate: an unavoidable automatic warning immediately before stall speed known as "stick-shaker."

The atmosphere in the cockpit remained calm enough—all involved were highly experienced C-5 crew. The audio recording of the cockpit

2 Number 3 engine idle

microphones reveals an oddly languid, unenergetic atmosphere that transcends the expected ethos of cool-under-pressure and seems rather fatalistic, even indifferent. Around fifteen seconds prior to impact, Lafreda allows only one vocalized concession to the inevitable consequence of the slow speed and heavy weight: "Guys, I'm concerned."

In setting the flaps to 100 percent early in his approach, Lafreda had slowed the plane to such a degree that max thrust on two engines was not enough to regain the required minimum airspeed of around 153 m.p.h.

In reaction to the warnings going off all around, Lafreda moved his flaps to 40 percent. But it was too little, too late: less than a mile out from the runway over empty grassy fields, the C-5 began to sink: nose high at least 20 degrees and tail low.

The first impact was the low-hanging tail flattening a telephone pole: "At 0639 the mishap aircraft struck a wooden utility pole approximately 185 ft prior to initial ground impact shattering the pole." The collision ripped away the entire tail section of the jet intact, a single piece of debris that spun away and crashed to the ground as the stricken, now-uncontrollable jet stalled and plowed into the scrubland with an impact force of 30-G.

Careering on its belly through the uneven field for almost 2,000 feet, the jet continued to skid and spin to the right as the left wingtip broke away, and the complete and intact nose and flight-deck section severed from the remainder of the fuselage and wings. When the wrecked plane came to a standstill it was within yards of—and in clear view of—the near end of the Dover runway.

Within minutes the previously alerted emergency vehicles were on the scene. USAF first-responder firefighters soaked the wreck with fire retardant foam as the seventeen aboard (which included some PAX passengers with seats on a "space available" basis hitching a ride to Ramstein) scrambled or were carried to safety. Many of the survivors were airlifted to civilian hospitals within the state of Delaware. There were no fatalities.

A few days later the crashed plane was declared unrepairable and was logged as destroyed.

The flight deck nose-cone was essentially intact and was the one section that was salvaged complete: it was shipped to Robbins AFB in Georgia, where it became (and remains) a unique and absolutely realistic C-5 flight simulator, albeit one with a rather distressing history.

As the official Accident Report later clarified, "The primary cause of the mishap was the pilots' and flight engineers' failure to use the number three, fully operational, engine."

3 Landing strut

Location: Ali al Salem Air Base, Kuwait
Date: 13 February 2003
Aircraft type: MH-53 Pave Low
Fatalities: none
Cost of damage: in excess of $15 million

The missions handed to U.S. Special Operations units will often require entry into hostile territory covertly—particularly a "direct action" type mission, which is defined as "a short-duration strike or other small-scale offensive action conducted with specialized military capability to seize, destroy, capture, exploit, recover, or damage designated targets in hostile, denied, or diplomatically and politically sensitive environments."

Very often, the best transport solution for such a mission is a helicopter—or a group of helicopters—to get the Special Ops team in close to their target, and to get them out again. These activities are known as infiltration-exfiltration or insertion-extraction. As Col. Rod Reay has noted, "A helicopter can land practically anywhere that it can avoid obstacles."

Through 2008, one of the main USAF helicopters modified for Special Ops use was the MH-53M Pave Low. The Pave is a ferocious-looking bulky and boxy single-rotor aircraft originally designed for combat search and rescue operations (in its rescue role it was nicknamed the "Super Jolly Green Giant").

Many of the Pave Lows were first delivered to the USAF in the early 1970s, but they were regularly overhauled and upgraded—fitted out with a spectacular amount of high-tech computer-based equipment. A forward-looking infrared camera system enabled crew to see the terrain ahead in real-time in an infrared-based image video-feed, i.e., to see ahead in complete darkness. Other avionics devices included Doppler radar, which enabled crew to fly at extremely low altitude, "hugging" the ground below. The cockpit of a Pave Low was replete with an array of super-high-tech color display screens and instruments.

In February 2003, U.S. Special Ops teams were involved in missions into Iraq, with the infil-exfil often being provided by Paves.

During spring 2003, the 20th Special Operations Squadron was on deployment from its home base, Hurlburt Field in Florida, to Ali al Salem

3 Landing strut

Air Base in Kuwait, west of Kuwait City—one of three strategic U.S. bases in Kuwait. The other two are Ahmed al Jaber Air Base (south of Kuwait City) and designated portions of Kuwait International Airport.

Al Salem is only twenty miles from the border with Iraq and so was—and remains—an important U.S. base set in an essentially hospitable country.

Upon arrival into the desert terrain and in advance of the invasion, the 20th were flying training missions in Kuwait using Udairi Training Range, in order to "spin up" or get prepared for upcoming operations. Udairi is an area of around twenty square miles of mainly desert in Kuwait and usually used for live-fire training.

On the evening of 13 February 2003, one particular Pave Low pilot, Capt. Shannon Woodworth, and his regular cockpit crew or "hard crew"—copilot Capt. Brian Reece and flight engineer Sgt. William Kerwood—along with three cabin crew—left scanner, right scanner, and tail scanner—were handed a night-infiltration training exercise scheduled for 19:30 takeoff time. The training mission was only their third time out since deployment and arriving "in country." They were all still getting used to the desolate desert terrain—it offered fewer obstacles than usual, perhaps, but equally fewer landmarks for orientation.

The mission briefing clarified the activity for the sortie: Woodworth's Pave would be flying as RAKE16; all involved would be wearing NVGs—night-vision goggles, helmet-mounted imaging devices which are more like binoculars than goggles. The mission requirement was to insert a Special Operations unit of eleven men, along with their motor vehicle, at a certain spot in the desert, and then return to base to await the call to commence extraction. Those briefing further clarified: there would be four helicopters going "a four-ship" consisting of Chalks 1–4. All four Chalks would land simultaneously. Each helicopter had its own designated specific landing spot, but, as one commander leading the pre-briefing noted, if any one of them were to miss its precise landing zone, no matter, because "it's a parking lot out there," meaning any spot is really as good as another in a stretch of featureless desert.

The one problem that evening was the thunderstorms overhead—with lightning and high winds making the weather too poor to proceed at first. The crews waited in a state of delay for four hours, until, at around 11 p.m., the call came through for the four crews to "step," or make their way to their aircraft.

Because of the great number of operations ongoing and being planned at that time, it was really a luxury for the training mission surveyors and planners to actually have "eyes on" the selected landing zones: many were picked using just maps and aerial sat photos—as was in fact the case with the zones given on the night of the 13th.

By eleven-thirty, Woodworth and his crew were *en route* on the twelve-minute-long flight to the specified location. As the four helicopters arrived at the vicinity of the insertion location, RAKE16 took up formation and began to land—descending at around 150 feet per minute.

Woodworth and his cockpit crew, having only recently arrived into the operational environment, were still getting acclimatized to the terrain and at that time they were executing every landing as a brown-out or dust-out. A brown-out landing in a helicopter is required when the landing surface is loose soil or sand. In such circumstances the air blown downwards from the helicopter's own main rotor will tend to create an intense dust cloud that reduces visibility in the helicopter to zero. A brown-out landing is coordinated between the cockpit and cabin crew members with each calling out and constantly checking the helicopter's position and progress through a descent which is executed "blind" by reference to instruments alone.

If Woodworth and his crew had been a little longer "in country" they might have realized that even in the arid deserts of Kuwait, immediately after heavy rain and thunderstorms, a brown-out landing would not always be necessary.

As they landed, the crew were coming in completely blind: on one hand they were trusting solely in their instruments for the descent, and on the other, they relied on the operation planners and their map, for the adequacy for landing of the terrain below them.

As it happened, RAKE16 was actually coming in to land about 600 feet from the exact landing spot given. There was not much thought about this, given the perception that had been voiced in the briefing, "it's a parking lot," etc. The only thought was the gripes from the Special Ops teams who would often moan if they were set down even $\frac{1}{10}$th of a mile from their expected insertion point.

It is normal procedure in a brown-out landing to touch down with a slight forward speed so as to offset any tendency for the helicopter to roll. As RAKE16 touched down, the ground was much softer than expected—the rain might have been a factor—and the terrain was different actually 600 feet away from the surveyed site.

As the front landing gear made contact, it began to plow through and down into the soft ground, and with the continuing slight forward motion of the helicopter, within seconds the landing gear snapped. This caused the front of the helicopter to dip sharply enough for the main rotor tips to make sudden and alarming contact with the ground.

As the rotor made contact, the entire rotor structure broke away from the main fuselage and spun up into the air. The debris of the main rotor was thrown in an arc (front and right) extending 300 yards. The crew immediately shut down their engines, but the damage was done: the shuddering helicopter came to a standstill completely disabled with significant damage to various on-board systems. The expected training mission was called off as attention turned to managing the crash.

Chalk 2 was sent back to Base for a medical and recovery team. Quite quickly it was established that there were no major injuries—all of the eleven Special Ops and the crew of six had been able to walk from the stricken bird. It was soon agreed that rather than waiting for the medics to arrive, the crew of RAKE16 and their Special Ops passengers would be taken aboard the other chalks for the ride back to base.

Soon after daylight on the morning of 14 February, the wreckage at the crash site was inspected: the helicopter had actually landed "on the edge of inhospitable terrain," and was badly damaged. The wrecked fuselage was later shipped back to Cherry Point Naval Air Depot in North Carolina, where the initial damage repairs were estimated to be "in excess of $15 million."

In the official Accident Report, it is made clear that the main rotor's dipping down and making ground contact was most likely caused not by pilot error, but by the collapsing landing strut being forced into the mechanics of the aircraft and so causing *uncommanded* movements.

4 Caught a tailwind

Location: Baghdad International Airport
Date: 3 July 2005
Aircraft type: HH-60G
Fatalities: none
Cost of damage: At least $7.5 million

In the summer of 2005 the 41st Rescue Squadron were on deployment from their home at Moody Air Force Base, Georgia, to Balad Air Base in Iraq. The 41st's role is combat search-and-rescue missions. They fly HH-60G Pave Hawk helicopters—similar to the Army's better-known Black Hawk—a twin-engine four-blade.

A USAF crash-site photograph of the HH-60 that crashed near the perimeter of Baghdad International Airport during the morning of 3 July 2005 following refueling after a DVS (Distinguished Visitor Support) sortie.

Due to the search-and-rescue tasking, the 41st's Hawks are fitted out with state-of-the-art high-tech imaging technology. Front-mounted under the nose is a forward-looking infrared camera that can visualize the heat from a human body regardless of visible light, fog, smoke, etc. These cameras produce a live thermal-based video feed of the forward view ahead which is ideal for search and rescue missions in combat zones. The X-ray-like electronic eye can easily locate a living human in otherwise unpromising conditions.

Overall, the HH-60G is a super-agile human-being-finder. Rescuing a fighter pilot who has ejected from his aircraft in an emergency and landed in hostile territory is one example of a mission that that might be assigned to the 41st. For a mission the usual crew was five: pilot, copilot, flight engineer, gunner, and medic (known as a pararescueman).

On 2 July, in the late evening, one such crew—led by aircraft commander Major Peter Candelario—were in the chow hall at Balad, as they waited on call, or on alert, for any search-and-rescue requirement within the Iraq theater of operations.

4 Caught a tailwind

At around 11.30 p.m. a senior officer approached them. They were being handed at short notice a "DV," or distinguished visitor support mission, with a scheduled takeoff time of 9 a.m. the next morning. A DV could be a head of state or another such senior civilian; it might have been the serving president, George W. Bush, or another civilian diplomat or dignitary. Commercial planes carrying politicians, negotiators and the like require helicopter support, the presence of which is a mandatory precaution in case of an emergency.

This being so, the commanding officer requested them to return to their quarters in order to rest before the upcoming mission. In fact, aware of the limited time before the mission, he personally escorted them back to their quarters.

In relation to their combat-ready training and capabilities, this was an uncomplicated workaday mission. It was unlikely that that it would require the use of the infrared camera, or the skills of the parachutist paramedic on the crew.

The support mission (comprising two near identical HH-60s) commenced as scheduled at 9:00 a.m. on 3 July and was completed without incident.

Following the Distinguished Visitor detail, both helicopters made their way to the hot-refuel "pits" at Baghdad International Airport (essentially a U.S. air base at that time); the plan was to refuel before returning together to Balad, about sixty miles to the north. The "hot" refuel area—refuel with engines running—had two designated landing bays, both of which were unoccupied upon their arrival, and the two helicopters landed and began to refuel.

As the refueling was underway the weather conditions were in transformation: the temperature was rising steadily, as would be expected in Iraq in July, and so too the wind was getting up—a strong breeze around 6 Beaufort.

Upon successfully refueling, the first HH-60 (the lead one) took off, pulling cleanly away from its landing pad in a wide left arc.

As it departed, a radio call came in to Candelario's HH-60—still on the ground—noting a "stiff tailwind" for the takeoff.

Candelario and his crew had two obvious options at this point for takeoff: just copy the style of takeoff of the lead ahead, or opt for a more cautious one, which would involve taking off into a hover, slowly turning ("pedal turning") to the required direction, and only then setting forward motion.

Candelario might have considered this by-the-book safer option, but he did not take off that way. Instead, he attempted to follow closely the takeoff of the lead, pulling straight up away in a wide left turn.

As Candelario's helicopter began to ascend, the required power to move swiftly away from the landing pad (as the lead had) was lacking: the combination of strong wind and rising air temperature was reducing their movement through the air. They were also about five percent heavier than the lead too, it later transpired.

The low-hovering helicopter began to drift towards the perimeter fence nearby, with its two engines on high throttle setting. Power required was exceeding power available—a rotor-droop situation. At the sight of the perilously looming obstacle, the flight engineer asserted: "Rotor! Rotor! Rotor!"

Candelario replied with the command to lockout: "Lockout! Lockout! Lockout!"

The copilot immediately complied: maximum and extraordinary rotor speed can be achieved by manually placing the two engine throttles temporarily to, as it were, *turbo* power, or lockout setting—super-maximum power that can be sustained only for a limited time.

Even with the extra power now available, the helicopter remained in its hover, still drifting around the airport perimeter and over an area of loose soil and scrub. The pilot could have used his extra power to pull decisively away from the several looming hazards, but he did not.

As the Pave continued to drift at an altitude of only about twenty-five feet, on-board visibility was suddenly reduced to zero by a rising cloud of dust and sand caused by the helicopter's location and low altitude: a brown-out. "The aircraft drifted slowly to the left towards the corner of the fenceline and was completely engulfed in a cloud of dust."

In the context of the brown-out, while still flying in lockout approaching the eastern fenceline, there now came a sudden loud bang reverberating through the cockpit.

Startled, and perhaps in part due to the perilous brown-out conditions, the crew did not correctly interpret the banging sound as an auto-flameout. The noise was the sound of an unavoidable automatic engine restart following a lockout. Lockout is only a short-term action and places intense strain on the engines, which auto-restart to avoid mechanical malfunction.

Some aboard assumed the sound was gunfire! The flight engineer looked over at the gunner to see if his weapon was in use: it wasn't. Then came a second cockpit-crew reaction, and again incorrect: a diagnosis of engine malfunction, or compressor stall.

In these moments the flight engineer called: "Compressor stall! [Engines] burning up, pull 'em back!" That is, he requested an immediate reduction in engine power. The pilots immediately reduced power (at 13:20 p.m.), causing the helicopter to rapidly lose altitude and crash-land on a raised bank, or berm, near the perimeter of the airport.

The descent from twenty feet caused significant damage to the high-tech equipment mounted under the nose. The force of the hard landing crushed the landing gear and badly damaged both the forward-facing infrared camera and the on-board weather radar. The damage was later estimated at a minimum of $7.5 million in repairs.

On the other hand, injuries sustained by the crew were minimal: one case of bruised coccyx ("tailbone") and two "bruised chins."

The later official Accident Report was explicitly critical of the crew's actions that afternoon. They were *overconfident* (in the aircraft's ability to perform at Georgia-equivalent altitudes in Iraqi heat and replicate the high-risk tailwind takeoff maneuver they had just witnessed their flight lead accomplish); *complacent, distracted* (from a critical task), and tended to channelize attention (unduly focusing on only one factor or task during a sequence of events).

5 Fly-by

Location: about 30 miles northwest of Guam
Date: 21 July 2008
Aircraft type: B-52
Fatalities: 6
Cost of damage: $84 million

The Boeing B-52 Stratofortress is an eight-jet-engine heavy bomber that can carry a payload of thirty-five tons of conventional bombs on a single mission.

The plane has a tapering fuselage and narrow swept-back wings that span a hundred and eighty-five feet. The design of the jet is iconic and enduring: it has a modernist-minimalist appearance, and were it not for the implicit immorality of bombing machines, it might have become an accepted classic of twentieth-century design. The B-52 entered service in 1954 and will still be in service in 2044, its design unchanged through ninety years.

One of the definite qualities of the B-52 is redundancy: in the case of a mechanical failure, each critical system has a separate and alternate back-up. For example, the flight-control surfaces can be operated by two completely separate hydraulic systems, and if both of these were to fail, the plane could still be controlled manually. So, too, the B-52 remains airworthy with up to four of its eight jet engines "out"—damaged or otherwise nonfunctioning.

B-52s complement other jets as such as the B-2 Spirit (a high-tech "stealth" bomber) on deployment as components of the USAF's continuous strike-ready force, which includes those stationed at "forward bases" outside of the U.S., in Europe, and in the Asia-Pacific region, among other locations. B-52s on forward deployment to Asia-Pacific are often posted to Andersen Air Base on the remote Pacific island of Guam. Guam really *is* remote, with no significant landmass in any direction for at least a thousand miles.

The U.S. first took control of the island in 1898, capturing it from the Spanish as part of the settlement of the Spanish-American War of that year. The first U.S. Army barracks was established in 1901. In 1941, concurrent with the attack on Pearl Harbor in Hawaii, the Imperial Japanese Army invaded and captured Guam, which was not heavily fortified at that time and had no significant military base.

In 1944, the U.S. recaptured Guam, and since that time its strategic importance has evolved. Now 30 percent of the island (seventy square miles) is taken over by U.S. military sites—with Naval Base Guam, at Santa Rita, and Andersen Air Base being the two main hubs of activity. There are several other U.S. military sites including test ranges and training areas, all of which are restricted areas off-limits to civilian islanders. Around seven thousand U.S. troops and servicemen are stationed on the island at any time.

The atmosphere between the U.S. and Guamanians is often fractious. Many local residents resent the presence of the U.S. as outrageous colonialism by an imperial power. This being the case, the U.S. tends to make a big deal of its successful liberation of the island from the oppression of the Japanese occupation.

The U.S. armed forces restored peace and liberty to Guamanians. To underline this—and encourage a little gratefulness and largesse from the locals—each year there is a big celebration of Guam Liberation Day, on 21 July. The day is marked with full ceremonials and speeches happening in Hagåtña, the capital of the island. To round things out and to add some extra *gravitas*, there is usually a USAF fly-by.

5 Fly-by

On 21 July 2008, the fly-by for Liberation Day was arranged to be a USAF B-52 heavy bomber with two F-16 fighters following one minute behind. The three jets were scheduled to pass overhead of the ceremony at 10:15 a.m. in the vicinity of the World War II Park and the Governor's Compound.

Such a duty is known in airman's parlance as a "fly-by" or a "fly-past," which might imply that it is not of any great significance, but in fact the opposite is the case. Any such mission is always afforded—and requires—the same level of detailed planning and respectful consideration as any other flown USAF sortie.

On this occasion the mission was handed to a B-52 crew of five—led by the pilot, Major Chris Cooper—all of whom who had been on forward deployment since mid-June from Barksdale Air Force Base, near Shreveport, Louisiana.

The other crew on the mission that morning were: Captain Michael Dodson (copilot); Major Brent Williams (radar navigator); First Lieutenant Joshua Shepherd (navigator); and First Lieutenant Robert Gerren (electronic warfare officer). A sixth man, Colonel George Martin, a USAF surgeon, had been invited aboard for a ride-along and would be sitting in the available sixth seat.

During the three weeks or so that the crewmen had been on deployment, they had flown several training sorties and were well settled into the routines of life at Andersen.

The scheduled show time for the crew (time given to report ready for work) was five o'clock in the morning, with takeoff to follow at 9:00.

During the pre-flight checks there were some minor gripes reported, but mechanically and operationally the plane was inspected and tested as fully operational and airworthy. The issues reported to the ground staff by the crew were minor indeed: a partially torn curtain and a noisy air-conditioning fan were looked at.

The setup that morning was for the B-52—flying as RAIDER21—to take off from Andersen and fly out over the Pacific to a holding position, or holding "orbit," at 14,000 feet, around thirty miles northwest off the coast of Guam. Then, a few minutes before the fly-by appearance, and on a word from the point-of-contact parade organizer, the plane would turn left, away from its holding circuit, and descend towards Hagåtña for a dramatic fly-past at 1,000 feet.

The B-52 took off at 08:59 a.m. and climbed out to the agreed altitude before taking up its holding pattern of counterclockwise circuits over the sea.

At 9:25 a.m. the point-of-contact parade organizers made a radioed request to the B-52 to bring the fly-by forward fifteen minutes, from 10:15 a.m. to exactly ten o'clock. The request was acknowledged and accepted.

At 9:48 a.m. the B-52 crew radioed in: they were about to leave the holding area and begin their inbound journey towards the parade.

At 9:53 a.m., about five minutes after the "on our way" radio message, the jet left its holding pattern and began a descent, but it was not at all as planned.

From its altitude of 14,000 feet, rather than turning back towards Guam, the plane entered a sudden and unexplained thirty-degree nose-low dive headed straight down towards the Pacific below.

There was no mayday call from the flight deck or any in-flight emergency declared (air traffic were making repeated proactive efforts to contact the plane at this time).

The jet began to dive with an airspeed of around 280 m.p.h., but it was accelerating as it went—seemingly at full-thrust. Within one minute the jet had descended 10,000 feet to 3,000 feet (the lowest altitude from which the plane could have realistically pulled up and recovered), with the rapid descent continuing now at 470 m.p.h.

Fifteen seconds later, the diving B-52 crashed "at a steep angle" into the sea with an airspeed faster than its stated maximum of 650 m.p.h.—and close to supersonic speed. At the moment of impact, the wing flaps (used to slow a aircraft) were retracted, and the speed of the plane as it descended into the sea was commensurate with its being flown at full throttle.

All six crew were killed or presumed killed on impact.

Much of the wreckage of the B-52 sank to the bottom of the sea. Some debris was recovered during a search-and-rescue operation that included twenty-two separate ships searching for survivors.

Attempts to reach and salvage the wreckage from the ocean floor carried on from 6 September through 27 October. The Navy provided two remotely operated submarines with which some debris was recovered, but with the main fuselage sitting at around 12,000 feet under water, the possibilities were limited. The one item that would have been sought in the case of a commercial aviation disaster was not present: the crashed B-52 had no crash-survivable flight-deck recorder, or "black box," as these devices are often known.

Given the small amount of wreckage that was recovered, the Investigation Board could only suggest what might have happened. They concluded that the accident was probably caused by an incorrectly set—and stuck or jammed—stabilizer trim. Although the trim could have been positioned manually, even after a complete loss of cockpit power, it was thought that it might have taken valuable seconds for the trim issue to have been initially recognized and diagnosed.

The truth is that the cause of the crash remains basically a mystery.

The crew made no radio contact with air traffic control during the events. And there were no eyewitnesses.

The lost jet was valued at $65.7 million, although a from-scratch replacement jet for the fleet is listed as costing $84 million.

6 Zero-G parabolas

Location: near Edwards Air Force Base, California
Date: 21 May 2009
Aircraft type: T-38
Fatalities: 1
Cost of damage: $6.4 million

Test-pilot work has always had a special romance associated with it. The test pilot is often glamorized as a rare breed among airmen whose job requires flying unproven prototype planes that quite possibly may develop a midair fault or malfunction. Equally, engineers and designers on the ground are relying on his feedback to hone and enhance a developing aircraft. The test pilot must be an outstanding precision pilot, resilient and quick-thinking in an emergency, possess a subtle analytical mind, and be also an excellent communicator.

The reality of test-pilot work is that it is not particularly glamorous. The work is involved with meticulously documenting, both quantitatively and qualitatively, aspects of a given aircraft's performance, often flown as extremely laborious and repetitive sessions of recording the parameters and findings across a range of slight increments to one flight control under certain circumstances.

One of the bases where much testing is carried out is Edwards Air Base, in southern California. The name of the base and its association with test pilot work was popularized by a 1983 movie *The Right Stuff*, starring Sam Shepard, and by the bestselling book by Tom Wolfe the movie was based on.

In the late spring of 2009, a group of Edwards Test Pilot School recruits were getting involved in learning the basics of their trade. The group had been given an extensive grid of blank flight parameters to fill in. In this case the filled-out grid would consist of a comprehensive overview of the pressure required to be applied to the main control stick of a T-38 to cause certain movements through the air at numerous altitudes and air-speeds. The T-38 Talon was the designated inexpensive-and-stripped-down trainer jet being used by recruits. The mission required hours of laborious—some would say tedious—work from each of the group, who were operating as crews of two in the two-seat T-38s.

One of the indispensable tools of the test pilot's work is a small device that rests in the hand: the control-stick pressure-gage, used to measure at any given moment the amount of force required to move the main cockpit control stick to achieve a certain flying outcome. The device looks something like a hiker's compass with two metal lugs on a short stem.

Two of the recruits from the recent intake cohort were experienced pilots: Major Lee Jones, a Boeing RC-135 (reconnaissance aircraft) instructor-navigator with 1,800 flying-hours logged; and Major Mark "Dash" Graziano, a thirty-year-old pilot who had been a KC-135 Stratotanker instructor pilot for many years—the KC-135 being the USAF's main air-to-air refueling plane. Graziano had also flown U-2s and had become an instructor in that plane too; overall he had logged 2,900 flying hours.

On May 21, 2009, Graziano and Lee were handed their training mission for that day: flying and documenting a sequence of maneuvers around negative and positive G-force including the midpoint between the two—zero-G.

One of the main flying maneuvers for the sortie was zero-G "pushovers" or parabolas—or, to some civilians, *whoop-de-whoops*. The exercise profile *is* somewhat comparable to a roller-coaster ride. The pilot climbs rapidly at a 45-degree angle and then "pushes" over the top of the altitude gained (he literally pushes the control stick abruptly forward), after which he descends in a rapid swooping dive. As the plane goes over the top of the curved arc, it will pass through zero-G for a few seconds—with anything that is not secured in the cockpit floating up as if the jet were temporarily in outer space. (Very similar roller-coaster-like parabolas are flown in large adapted cargo aircraft to simulate space conditions for trainee astronaut acclimatization.)

On this particular training flight it was Graziano flying the plane up front, and behind him was Lee in the navigator role.

The mission began at around 11:20 a.m. in typically laborious Test Pilot School fashion with the pilot being required to gather data using his

6 Zero-G parabolas

control-stick pressure-gage to take note of and record his on-the-ground stick pressures. When Graziano attempted to save his pressures onto his memory card, he was getting an error message, and a technician came out to the jet to sort that out.

After the minor delay, the two departed Edwards and ascended into one segment of the restricted airspace surrounding the base to continue their data-recording mission. Pilot Graziano proceeded to around 20,000 feet and flew several pushovers.

As they went over the top of one of them, Graziano's stick-pressure gage floated up and got lodged somewhere behind his seat, which was annoying as he needed it throughout the mission. One very popular way for a fighter pilot to retrieve just such an item (pen, pencil, sunglasses, etc.) that has floated out of reach during zero-G is to do a mini-pushover, by which it will float up again and can be grabbed. Graziano came on the intercom to let Lee know that he was about to get his gage back, to which Lee replied, "Okay."

It might have been that Graziano was attempting a nose-down mini-pushover, or it might have been that he was physically reaching behind him to retrieve the gage. Lee, when considering it later, was not certain. Either way, within seconds of the radio message about retrieval, Lee became aware that the jet had entered a steep nose-low dive which was unlike any of the maneuvers that morning. He was not certain because as the jet had gone "over the top" he himself had risen up in the zero-G conditions, and with the sudden nose-low change had hit his helmeted head sharply on the canopy above him; the blow was so sudden and abrupt that he had temporarily lost consciousness.

As he came around—he must have been out cold for only five seconds, or around that—he was aware of having seen Graziano also rise up from his seat in front and possibly hit *his* head on the canopy roof too. Recalling these events later, Lee's memory was inconsistent, with notable events occurring at different places in the narrative timeline each time he told it—a recollection pattern consistent with concussion.

Lee was woozy and somewhat dazed and "seeing white." Even in this hazy and confused state he was aware enough to realize that his jet was 80 degrees nose-low diving towards Earth at more than five hundred miles per hour with its airspeed rising. The jet was rolling, seemingly uncommanded as it went.

Lee called for Graziano, but there was no intercom reply from the motionless figure ahead of him. Lee flicked over to rear-cockpit control and turned the jet-engine throttles to idle. Then he snatched his control stick and attempted to pull up, but he felt no reaction to his inputs. He felt like the plane was not responding at all to any of his stick movements—any movement to the control stick just did nothing.

As he passed through 10,000 feet (the lowest altitude at which he could reasonably pull up) Lee declared on his intercom: "Bail! Bail! Bail!" He then reached down and pulled hard on his ejection lever.

Within one second, the navigator was blasted clear by his under-seat ejection catapult into a seven-hundred-miles-per-hour wind rush, causing him survivable head and neck trauma.

The diving and rolling of the jet, and the unsafe-to-eject high speed, caused various malfunctions and tangles of his ejection drogue and parachute, but it was still effective in saving his life.

In many two-seat fighter jets like the F-15, the default ejection-seat setting is "auto," and in this position either one of the two flight crew pulling the ejection handle will remove both occupants (with a half-second delay between them) from the cockpit near instantly. In the case of the T-38 (as of 2009), there was no equivalent one-for-both ejection setting.

No more than five seconds after Lee ejected, the T-38 crashed nose-down in desert scrubland twelve miles north of Edwards with the unconscious and incapacitated Graziano still in the pilot seat.

The Accident Investigation forensic teardown of the crashed jet found that the jet's tail rudder (similar to the rudder on a boat) was deflected to a crazy angle of 30 degrees, when the maximum deflection available is six degrees. The accident—and fatality—had been caused by a mechanical breakdown of the rudder operating mechanism, possibly the connector rods.

Although it could not be definitively ascertained as to how this mechanical breakdown occurred, the Accident Investigators were able to pinpoint and highlight a number of failings as regards the arrangements for mechanics. The documentation of certifications of proficiency and documentation of qualifications for the mechanics working on T-38s at Edwards were found to be incomplete and confusing. Some of the mechanics were vague and unsure as to what their level of proficiency allowed them to work on, e.g., CSM—Critical Safety Mechanisms.

7 Arctic Thunder

Location: near USAF Joint Base Elmendorf-Richardson, Alaska
Date: 28 July 2010

7 Arctic Thunder

Aircraft type: C-17 Globemaster
Fatalities: 4
Cost of damage: $184.6 million

The Boeing C-17 Globemaster is an imposingly dense and menacing jet, squat and low as it rumbles along a runway with its enormous T-design tailplane rising 55 feet above the ground. And below the tail, a large aft door opens on to the stark and austere cargo compartment—with a capacity of around eighty-five tons of palletized cargo on a standard airlift mission.

The role of the C-17 is "rapid strategic delivery of troops and all types of cargo to main operating bases or directly to forward bases in a deployment area ... [in addition to] tactical airlift and airdrop missions."

The C-17 has also become the plane of choice for U.S. Special Operations units requiring rapid lights-out infiltration-exfiltration into hostile territory. As Navy SEAL Robert O'Neill recalls, for example, in his memoir *The Operator*: "Taking off in our two C-17 transport planes, carrying two speedboats. Time was of the essence, and we all knew it." Or elsewhere: "A C-17 is just this big open bay with benches on either side and about a half dozen of our huge shipping boxes lashed down tight" (O'Neill, 2017, Loc: 3493/2023).

A video-capture of the "max perform" forty-degree nose-high takeoff executed by Maj. Freyholz from the runway at JBER on 28 July 2010. One minute later, the plane crashed into woodland, killing all four on board.

The C-17 can land or take off on a short runway or an improvised landing strip and can rapidly climb away to safety: during a full-performance takeoff, the C-17 will climb out 40 degrees nose-high. In other words, the C-17 is not only a lumbering, schlepping freighter, it is also a plane that "wants to fly."

A number of USAF C-17s are stationed at Joint Base Elmendorf-Richardson, a busy U.S. air base near Anchorage, Alaska, known to airmen as J-BER, pronounced "Jayber." Much of the military activity at JBER is carried on in support of U.S. operations in the Asia-Pacific region. The base is only five hundred miles from the Bering Strait, and the coast of Russia.

Each July, towards the end of the month, the base opens its gates to the public, for a popular once-per-year airshow: Arctic Thunder—an event that often draws in tens of thousands of spectators. In 2010, in late July, plans were well underway for that year's airshow. One of the spectacles for the upcoming show was to be a C-17 demonstration: a full-performance takeoff followed by a low pass over the main spectator area.

Flying a demonstration—in front of a crowd or for another other reason—is something that can be required of a pilot of pretty much any U.S. warplane, and this being the case, some options for such a display are published as official *demonstration profiles*. If a demonstration is required, then one of profile options for that plane is selected, and the pilot's mission for that particular day's duty will be to fly the given profile.

On 28 July, Major Mike Freyholz had been handed a practice session for the C-17 segment of Arctic Thunder. He was to practice "standard profile 3." Freyholz was a very experienced C-17 pilot with three thousand flying hours recorded. He was in the Air National Guard in 2010, but had been formerly an active service pilot with three hundred hours of airlifts in Iraq and Afghanistan completed. Freyholz was also an instructor for the C-17. All this being the case, there was really no great need for Freyholz to practice the demo set, as it was all rather straightforward: a full-throttle takeoff and climbout up to 1,500 feet, and then a 260-degree turn before swooping back down to a high-speed pass over the gathered crowd. That was it—nothing more to it.

The jet that day had a crew of three: Freyholz; his copilot, Major Aaron "Zippy" Malone; and a loadmaster, Sergeant Thomas Cicardo. In addition to the crew, also aboard was Capt. Jeffrey Hill—officially logged as flight surgeon and-or safety officer, who was on a ride-along.

For Mike Freyholz, the personal satisfaction to be found in flying this brief routine—something he also emphasized to his students when instructing—was to execute the set absolutely crisply. For him it was the overall precision and sharpness of the maneuvers that were impressive and helped therefore to "put on a good show for the crowd."

The practice mission-sortie that Wednesday began in the early evening soon after six o'clock as Freyholz and his crew did a "hot" crew-change—that is, they took charge of the jet by swapping over with another crew as the jet idled on the runway its engines still running.

Flying as SITKA43, Freyholz took off at 6:20 p.m. He rotated full-throttle and pitched his C-17 40 degrees nose-high, roaring up and away from the runway. The jet was not really traveling off-base and was to remain in visual sight of the control tower for the few minutes duration of the display maneuvers.

The demo set required Freyholz to climb out rapidly to 1,500 feet and then position for the 260-degree right-hand turnaround. On *this* practice run, however, instead of going all the way up to 1,500 feet, Freyholz decided to gain only 850 feet before leveling off and setting up for the turnaround.

The way that Freyholz liked, or rather insisted upon, while flying the 260 was not strictly by the book. He would keep the jet at full throttle (as per the climbout) and complete the turn using only his rudder. In effect he was using only two controls: the throttles (which he kept on max from the moment of brake release on the runway) and the right rudder—turning on the rudder being the tightest possible way of turning the plane (and many other planes) around.

The bald fact was that, beyond the stated urge to *put on a show* for the general public, Freyholz was executing the demo as an opportunity to fly the jet "max performance"—to fly it to the edge of its envelope, pushing it to its limits, as a challenge and as a thrill. Of course, "maxing" this way is officially forbidden in the USAF.

As the jet entered the banking turn, it began to slow. On this occasion, as Freyholz was completing his turn—using his technique—he had an airspeed of only 216 m.p.h. (222 m.p.h. being the recommended minimum), and this caused the in-cockpit stall warnings to kick in—audible cockpit warnings and on-screen messages.

Freyholz was expecting to get the warnings, and so his reaction to them was actually nothing. He was used to hearing from "bitching Betty," the female-voiced audible caution warning system, in any such tight turn: "Warning, warning.... Warning, warning.... Warning, warning..." Freyholz's attitude was to disregard such auto-safety features insofar as he was well aware that flying max performance would inevitably cause various in-cockpit warnings to sound. These he habitually and studiously ignored: he was focused rather on his maneuvers.

As Freyholz had explained to several of the pupils he had instructed, these stall warnings were "something of an anomaly" and could be disregarded if executing a very tight turn. It was only momentarily that the plane was touching stall speed, and as it came out of the turn, airspeed soon increased again.

As the warnings came on, Zippy Malone was suddenly not feeling as confident as Freyholz, and he called out: "Not so tight, brother!" Then Jeff Hill—sitting just behind the two front seats—also called out. Three times he exhorted: "Watch your bank! Watch your bank! Watch your bank!"

In this instance, unlike all the other times, rather than quickly regaining speed as it came out of the banking turn, the plane actually entered a full airstall, and began to lose altitude at the alarming rate of 150 feet per second. Since the plane had begun its stall at only 850 feet up (rather than the requested 1,500), the situation was instantly critical: there was so little altitude available in which to mount a recovery. (The basics of stall recovery are obvious enough: increase throttle to maximum available and level the wings.)

Freyholz began his recovery procedure, but it was too little, too late, and seconds later—and just over one minute after takeoff—the C-17 crashed back to earth. "The aircraft impacted wooded terrain northwest of the airfield at 63.6 degrees of right bank, 16.0 degrees nose-low at 211 m.p.h. on 28 July 2010 at 18:22." The four airmen aboard were killed in the crash.

Freyholz had trimmed all margin of error from the demo profile. He had left himself nowhere to go if he got into trouble. This might have been acceptable if it were only his life and his property at stake, but it wasn't: it was the lives of three other men, and a USAF jet valued at $200 million.

Upon impact the C-17 exploded and the post-crash fireball ignited a forest fire that burned out of control for thirty-six hours. The post-crash fire burning in dense forest was inaccessible to the rescue crews who arrived on site within seven minutes but were unable to contain the ferociously blazing fire for many hours.

8 C-Bleed hot

Location: Talkeetna Mountains, Alaska
Date: 16 November 2010

8 C-Bleed hot

Aircraft type: F-22 Raptor
Fatalities: 1
Cost of damage: $147 million

The F-22 Raptor is a formidable and extraordinary flying vehicle. "Its combination of stealth, supercruise, maneuverability, and integrated avionics ... make it the world's most advanced fighter."

The overall look of an F-22 is minimalistic: every component is boxed in—much as the fairing shell of a racing motorcycle disguises the mechanics beneath. It is the design-shape that is emphasized: a series of flat interlocking diamond shapes.

In a full-performance afterburner takeoff—usually for public demonstration—the F-22 can pitch nose-up 90 degrees high almost immediately after wheels up and depart in a manner redolent of a space-rocket launch.

The overall visual impression of the F-22 as alien and otherworldly is redoubled by its dull-matte nonreflective RAM (radar-absorbent material) cladding. The RAM cladding, together with other design and avionic-based features, gives the jet its crucial "stealth" capability. The Raptor essentially defeats its own image: the plane will appear on enemy radar,

Crash site in the Talkeetna Mountains in Alaska. The impact speed of the F-22 Raptor was such that the entire jet entered the Earth nose-down and was completely buried at ground level. The crash site was only visible as a crater.

if it appears at all, with the "signature" of an object with dimensions of less than one square foot. (It is said the Raptor pilot's helmet returns more radar waves than any other part of the plane.)

The Raptor's through-air maneuverability in the case of a *dogfight* is enhanced by the pilot's numerous real-time video streams, which allow her-him to fly with near 360-degree visibility. In a worst-case scenario, an F-22 under attack from an already-launched enemy air-to-air missile can simply outrun most such missiles at Mach 2, or up to 1,700 m.p.h.

The basic use of the F-22 in a conventional combat setting is in the very early stages of a warfare campaign, and in particular during the instigation of air dominance over a specific geographic territory. As of 2017, at least one hundred USAF F-22s could enter *en masse* any designated "hostile" airspace over Earth, on missions to degrade and destroy enemy radar installations, missile shields, runways, and other targets (missions that would likely use surprise as a component of the tactical planning).

The F-22 is a vital attack weapon for the USAF: it is a weapon that no competing air force can match (Russia is the only state operator that is competitively attempting to respond to the F-22). In other words, an F-22 pilot flies alone, high above the Earth, as a near-invincible, super-high-tech warrior.

The USAF Air Base JBER ("Jayber") in Alaska (in full, Joint Base Elmendorf-Richardson) is a key strategic base for the U.S. military. Geographically, it is a main base in the goal of ensuring peace in the Asia-Pacific region, and equally important, the base is close to Russia. Those who imagine the threat from the Russian military to the U.S. evaporated absolutely with the fall of the Berlin Wall might refer to the at least fifty instances of Russian warplanes intentionally entering the U.S. Air Defense Identification Zone (the zone immediately preceding U.S. airspace) off the coast of Alaska since 2010. In each instance, known as "buzzing," the Russian jet or jets—often a Tu-95 bomber flying in formation with Mig-31 fighter jets defending it—have been successfully air-intercepted and *escorted* away from the direction of U.S. airspace.

At least twenty F-22s are stationed at JBER. The Alaskan airspace around JBER is restricted to civil aviation, and the extensive restricted zone is divided into a number of sectors for organizational purposes.

On 16 November 2010, a night practice mission was taking place in the skies around JBER. The mission had been set up with four F-15s flying in as "red air" simulated hostiles: these would be simulating a surface attack on certain ground targets. In response to the incoming hostile jets,

8 C-Bleed hot

the Air Force response was to be two sets of three Raptors—a set of three being known as a "three ship."

During late afternoon and early evening, the planning for the sorties was carried on rather uneventfully: such practice missions at night are just an ordinary part of the fighter pilot's working week. All pilots involved that evening were wearing NVGs—infrared-based night-vision devices—and were wearing, for the first time that winter, cold weather attire including the classic MA1 flying jacket.

It was a clear night with "unlimited visibility and 74 percent moon illumination over snow covered terrain," as the two groups of fighters, with afterburners roaring red-hot, streamed into the sky a little after six. The intercept-and-kill mission was carried out very much as been planned.

One of the Raptor pilots that evening, flying as ROCKY3, was Captain Jeff Haney, an experienced F-22 pilot with three hundred hours in and F-22 logged, at least forty of those hours wearing NVGs. Shortly after seven-forty, during a series or regrouping maneuvers, not long after the main mission objectives had been accomplished, Haney's jet developed a malfunction.

Haney was a hundred and twenty miles north of his base, flying at 540 miles per hour and around thirty-seven thousand feet over the Talkeetna Mountain range, when he observed on his in-cockpit head-up display screen a blandly worded caution message informing him of an issue: "C BLEED HOT."

Haney's on-board fire protection systems had detected a "bleed air" leak. Bleed air is the supply of compressed air that is siphoned off, or bled, from the jet engine's compressors for use elsewhere in the plane, including the air that is conditioned and routed to the pilot's oxygen mask.

To the F-22's computer sensors, a bleed air leak is a substantive malfunction in that compressed air reentering the precision of a $30 million engine may ignite an engine fire. The on-board systems immediately shut off the pressurized air-supply system as a precaution.

One consequence of the on-board bleed-air system's shutting down was the cessation of any air supply through the pilot's oxygen mask. This cutoff was indicated to the pilot initially as another advisory warning or caution message on his head-up visual display: "OBOGS [On Board Oxygen Generating System] FAIL." In these moments, the pilot would have become aware of the failure of the air supply through his oxygen mask, which leads to "severely restricted breathing," and with a "sense similar to suffocation."

Immediately upon recognizing the in-flight emergency, Haney retarded his jet's throttles to idle and began to descend to a lower altitude.

As would be expected, the jet's angle in the air changed to 30 degrees nose-down: a sharp descent was underway.

In this situation Haney had two really immediate and actually pressing options: to eject from the jet and parachute away to safety, or to successfully start up the emergency oxygen from a supply canister to the left of his seat. In the F-22, as in several other fighters, the canister is fitted with a large circular bright apple-green aluminum pull-ring. It is designed to be very obvious. It is activated manually with around forty pounds of forward-and-upward pulling force.

Probably the least dramatic outcome of this incident would have been for Haney to open the emergency oxygen and head for an urgent RTB (return to base). He could also have been on an any-runway-you-care-to-nominate approach with a declared emergency within five minutes. It would have been expected for Haney to manually open his emergency oxygen supply at this moment and then make his next decisions. For some reason he did not open the oxygen canister supply.

As the diving descent was continuing, several aircraft control inputs were recorded, but these were so random, and with no obvious purpose, that they were probably carried out inadvertently, possibly as the pilot struggled in the cockpit to manually start his emergency oxygen supply. Also, the jet had rolled so that it was diving inverted, an awkward and unconventional position, or "unusual attitude."

As the jet gathered speed, its nose dipped until it was diving—arrowing—towards Earth at a speed of at least seven hundred miles per hour.

Fifteen seconds later, with the plane passing through only five-thousand-feet altitude, the pilot suddenly made a definite attempt to pull up and out of his nose dive—an extreme maneuver that would have placed at least an eight-G-force strain on his body. The speed and angle of descent of the jet were too determined: three seconds after his pull-up effort, Haney's plane crashed nose-first at a speed of at least nine hundred miles per hour.

The plane had the characteristics of a high-speed dart: the crash site at ground level left a water-filled crater about fifteen feet across, with the plane buried deep in the ground nose-first. The pilot was killed on impact in the crash, which caused the complete destruction of his aircraft—later officially valued at $147 million.

In terms of the pilot's personal psychology, although it cannot be said with any certainty, a panel of experts decided that after he lost his air supply the pilot's thinking probably became distorted by a phenomenon known as "channelized attention." That is, his conscious interests narrowed: he became fixated on starting his oxygen supply and was no longer thinking of the equally pressing matter of flying his plane safely.

The later engineering inspection of the wreckage and computer data analysis showed that Haney had not attempted ejection.

The Investigators speculated that the large pull-ring for the oxygen got somehow stuck down the side of the chair and it was this action of trying to urgently retrieve the tab which was preoccupying the pilot during the fifteen seconds of "unusual attitude."

9 Ground-rush in Germany

Location: near the village of Laufeld, Germany
Date: 1 April 2011
Aircraft type: A-10 Thunderbolt
Fatalities: none
Cost of damage: $16.1 million

The A-10 Thunderbolt is a "highly accurate weapons delivery platform" designed for close air support of troops on the ground. The A-10 is very often the jet that arrives when those under fire on the ground "call in an air strike." For this reason, the A-10 is one of the jets that U.S. army troops are familiar with, and fond of—often nicknaming it affectionately the "warthog" or simply the "hog," in reference to its somehow lumpish and inelegant visual appearance.

The lumbering "long-loitering" plane is designed to fly at low ceilings—under 1,000 feet. At such altitudes an A-10 pilot can observe his targets on the ground with the naked eye. Upon acquiring, he advances, aiming his General Electric GAU-8 Avenger hydraulically driven, seven-barrel, Gatling-type cannon, a machine that fires 30mm shells in short bursts at a speed 4,000 rounds per minute. The A-10 is sometimes dubbed simply the "flying gun."

If the cannon alone is not sufficiently devastating to enemy forces, then the pilot will likely turn to the missiles and bombs loaded up in a long row on his eleven under-wing and under-fuselage pylons. In this regard, the jet is literally an airborne weapons-delivery platform.

Of course, flying in so low and slow over a field of battle also makes the A-10 a ready target for hostile forces on the ground, and A-10 pilots are often esteemed as exceptionally fearless. An A-10 on any ordinary ground support mission is likely to take fire, so the plane is designed to be return-to-base airworthy even with quite extreme battle damage.

The USAF has A-10s stationed at many bases around the world: the A-10 has to go wherever battle is to be joined.

Spangdahlem Air Base in Germany is one of the bases where A-10s are stationed. The base is *in the heart of Europe*, close to the western border of Germany—and only fifty miles from Holland, Luxembourg and France. U.S. forces in Germany are tasked with supporting NATO forces, but the activities at the U.S. bases in Europe (as elsewhere) are absolutely autonomous and independent of the host state's military activity. Of course, USAF air traffic is constantly coordinated across a number of European airspaces.

As with any squadron of warplanes, an ordinary day-to-day activity is maintaining battle readiness. One basic means of sustaining fighting preparedness is the training sortie: a planned mission to attack a simulated target on the ground or in the air.

On Friday, 1 April 2011, at Spangdahlem, one such training mission was scheduled. Two A-10s were to fly out over Holland into an airspace nominated and designated by the USAF as Training Military Area D—in Dutch airspace—where they were to carry on simulated attacks on each other. Dogfight maneuvers are designed to practice defending and attacking against an airborne threat from another fighter at close quarters. Both planes would have practice missiles and target-practice ammunition.

It was a rather typical northern European afternoon, drab and gray with plenty of cloud around, and the pre-flight briefing included a discussion of the weather: there was cloud from around 1,500 feet up to around 5,000 feet. Above that, visibility was excellent.

Flying through clouds, especially during takeoff and landing, requires pilots to fly by "instrument rules," that is, they must fly without reference to what can be seen from the aircraft (often, all that can be observed is clouds as fog). Flying under instrument rules, the pilot flies his plane solely by reference to the flight-deck or cockpit instruments. Given the clouds, for the sortie that day, RTB—return to base—was to be an instrument landing for each of the two A-10s.

The two Thunderbolts departed Spangdahlem about ten minutes later than scheduled, at just after ten past two in the afternoon. One of the A-10 pilots on the sortie that afternoon was Colonel Scott Hurrelbrink. Hurrelbrink was a very experienced pilot with at least eight hundred hours

9 Ground-rush in Germany

logged flying hogs. On this particular sortie it was Hurrelbrink's partner, his "wingman," who was the mission commander.

The practice session in the skies over Holland passed uneventfully, and by three forty-five p.m. the two—flying in close formation—were beginning to ready for the approach back into Spangdahlem Base. In order to land, it is necessary to "configure" a plane, meaning lower the wheels, set the speed brakes into position, and extend the flaps on the wings (making them larger and so adding stability).

At 15:47 Hurrelbrink turned his attention to preparations for landing, and during these moments, at around 5,000 feet up, the two A-10s entered an area of cloud.

Turning his attention back from a focus on his landing configuration, Hurrelbrink realized that within the last few moments he had lost track of his wingman—a hazardous situation during close-formation flying as the planes typically retain less than ten feet between wingtips.

As soon as he lost his sense of the mission commander's position, Hurrelbrink made a radio call to that effect: a "lost wingman" alert. The other jet's pilot heard the alert, and in response, rather than immediately assert his precise altitude and position (as was standard procedure), communicated instead an instruction to Hurrelbrink: "Two's continuing the approach; clean up and climb." Meaning the second plane should retract landing configuration ("clean up") and climb back up above the cloud before making his approach alone.

As he continued through the clouds, Hurrelbrink followed the mission commander's instruction to clean up, but rather than climb decisively up out of the cloud, the pilot instead followed correct standard lost-wingman procedure: roll way 15 degrees for 15 seconds, then resume heading, and if landing request separate clearance.

As he continued through the clouds, now out of formation and essentially independent of his wingman, Hurrelbrink's jet began to take up an unusual attitude. The plane became inverted 180 degrees and, alarmingly, 60 degrees nose-low (sharply down towards the ground). For some reason that cannot be explained other than as "spatial disorientation," Hurrelbrink was simply not aware of the jet slowly turning into its extremely perilous *unusual attitude*.

Then, still in this awkward and alarming orientation, Hurrelbrink's A-10 exited the "pretty thick" or "very thick" cloud cover, revealing quite starkly to the pilot his predicament. The sudden reveal of the Earth, only 1,000 feet below him, struck Hurrelbrink with a shock force: the ground seemed to the startled pilot to be surging towards him. The result was a debilitating and horrifying psychological distortion—"a visual misperception of how quickly the ground is approaching"—known as "ground rush." It is at around 1,000 feet up that ground rush tends to affect perception, particularly with skydivers: this is the altitude at which perception of the ground below will tend to shift. It is at this altitude and below that geographical features and structures on the ground become recognizable, distinct, and imposing. (At 1,000 feet the skydiver is no longer falling through the sky, but falling dramatically towards the fast-approaching surface of the Earth.)

Hurrelbrink, in his agitated state, was still aware enough to begin to take action to pull up his jet out of its dive, or so he thought. But in fact, his attempted recovery maneuver—pulling hard aft on his control stick—only further increased the dive, from 60 degrees nose-down to fully 90 degrees nose-down. He was arrowing directly down towards the ground, nose-first, at around 230 m.p.h. with not more than five seconds to impact. At this moment Hurrelbrink realized the futility of further recovery efforts and made the decision to perform ejection: he located and then pulled hard on his ejection-seat handle.

Ejection commenced: it takes a modern ejection system about two seconds to remove a pilot from his jet. As fast as that might seem, in this case it was only just fast enough: three seconds after successful pilot ejection, the A-10 crashed into the "gently sloping ridgeline" of rural farmland (still in its inverted 90-degree nose-down attitude), near the German village of Laufeld, and was destroyed.

The ejection was successful, but not ideal—the pilot was simply too close to the ground for his parachute to fully deploy. However, Hurrelbrink survived, floating down on his parachute, only 100 feet from the wreckage of the crashed plane which was engulfed in a blazing post-crash fire.

As is often the case with non-combat crashes occurring near a U.S. base in a host country, it was concerned locals and local first-responder emergency services that were first to arrive on scene. On this occasion it was a rescue helicopter owned by the German Auto Club ADAC.

The responders found the pilot complaining of pain in the shoulder and back but able to move all his limbs. Within eight minutes the helicopter took off en route to Trier Hospital. Hurrelbrink was later assessed to have only minor injuries.

As of 2017 Hurrelbrink is Vice Commander, 36th Wing, Andersen Air Force Base, Guam. The value of the lost jet was later estimated at $16.1 million.

10 Flameout Volk

Location: New Chester, Wisconsin
Date: 7 June 2011
Aircraft type: F-16
Fatalities: none
Cost of damage: at least $25.7 million

Air National Guard airmen generally work two days per month for the USAF—48 days per year—while also keeping a civilian job. The ANG is a secondary force which is additional to the main USAF capability.

The organizational setup with the ANG is that it is administered by each U.S. state individually. Of course, for deployment in an emergency, any ANG squadron may be placed under the jurisdiction of a central operational command.

In 2011, Lieutenant Colonel Glen Messner was a member of the ANG based at Truax Field, a component of Dane County Regional Airport, in Wisconsin. Messner had been an A-10 Thunderbolt pilot before he moved to flying the F-16 Fighting Falcon.

The F-16 is a single jet-engine fighter aircraft which forms the backbone of the USAF fighting force with over one thousand on the inventory (as of 2017). Many F-16 engines are Pratt and Whitney F100 type engines that may be valued at approximately $20 million apiece. The F-16 can fly at Mach 2, or around 1,700 m.p.h.; it is also highly maneuverable.

On June 7, 2011, Messner was flying one of his usual twice-per-month "active duty" days. On this particular day, Messner's sortie was a 2-ship: two F-16s—callsigns ROCK31 and ROCK32—would be going out to practice certain maneuvers. The two were going to do some simulated "dogfight" exercises—air-to-air attack-and-defend. They would be taking it in turns to simulated-attack one another. In the face of attack, each pilot would then defend his aircraft with maneuvers such as performance turns, jinking, and S-bends, and then use simulated air-to-air missiles to go for a "kill" on the other.

The other activity that the two had planned for that day's sortie was simulated flame-out approaches. A simulated flame-out approach is a practice activity in which the pilot controls his jet and attempts a landing approach as if his jet engine has ceased to function (known as "flame-out" or "engine-out"). In such a situation, the pilot nominates an airstrip or runway and carries out a landing approach by gliding in only—as if experiencing an engine-out emergency. The pilot will advance towards the nominated runway with his engine throttle set to "idle," gliding down towards the runway, then, before actually landing this way, he brings back up the throttle-thrust and ascends again (known as a "go around").

Every USAF warplane has a some glide-potential or glide ratio, which is different for each plane. For the F-16, a very rough estimated glide ratio is one mile for each 1,000 feet of altitude. In other words, an F-16 going engine-out at 20,000 feet needs to find somewhere to land not more than twenty miles away.

ROCK31 and ROCK32 departed Truax at 11:50 a.m. Messner used "military power" for takeoff—high power but short of a full-performance afterburner takeoff. The two F-16 pilots climbed out and made their way from Truax to Volk Field, a small ANG air field also in Wisconsin, about eighty miles northwest of Dane County Airport.

In the sky above Volk, Messner practiced several times his flame-out approach—each time setting his engine throttle to idle and then gliding in, down towards the runway. After the simulated flame-out sessions, the two moved on to their air-to-air dogfight maneuvers, which continued uneventfully, always in the same general airspace between Truax and Volk.

Soon after 1:00 p.m. the two jets were getting low on fuel—Bingo fuel, as this is known—and came back into formation for a return to Truax. As the two were doing a visual battle-damage check on each other (flying close by to check the external condition of the other's jet following dogfighting), Messner's jet suddenly lost engine power. His engine had flamed out, and he heard the unmistakable sound of the turbine "winding down."

Messner was at 9,000 feet flying at 350 m.p.h. At 13:13:12, the pilot transmitted over the auxiliary radio to his wingman: "Knock it off, knock it off.... ROCK 31, knock it off ... just lost my engine." And at this, he commenced towards Volk Airfield—where, irony-of-ironies, not more than one hour before he had been practicing flame-out forced landings. Messner had a real in-flight emergency that mirrored precisely the eventuality he had just been simulating.

Messner checked his position. Unfortunately he was about thirty-seven miles from Volk with a glide potential of just under ten miles. He just would not have the glide range necessary to make it in to land at the nearest runway. This being the case, Messner turned his attention to restarting his failed engine, knowing that at some point, if he could not successfully achieve this, he would have to go for an ejection.

With his engine restart efforts continuing, Messner was also seeking

10 Flameout Volk

to locate a rural unpopulated area on the ground below. Minimizing potential civilian casualties and on-the-ground damage is a pilot responsibility in the case of an ejection.

As he hunted for a woodland area, Messner simultaneously made repeated attempts to restart his engine. As Messner later described it: "It was automatic. I never had time to be scared, [or] to freeze up."

It was futile: the engine was absolutely out, and during the restart attempts the F-16 had descended to well below the minimum recommended altitude for ejection. The jet was now only 1,500 feet up. At 13:15:38, two and a half minutes after his initial engine wind-down, Messner ejected, and parachuted safely to the ground.

The uncontrolled and unmanned F-16 continued its perilous and doomed flight for around twenty seconds before it crashed, nose-low 80 degrees, into a vacant holiday cottage off Elk Avenue in the village of New Chester, Adams County, Wisconsin. The home was owned by Jack and Becky Weslowicz. As Barry Adams of Madison.com reported: "Wesolowicz bought the 10-acre, $150,000 wooded property about seven years ago [2004] as a weekend and holiday getaway. His family, which includes his wife, Becky, and two children, Nicholas, 10, and Katie, 7, liked its wooded setting and the close proximity to Wisconsin Dells. They also spent Thanksgivings and Christmases at the home."

As Tabitha Koback, an eyewitness, recalled: "All of a sudden I just looked back toward the truck and then looked over and saw this huge mushroom cloud of smoke and I just looked at my husband and said 'Oh my God, that plane crashed.'"

Koback and her husband drove towards the crash site and soon located the pilot: "Four hundred or five hundred yards down the road [from the crash site] there he was standing in the ditch with his parachute and gear," said Tabitha.

The crash and post-crash fireball destroyed the plane and the property. The impact crater was nine feet deep and thirty feet across. The lost jet was later valued at $25.7 million.

The post-crash investigation engine "teardown" revealed one highly likely cause for the catastrophic loss of the engine in-flight: the presence of a large foreign object lodged inside the main oil supply line that had blocked oil circulation to the engine. The object recovered was approximately nine inches long by three-inches wide.

The foreign object was a piece of Teflon—a low-friction material with many uses in aeronautics—which could only have been left inadvertently in this pipeline by a mechanic servicing the jet engine.

The later Accident Report noted that the jet engine had in fact been partially dismantled on 24 January 2011, for the express purpose of conducting "a search for a piece of missing safety wire dropped during engine maintenance." The report does not mention if it was located at that time, but it does document several problems with the engine between February and June in the lead-up to the doomed flight. It is quite likely that the foreign object located during the teardown was exactly the one that had been missing, as "safety wire" is often Teflon-based.

A second probable cause of the accident was the failure of bearings (or the use of incorrect-size ball bearings) in a secondary gear-box mechanism. These two issues were observed, in addition to the presence of a substantial quantity of sand-blast residue used during major overhaul-type maintenance. The overhaul had been carried out at Oklahoma Air Logistics Complex at Tinker Air Force Base, east of Oklahoma City.

11 Mist-up AirVenture

Location: Wittman Airport, Wisconsin
Date: 28 July 2011
Aircraft type: F-16
Fatalities: none
Cost of damage: $5.4 million

During the 1940s, in the U.S., racial segregation was rife. The laws enforcing racial segregation are often referred to as the Jim Crow laws. During the years leading up to and during the U.S. entry into World War II, there were separate pilot schools for African American pilots in the USAF. The largest training center for African American cadet pilots was Tuskegee University and Moton Field, in Alabama.

During the last week of July each year at Wittman Airport in Wisconsin (close to Oshkosh), there is a large convention and airshow for aviation enthusiasts: AirVenture. Diverse events take place over a number of days with many fly-ins, fly-bys, aerobatics displays and more—including numerous USAF aircraft, both historical and in-service.

AirVenture is a very popular event attended by around two hundred thousand spectators and aviation enthusiasts over the week. Many of the attendees stay through the week with permits to camp out at Wittman in tents; the event is something of a festival.

11 Mist-up AirVenture

The F-16 that departed the runway at Wittman during the AirVenture airshow in 2011. The aircraft's front landing gear collapsed when the aircraft careered off the runway and into the grassy surrounding area. As a result, the jet engine sucked in large quantities of soil and grass through its front air inlet before it was shut down.

In 2011, one of the events was a celebration of Tuskegee Airmen, scheduled in for 28 July. In support of this Tuskegee event at Wittman, two pilots based at the Air National Guard, U.S. Base at Dannelly Field (directly adjacent to Montgomery Regional Airport, in Alabama) had been tasked to fly two F-16s up to Wittman.

The requirement was not a training sortie as such but rather a "cross country," a straightforward tasking to fly a jet from one airport or air base to another. The two pilots had meticulously planned out their "cross-country" route. They had familiarized themselves with the projected weather conditions (excellent visibility was forecast); they had looked at the details for landing at Wittman including getting hold of a copy of the "Chicago Sectional" for a visual-landing rules (VLR) landing at Wittman; and they looked at specific guidance published by AirVenture for pilots on fly-ins (several hundred planes fly into Wittman during the airshow week).

On the morning of 28 July the two airmen arrived at Dannelly for a 7:15 a.m. "showtime" (time required to report ready for work). After having thoroughly checked over their aircraft, the two F-16s departed Dannelly at 9:50 a.m., and soon climbed to their cruise altitude of 28,000 feet.

The nine-hundred-mile flight took the two due north over Tennessee,

Kentucky, Indiana and Illinois. The flight was unremarkable and not especially noteworthy. As the two descended towards Wittman on visual flight rules, there was some low cloud around, causing the two to be positioned very slightly low and fast for final approach.

The first of the two F-16s landed successfully at 11:15 a.m., and then it was the turn of the second pilot, Major Colin Aitcherson, to land. As he made final approach to the runway, he made certain adjustments to his flight path and airspeed, but even so he landed fast. The correct landing ground-speed at touchdown was 160 m.p.h. but in this case Aitcherson touched down doing 200 m.p.h.

At this moment, immediately after touchdown with the plane's rear landing gear down and the nose-high (the front landing gear having not yet made contact with the runway), the obvious and correct action would be for the pilot to deploy his airbrakes. On an F-16 the airbrakes are at the back of the plane on either side of the main exhaust-nozzle: two sets of two flat-panel flaps (each the size of a door) that can be opened in order to intentionally defeat the jet's aerodynamics when required.

Aitcherson, however, did not deploy his airbrakes. Just as he was landing—in the most crucial and precarious moments of any flight—the pilot's cockpit interior was, astonishingly and alarmingly, enveloped in thick fog. It was so dense that he literally could not see his instruments inches in front of his face. He lost sight of his main head-up display and his nose-wheel steering indicator and the angle-of-attack gauge.

The effect of the sudden in-cockpit mist-up for the pilot was intense and overwhelming. He later said it was "like having a white plastic bag placed over his head." Aitcherson "reached for the DEFOG lever and shoved it full forward." Several times the hapless pilot "recycled," pushing his DEFOG lever to max, but each time there was no effect—the cockpit remained shrouded. (The DEFOG option usually works by supplying warm air—at 158 Fahrenheit—into the canopy area for three minutes.)

As the jet's nose-wheel contacted the runway (and with the plane at least forty miles per hour faster than expected on the tarmac), the pilot experienced a sensation of vertigo and disorientation, "almost a tumbling sensation." In this confused state, with the "loss of total visual," Aitcherson's F-16 continued at speed along its runway with the pilot braking as hard as he could using his main landing-gear brakes.

At such speed, and without the use of airbrakes, the F-16 quickly used up the full length of the runway available. With the pilot helpless to stop it, the plane careered off the end of the end of the prepared tarmac surface and into the grass beyond (in full view of hundreds if not thousands

11 Mist-up AirVenture

of picnicking aviation enthusiasts). The jet bumped through the grass for about a hundred and fifty feet before the front landing-gear strut collapsed, causing the F-16's nose to drop to the turf. Still standing on its rear wheels, the fuselage inclined about 20 degrees—with, if you like, its butt in the air.

Aitcherson, still with no visual references, "felt a bump and rumbling, and then the nose dug in." At the moment the jet came to a standstill, Aitcherson's only thought was to get out. He carried out his emergency egress and jogged away from the plane with spectators all around within fifty feet of the jet. Referring to amateur videos of the accident, it can be seen that the spectators around did not react very much to the accident; the sight was perhaps more comedic than dramatic to a casual look. Only when a few flickering flames and a plume of smoke begins to issue from the tailpipe is there any reaction at all.

The problem with Aitcherson's egress was that he had not shut his engine down. He had abandoned his jet so hurriedly that he had left the throttle to his $30 million Pratt and Whitney F100 engine set to IDLE mode—in neutral but still cycling, and with the air intakes still drawing in not only air but also "dirt and sod" from the field. Some of this matter was passing through the engine and being sprayed out behind, making the plane appear as something like a high-tech agricultural cultivation machine.

Minutes later, Wittman emergency services took control of the scene. Fortunately there was no major post-crash fire, and the airshow schedule was not really affected.

Mechanics later estimated repairs required to remedy the damage to the jet to be at least $5.4 million.

Aitcherson later explained to the Accident Investigation Panel: in the moments of landing his jet, he was completely blinded and suffering vertigo-like disorientation due to the mist-up. This being the case, he was distracted from deploying his airbrakes. He was "preoccupied with … other stuff going on in the cockpit." Also, he could not see the instruments or display in order to evaluate his angle of attack or his nose-position height.

Engineers later suggested that the mist-up malfunction "could be caused by an environmental control system anti-ice valve that was faulty or was otherwise prevented from adding warm air to the cold turbine output; a faulty Cabin Temperature Control Valve; the warm air mix components system; and maybe a fault in the MAX DEFOG circuitry."

When the jet's air-con system was tested for malfunctions, over a series of at least twenty tests it was not possible to recreate the unexplained and apparently one-off mist-up.

Due to the number of avid aviation enthusiasts around the accident as it was taking place, the Accident Investigation Panel were able to gather a number of photos and videos of the landing and overshoot, and these do indeed clearly evidence an extreme mist in the cockpit in the moments of landing.

The incident, if not a mystery exactly, remains at least anomalous and freakish.

12 Warthog seizure

Location: near Moultrie, Georgia
Date: 26 September 2011
Aircraft type: A-10
Fatalities: none
Cost of damage: $14.7 million

The A-10 Thunderbolt is a U.S. warplane that provides close air support to infantry troops in battle as they advance in hostile territory. The Thunderbolt flies slow-and-low—it has ability to "loiter" menacingly above a battlefield.

The A-10 is a tough and rugged jet, a "flying tank," able to return to base "all shot up," recalling the tradition of the classic World War II planes and their intrepid pilots—like the B-17 Flying Fortress. The A-10 is renowned as a "badass" jet—a flying beast, if you will—and hence its nickname: the Warthog or just Hog. A partial aesthetic explanation for the fairly disparaging nickname is that the A-10's twin jet engines are mounted close to the fuselage and above the wings, and so give the jet a rather unaerodynamic look; the engines are pitched up 9 degrees off the aerodynamic line.

The Thunderbolt is designed around parameters and expectations that are really the reverse of the high-tech stealth fighters. Rather than avoid detection and enemy fire, the Thunderbolt expects it, presumes it, and is ready for it: the cockpit area is clad in three-inch-thick titanium armor plating; the wings and fuselage are constructed using cellular honeycombed composite materials that soak up enemy fire. In every way the plane is built for survivability—remaining airworthy with one engine

12 Warthog seizure

Aerial view of the crash site about twenty miles northwest of Moody Air Force Base in a deserted quarry between Moultrie and Valdosta in Cook County, Georgia. An A-10 Thunderbolt was completely destroyed in the accident.

destroyed, or chunks of wing or fuselage missing, or with the hydraulics for the flight control surfaces out of action, for example. The plane is also designed to be amenable to running repairs—particularly repairs carried out at short notice and with improvised ad hoc materials. A Thunderbolt can and will get patched up in the heat of battle. In addition, it can take off from an improvised runway: any reasonably flat short stretch of highway will work.

The Thunderbolt's two TF-34 jet engines are extremely robust, as aviation journalist Joakim Balle has noted: "In service, the TF-34 has proven to be a highly reliable and maintainable power-plant with low operating costs. General Electric has delivered approximately 2,100 TF-34 engines [to the USAF] that have accumulated more than thirteen million flight hours." The TF-34 engines fitted to an A-10 are specifically designed to withstand extreme foreign object damage—such as shrapnel and debris being "ingested" or sucked into the gas turbine system.

Observed by enemy positions on the ground, the Warthog must be a daunting and depressing sight: some planes will fly straight over a battlefield on missions further into hostile territory, but this is not the case for the Thunderbolt. If enemy ground positions observe Warthogs moving towards them at 1000-feet altitude, then they can be reasonably sure that they are about to come under a horrifying barrage—a fact that is emphasized by the visible sardonic shark-teeth smile often painted onto the nose of A-10s in active service. Conversely, to beleaguered allied troops on the ground, the sight of an A-10 advancing implacably towards them during a dicey firefight must be a wonderfully welcome and probably unforgettable sight. As Robert O'Neill recalls in his memoir *The Operator*: "Those are badass attack planes, a flying arsenal. They came in low, just tearing the sky apart, and opened fire right over our heads with their four-thousand-pound, seven-barrel Gatling guns. We could hear the bullets going supersonic: we heard them hit before we heard them shoot. It was all backward. Just insane. It sounds like a big dragon flying over you, screaming and spitting fire."

On Monday, 26 September 2011, an unnamed pilot based at Moody Air Force Base, Georgia, had an FCF to carry out on an A-10 that had just been through a major scheduled maintenance. An FCF is a "Functional Check Flight" and involves taking a flight in a plane and carrying out a range of functionality tests—no different from a garage mechanic taking a car that he has been working on for a test drive to see how it is handling after he's worked on it.

An FCF requires the pilot who is testing and checking to get airborne and then work through a set checklist of operations at several altitudes. The FCF is a rather hair-raising tick-box exercise in that it is necessary to check, for example, if the jet's stall warnings are working—audible in-cockpit and control-stick vibration. This being the case, it is necessary to slow the jet being tested into a midair stall in order to observe and hear if the warnings are sounding.

FCF work requires pilots who can fly and control a jet at close to the edge of its sustainable-flight parameters, or "envelope," and simultaneously meticulously fill in a checklist form with comments as required. The FCF is not particularly glamorous work, but nevertheless requires experienced pilots with a definite ability to multi-task. On the other hand, such a flight is absolutely routine and will usually be designated "low risk" on a risk assessment grid.

The A-10 going through FCF on 26 September 2011 departed Moody at approximately two o'clock in the afternoon, flying as callsign DYNO51.

The way an FCF is done—in the USAF at least—is to work through the same checklist of operations at several different altitudes. The pilot

12 *Warthog seizure*

soon climbed out to his first agreed altitude—10,000 feet—in a restricted military airspace above Georgia, designated as Corsair Military Operating Area. Following the testing at 10,000 feet, there was only one query noted: no audible warning for landing gear down.

Next, the pilot ascended to 18,000 feet. On the query list this time: the front-of-wing slats were observed to extend only after a slight delay rather than immediately. Also, the in-cockpit audible stall warning messages seemed to be playing up—either not working at all or working only intermittently. This meant that the pilot, *as he continued about his work, would need to keep an especially watchful eye on his airspeed, since he already knew that the automatic audible warnings were unreliable.*

At around two-thirty p.m., the pilot began to ascend for his final checklist session—now at 35,000 feet, a high altitude for an A-10, which usually flies low (its maximum is only 40,000 feet).

It was also a high altitude for this particular pilot, who had never actually flown an FCF above 23,000 feet before.

After the ascent, the pilot began working through his checking chores. All progressed well up to the point that he was checking front-wing slat extension. In order to check slats—usually used when landing—he had to slow his jet substantially. The pilot "retarded throttles," then extended his slats and looked over his shoulder to visually check—by looking out through the canopy glass—that the slat had moved position. In order to do this, it was inevitable that the pilot's attention would be temporarily away from the main flight controls and cockpit instruments.

Having observed the slats, the pilot turned back towards the flight controls and instruments, at which moment he immediately realized that he had entered a stall. At this, the pilot began a standard stall recovery: level the wings, nose level, and throttles to maximum available.

Unfortunately, as the pilot looked down at his two engine r.p.m. gauges, he saw that both needles were not indicating increased engine power, but in fact both were "winding back" towards idle, with all other relevant gages also decreasing (tachometer, turbine air temp, etc.).

At this, the pilot began to presume that somehow or other he had had both engines flame out on him simultaneously—meaning both had turned off for an unknown reason and so should be restarted.

As he went through flame-out or compressor stall restart, it began to dawn on the pilot that he had lost both his engines, at which he went through an emergency restart—his "boldface" emergency procedures—but it was no use; the engines were not restarting at all.

All the while the gliding jet was descending.

After a number of further restart efforts—last time he tried he was at only 2,600 feet—the pilot began to resign himself to an emergency ejection and the requirement to ditch his plane.

At first he began to maneuver his gliding jet towards a designated official bailout area over U.S. military land, but within seconds he realized that there was not the time available: he was going down fast.

The pilot looked down in search of uninhabited land and saw below a deserted sand quarry between Moultrie and Valdosta in Cook County, about twenty miles west of Moody.

With crash-course set down towards the quarry, the pilot checked his emergency egress seating position and firmly pulled his ejection handle.

Seconds later, at around a quarter to three, his $15-million A-10 crashed to earth in the sand quarry and burst into a post-crash fireball.

Larry Taylor, a nearby resident, rode out on a golf cart with his nephew to check on the accident. At the scene he found the pilot unharmed with his parachute next to him.

Larry Taylor: "He [the pilot] said that both engines quit; he said he coasted for two miles apparently. He seemed shaken up, but was laughing and carrying-on. He was shaken up, but that seemed natural considering what happened."

Taylor used his golf cart to transport the pilot to the nearest main road.

Colonel Billy Thompson, Squadron Commander of the 23rd Wing at Moody Air Force Base, said immediately after the crash: "The A-10, as a whole, is a highly reliable aircraft. The A-10 is a wonderfully reliable aircraft. All of our aircraft are obviously inspected before each flight, but I don't have any further data at this point."

The ensuing investigation concluded that the only possible explanation was a double engine-core seizure, something unknown to the A-10. In fact, the Investigators could find only one comparable such case, and this in civil aviation.

Although it was deemed a noncausal factor by the Investigators, it is worth noting that the pilot tested positive for amphetamines or speed. He had taken "go pills" before the flight, a factor which was not troubling to the Investigators, as the taking of such pills by USAF crews is somewhat entrenched—particularly for early-start missions.

13 Walan Rabat

Location: Walan Rabat Landing Zone
Date: 18 December 2011
Aircraft type: M-28 Skytruck
Fatalities: none
Cost of damage: $12.3 million

A significant component of modern warfare as it is carried on by the U.S. military is relentless small one-off clandestine missions.

These missions are not necessarily briefed in the context of any particular "hostility," but rather with no end or beginning: as responses to threats uncovered by intelligence gathered by satellite, by overflying, and from the work operative in the field, i.e., spying.

Many U.S. military operations carried out around the world—countless individual missions—are Special Operations. "Special Ops" forces

The wreckage of a PZL M28 Skytruck in use by U.S. Special Operations. The accident happened as the M28 landed at the remote Walan Rabat Landing Zone in Zabul province, Afghanistan. The LZ was a "semi-prepared" 1500-foot-long stretch of bare light-brown soil and sand over smooth rock on an incline of three degrees between mountains rising steeply all around it.

working clandestinely—their most famous mission in the 21st century being the secret mission into Pakistan to carry out the execution of Usama ibn Ladin—or Osama bin Laden, or to the U.S. military, ever ready with a new acronym, OBL—at his home or "compound" in Abbottabad on 2 May 2011. The mission *was* secret but many details were eventually made public because of the significance of the target.

Special Operations Forces operate with a very definite impunity: many Special Operations missions are only scantily documented, known about by a few higher-ups and those on the mission itself, and are far beyond the oversight of democracy.

Soon after the events of 9/11—the attacks on the U.S. by a group of terrorists, the U.S. launched a full-scale conventional ground invasion into Afghanistan with its stated mission being the removal from power and destruction of a quasi-state operator known in the west as the Taliban. The first missions began the day after 9/11.

A complete picture of U.S. operations in Afghanistan would include conventional military operations as well as the clandestine Special Ops missions ongoing through sixteen years (as of 2017).

Several USAF squadrons take on the task of flying Special Ops forces to where they need to be and flying them home again.

During December 2011, U.S. Special Ops were active in the Afghan province of Zabul—a remote and sparsely populated mountainous region of Afghanistan. On 18 December, a USAF Special Ops support crew, based at Kandahar Air Base, were tasked with a non-combat ferrying mission with four legs.

The crew of three—pilot; copilot; loadmaster—would be flying an unmarked PZL M-28 Skytruck—a commuter plane of Polish origin. (Unmarked means not recognizable or identifiable as a warplane in any way; the only evidence of its being in use by the USAF were modifications in the cockpit, including military avionics.) The M-28 is a rather bland-looking plane with the general appearance of an unremarkable small aircraft that might be spotted at any provincial-rural or metropolitan airport—white and marine-blue with a narrow sky-blue stripe along the length of the fuselage. The quality of the plane that makes it appealing to Special Ops—apart from its not being a recognizable military plane—is its STOL capability, or short takeoff and landing: the M-28 was designed precisely to land in remote locations on improvised landing strips.

The sortie required that four Special Ops be picked up with their kit from another U.S. base near Qalati Ghilj—known as Qalāt, Kalat, or, to the U.S. military, simply Qalat—and flown on to their destination in Zabul.

13 Walan Rabat

The arrangements for the drop-off in Zabul were that the M-28 should land on a bare-soil landing strip in the mountains designated as Walan Rabat Landing Zone. The landing zone or LZ was in no way a conventional runway, but rather a flat-enough stretch of land that had been sprayed and painted up with runway markings—actually only one week before the day of the mission. Operations in the Zabul area were intensifying, and the crew had flown missions out to Walan Rabat twice already during the preceding week.

Walan Rabat Landing Zone is a definitely austere and desolate place to land a plane: 5,000 feet above sea level; a 1,500-foot-long stretch of bare light-brown soil and sand over smooth rock; on an incline of three degrees rising. Beyond the runway, about a mile away to the north, is a 1,600-foot-high mountain.

Officially Walan Rabat is "a 31-foot wide, semi-prepared dirt strip with poorly defined boundaries." The Landing Zone was surveyed by U.S. forces and declared a usable airstrip on December 11, 2011, with a note in the survey-report highlighting the fact that winds often cause two inches of loose soil or "moondust" to accumulate on the strip itself—extremely light and uncompacted, sandy topsoil.

On the day of the mission, takeoff for the flight to Qalat was scheduled for two o'clock in the afternoon. The crew spent the morning involved in admin tasks as well as planning out the mission.

The wind at the zone, it was noted, would be a tailwind of around twenty miles per hour—close to maximum safe gusting speed for the small commuter turboprop.

All pre-flight activity progressed unremarkably. "The pilot awoke at 9:00 and went to the joint operation center, made a few phone calls, and ensured the day's mission was still on track. The pilot then went to the gym and returned to the M-28 planning room at 11:30."

The M-28 departed Kandahar at 14:09 p.m.—a nine-minute delay due to airfield congestion. The short flight to Qalat airstrip was carried out successfully, with the four Special Ops forces safely onloaded with their kit.

The second leg was the flight to the Walan Rabat zone—about 120 miles flying northeast out of Kandahar. This also passed off without incident up until the M-28 was about seven minutes out from the Zone.

As they were descending in on landing approach, there was some discussion about the winds. They were on the limit for a safe landing, that was known, but turning around and going back to Qalat was not under discussion. The copilot was somewhat remiss in that he had left his wind calculation charts in the back of the plane and could reach them in order to do any precise calculations for the pilot when requested to do so.

As the plane continued its descent in to Walan Rabat, both the front-cockpit crew were struggling to get any sort of visual on the LZ: as they flew in on the correct course, it was not possible to discern any marked-up airstrip.

About a mile out, the copilot commented to his pilot that that he was "still drugin' looking," for any markings on the ground. To which the pilot acknowledged with, "Yep, this one will be drug in."

Only thirteen seconds before landing, the pilot and copilot declared in unison "negative box": they could not get a visual on the landing zone's ground markings. At only three hundred yards out—six seconds before landing—both suddenly proclaimed: "Got the zone!" And the pilot clarified: "Coming back to centerline."

Then, "shortly after the cockpit voice recorder records the sounds of the aircraft landing for five seconds followed by a loud yell from an unidentified crewmember as the recording ends."

The plane came down hard. For two or three seconds the landing seemed good, but moments later the plane careered off the prepared stretch of land and into much bumpier ground—the strip was only 31 feet wide. As the plane entered the uneven terrain, it bounced over rocky ground until—within a few seconds—the front landing gear collapsed, causing the plane to "summersault [sic] forward, tail-over-nose, coming to rest upside down, just off the right edge of the landing zone at approximately midfield."

There were no serious injuries, but the plane was a hissing, creaking wreck of twisted metal, cabling, and pipework. The lost aircraft was later valued at $12.3 million.

The mishap crew and passengers (seven in total) exited the wreckage of the aircraft through the copilot's window with the pilot heaving himself out last.

A rescue mission was soon underway: an HH-60 Pave Hawk, Special Ops-specific helicopter arrived and landed close to the zone later that afternoon.

Unfortunately, as the rescuing HH-60 was departing Walan Rabat, with all seven rescued from the crashed M-28 aboard, it too crashed—during takeoff. Another hard landing: the four Special Ops and the three support crew had crashed twice in one day. For the second time in a day, all on board survived the crash with only minor injuries. The worst of these were suffered by the copilot, who was "thrown from the HH-60 during the crash and was partially pinned underneath some wreckage."

14 Overshoot Shank

Location: Forward Operating Base Shank, Afghanistan
Date: 23 January 2012
Aircraft type: C-17
Fatalities: none
Cost of damage: $200 million

In January 2012, the 437th Airlift Wing was on deployment from its home at Joint Base Charleston, South Carolina, to Al Udeid Air Base, Qatar, southwest of Doha—nominally a Qatar Emiri Air Force Base, but *de facto* a U.S. Air Base.

The 437th flies, among other aircraft, the Boeing C-17 Globemaster. This "massive long-haul military transport aircraft tackles distance, destination and heavy, oversized payloads in unpredictable conditions … it can carry large equipment, supplies and troops directly to small airfields in harsh terrain anywhere in the world." In addition, "the C-17 is capable of rapid strategic delivery of troops and all types of cargo to main operating bases or directly to forward bases in the deployment area … the inherent flexibility and performance of the C-17 force improve the ability of the total airlift system to fulfill the worldwide air mobility requirements of the U.S."

The C-17's cargo is loaded via a large rear ("aft") door: 85 tons per full load. And once loaded it can fly the load wherever it may be needed at 520 m.p.h. (mach 0.7). Each new C-17 costs the U.S. military $200 million; as of 2017 there were 187 on the inventory.

On 22 January 2012, a C-17 crew of six—pilot; copilot; first pilot; loadmaster 1; loadmaster 2; flying crew chief—were handed their mission for 23 January. It was to consist of three flown legs.

First, the designated C-17—MOOSE89—was to take off from Al Udeid Air Base and fly four hundred miles northwest up through the Persian Gulf along the coast of Saudi Arabia to Kuwait City International Airport. In Kuwait, fifty tons of cargo was to be onloaded (around 75 percent capacity), as well as twenty tons of fuel (bringing it to near max capacity). Second, the C-17 was to depart Kuwait City Airport bound for Forward Operating Base Shank, near Pul-E Alam, in Logar Province, Afghanistan— where the cargo was to be offloaded. Finally, the C-17 was to RTB (return to base) in Qatar.

The wreck of a C-17 Globemaster that overshot the runway and "departed the prepared surface" at Forward Operating Base Shank, in Eastern Afghanistan.

The U.S. Forward Operating Base Shank is an extremely desolate military outpost, at 6,600 feet above sea level on an area of flatland in mountainous and barren terrain in the wilderness of uninhabited rural Afghanistan. The base itself is rudimentary: there is the runway; a heavily fortified perimeter formed of two-foot-thick concrete-block wall-sections; a row of wooden cabins; and a concrete control tower. During the winter months, given the altitude, to keep it usable, crews working in shifts are required to clear snow from the runway and spray it with deicer chemical solution at least three times a day.

The 23 January cargo-moving mission was a graveyard shift job with takeoff from Qatar at 3:30 a.m. The C-17 thundered off en route to Kuwait, completing the flight in one hour and fifteen minutes.

The route for that early morning's cargo shifting is indicative of the USAF's transnational or trans-border ethos: that flight was *between U.S. bases*, and that these were located in three different sovereign countries and required passage through the airspace of a fourth (Saudi Arabia), was so ordinary that it was not remarkable. The USAF carries on this way around the world every day.

The onload at Kuwait took several hours: many metal Tricon containers full of U.S. materiel had to be forklifted in and securely strapped in place. It was not actually until after dawn that the hulking jet taxied out to the runway at Kuwait City—07:37.

14 Overshoot Shank

The jet passed into the nominally hostile airspace of Afghanistan mid-morning, at 11:00 a.m., crossing a time zone (plus one-hour-thirty) as they went. The pilot then briefed all crew for a Combat Entry. The Combat Entry discussion was in truth a technicality and was soon dealt with.

A more pressing matter, with the C-17 at 28,000 feet, and about to descend into Shank near fully laden, was the status and condition of the runway. And to find out more about this, the copilot began a discussion with the air traffic control tower on the ground.

The news coming back from the tower was that the beginning section of the runway was possibly closed for maintenance and that the surface was recently deiced. The tower at Shank was not in clear view of the entire runway, so some of the information was being provided to the incoming C-17 after calling on walkie-talkie to the supervisor of the Exelis contract team who were responsible for clearing snow and deicing.

After the radio discussion, the tower was still not completely certain of the current status of the runway and so asked the Pilot to take a view of the circumstances on final approach:

> COPILOT: "I'd like to confirm that the full length of the runway will be usable. We're going to need full length to land."
> TOWER: "That's a negative, sir, full length landing will be at pilot's own discretion due to personnel and equipment east of the tower, and that area is not visible from the tower."

The tower then suggested that it might be worth flying in the first time as a touch-and-go, and then do a go-around (immediately take off and circle around) in order for the copilot to familiarize himself with the landing conditions.

Then, one minute later, the discussion began again:

> TOWER: "MOOSE89 did you copy, full length will be at pilot's discretion."
> COPILOT: "Affirmative ... we'll need the full length. Did you say you can coordinate the [maintenance] personnel to be out of the way, though?"
> TOWER: "MOOSE89, stand by, we'll contact airfield management."

At this stage the C-17 was well into its descent towards the landing strip. As it leveled off at 17,000 feet the tower came back on the radio.

> TOWER: "They're basically saying the same thing, sir, they said you can do a low approach or a touch-and-go if you need to, sir, they would not move the equipment, they are unable to...."

At the end of the discussion with the tower, the pilot and copilot were also required to adjudge the runway condition, which they thought would be wet, probably with slushy snow on it in places. The runway was deemed "fair."

When the captain called "fair," it was incumbent on the copilot to transpose that to an RCR, or Runway Conditions Reading, of around 12, whereas a perfectly dry runway would be 23. Once this figure is punched into the mission computer, the display will flash up the length of runway-in-feet required to land. With RCR readings, if no number flashes back up, then it means: not enough runway available.

For some reason, immediately upon the getting his RCR number from the pilot's "fair," the copilot typed in his 12, but did not successfully enter it. It is unclear what happened in those moments to distract him, but the readings coming out of the computer were still based on a 23 setting—a bone-dry runway.

During these moments the pilot asked the copilot for his opinion on the runway-length-required issue:

> PILOT: "What's your thoughts on this runway thing he's talking about? We have to land 1200 feet down?"
> COPILOT: "They've been there the whole time, they are not on the runway.... I think ... if we see anything that looks fishy we'll go around."

As these conversations were completed—somehow quite inconclusively—the pilot was well into final approach, and all attention in the cockpit turned to visually acquiring the runway.

At 12:15 p.m. the copilot acquired the landing environment, but not the runway: "I'm not making out the runway yet though. I think I'm seeing it but it actually just looks pretty, like snow-covered, but I think it's just white."

Just before landing, the tower issued another "pilot's discretion" disclaimer, and the copilot responded: "MOOSE89 is gear down, cleared to land and understand all."

At 12:17 p.m. the cockpit conversation continued:

> COPILOT: "I've got the runway in sight so it looks like..."
> PILOT [finishing the copilot's sentence]: "Black [tarmac] and little pieces of white [snow]."

At 12:19 p.m. the C-17 touched down at Shank about 1,200 feet from the beginning of the runway (they had avoided the closed portion after all). The copilot turned on the thrust reversers of his four jets, opened the wing spoilers and applied the brakes: "Good, ground spoilers ... four blue ... brakes."

All was well except for the fact that required stopping distance, given the near-capacity weight and the snowy-icy surface, was further than the 5,925 feet of runway available. MOOSE89 actually needed a minimum 6,047 feet—if it were a clean and dry runway, which it wasn't.

Even with all ground-speed-retarding measures operational, the plane continued along the full length of the runway and simply continued traveling. As the leader of the salvage operation later pointed out: "For a combination of reasons ... the aircraft went over the end of the runway."

The jet sped on across 700 feet of semi-prepared surface until its forward motion was finally impeded by impact with a low ski ramp used for drone launches. When the jet came to a complete standstill, the copilot called: "Evacuate! Evacuate! Evacuate!" At which all aboard left the aircraft—some using the ditching hatch in the roof, since the plane was down on its belly. There were no serious injuries.

The C-17 sustained significant damage to landing gear, cargo floor, undercarriage, antennas, and other "main structural components." Initially the total cost of repair was estimated at $69.4 million; shortly afterward, the figure was corrected when the plane was declared unrepairable—bringing the total cost of the accident to $200 million.

15 Paddy field

Location: 150 miles south of Seoul
Date: 21 March 2012
Aircraft type: F-16
Fatalities: none
Cost of damage: $21.8 Million

During the Korean War, 1950–53, North Korea (backed by China and the Soviet Union) and South Korea (backed by a U.S.-led coalition) were at war. Since that time the U.S. has retained strategic air bases in South Korea. The main perceived threat is an attack on South Korea by North Korea—a bleak totalitarian pariah state with an unpredictable dictator ruling a population of around twenty-five million.

The USAF strike-ready force based in South Korea is permanent. One of the U.S. air bases in South Korea is Osan Air Base, "providing combat ready forces for close air-support, air-strike control, counter-air interdiction, theater-airlift, and communications, in the defense of the Republic of Korea."

In the spring of each year in South Korea, "Foal Eagle," a significant U.S. military training exercise, takes place. U.S. forces link with the South Korean military—including at least 200,000 troops—in a large-scale scene of simulated attacks. The simulations closely and transparently model likely scenarios in any potential future military conflict with North Korea.

Within the greater context of "Foal Eagle," on 21 March 2012, two F-16 pilots had been tasked to fly a "two-ship" training sortie—two jets going out as a pair. The mission was to train in "unopposed air interdiction," also called deep air-support—the process of overflying an enemy territory and attacking any structure or place which, although not explicitly a military installation, will still be of use to a hostile military operation during wartime. Targets might include civilian communications towers or bridges.

The two jets took off from Osan Air Base at 11:30 a.m., and the training carried on as expected for about thirty-seven minutes. At 12:07 p.m., while one of the two unnamed pilots was maneuvering for a simulated attack, flying at 470 m.p.h. at an altitude of 16,000 feet, he "heard a loud bang followed by subsequently quieter bangs and noticed rapidly decreasing jet-RPM and rapidly increasing fan-turbine-inlet temperature." The F-16 has only one engine.

The stricken pilot immediately spoke over his radio intercom to his wingman: "Knock it off! Knock it off!"—a formal phrase imparting an urgent need to cease a training exercise.

An F-16 has only one engine, but it can glide without power for a short distance, and it is possible, if necessary, to land "engine out," meaning without power—the only requirement being the presence below of a runway within range. As a rough guide, an F-16 can glide one mile for every 1000 feet of altitude. A jet at 20,000 feet will glide "engine out" for a distance of only about twenty miles in order to reach a suitable airstrip or runway to make a forced landing.

On the 21 March sortie, the malfunctioning jet was around a hundred miles south of Osan and actually quite close to Kunsan Air Base—the other principal U.S. air base in South Korea—when the engine died. The engine-out pilot quickly calculated: he was only thirty-four miles from Kunsan. At 16,000 feet, he was near but not near enough; his maximum safe range would be 16 to 20 miles.

Undaunted, the pilot set course for Kunsan, and as the plane continued to glide "engine out," he attempted several mid-air restarts—a procedure known as a "flame out" restart. Given the clanking-rumbling bang that he had heard, the pilot was well aware as he went through his windmill-restart and flame-out checklist that his jet was unlikely to restart.

15 Paddy field

Six minutes after the initial loud bang, at 12:13 p.m. the pilot crossed into the lowest safe ejection altitude of around 2,000 feet. He leveled his wings at 1,600 feet and 225 m.p.h, and pulled his ejection handle. He was blasted up and away from his now doomed aircraft.

One minute later, at 12:14 p.m., the F-16 at low speed and 20 degrees nose-low, crashed in rural farmland in the South Korean countryside. "The impact site was a semi-dry rice field consisting of wet clay ... located on the south side of a river," in the area of Hwachon-ri, Hwayang-myeon, Seocheon-gun, and Chungcheongnam-do, about 150 miles south of Seoul.

The ejection was successful with a "good chute," or parachute opening without complications. As the pilot regained his spatial awareness following the temporary disorientation during the moments of the blast-clear, he quickly became aware of a predicament: he was parachuting towards the ground from only around 1,000 feet with the Geum River below him. The Geum is one of the of the largest waterways in South Korea: it is more than a mile across as it passes farmland at Hwachon-ri, Hwayang-myeon, Seocheon-gun, and Chungcheongnam-do—the spot where the pilot was coming down. Fortunately the pilot was able to successfully steer his parachute: he "landed on the north bank of the river in a flat field." Upon landing, the pilot spent several minutes spreading out his parachute canopy on the ground in order to create an obvious visual cue for airborne search and rescue—as is required if conditions allow.

He was soon recovered by the 6th Search and Rescue Squadron operating out of Chong-Ju Air Base and was transported via HH-60 helicopter to Kunsan Air Base medical clinic for examination. It was determined that he had sustained no injuries.

The F-16 that crashed in to a paddy field was powered by a General Electric F110 turbofan engine. The Accident Investigation Panel examined the engine wreckage and the existing maintenance documentation.

Their findings were conclusive. In early 2011, about a year before the paddy field crash, the engine was installed on a different F-16 jet. In the USAF a jet engine is quite independent of any particular aircraft and has its own schedule of maintenance and installation history.

During this previous installation at Osan Air Base, there were some obsolete painted ground-markings that were required to be altered, including some "in and around" the F-16 hangars. These painted markings were removed by the use of shot-blasting equipment, which was rather effective, but which left quite a bit of residue of the highly abrasive tiny metal balls ("shot") that the system sprayed out. This residue was not *completely* removed from the floor of the hangars, and some of it had, unfortunately, been sucked into the main air intake of the jet engine that later became faulty.

Once it had entered the jet's air-movement system, the abrasive residue had in effect "shot blasted" the jet's delicate compressor-rotors, causing foreign-object damage that was identified during a routine borescope inspection. (A borescope is rather like a medical endoscope: a video camera on the end of a thin flexible cable for use in inspecting deep inside precision machinery.)

Once the shot-blast damage had been observed, the F110 jet engine was removed from that particular F-16 (on February 28, 2011), and time-tabled for restoration.

A significant portion of a jet engine is the machinery of compression: air is sucked in and intensely compressed before being mixed with combusting jet fuel in order to create the "thrust" that allows the aircraft its impressive forward movement.

To compress the air entering the jet, rings of spinning rotor airfoil blades are alternated with stationary rings, or stator vanes. In the case of the shot-blasting foreign-object damage to this particular engine, it was certain of the stator vanes which were requiring attention. And this being the case, once under repair in the shop, certain of the stator rings or "stages" were removed in order that some of its individual airfoils could be replaced.

At that time at Osan, the engineers assigned to the task at hand were somewhat underqualified: the leader of the team was fully qualified, but she had only one year's experience on F110s—which is considered marginal. The three other members of her repairs team were not sufficiently qualified to be deconstructing a $15 million jet engine. The first of the three had only recently finished technical college; the second was a "journeyman" and was not officially qualified to repair F110s; the third had very little experience and few verifiable engineering qualifications. His training as regards F110s had been in the form of "look-and-learn" or "on-the-job" training.

As the team went about replacing the damaged airfoils, one of the three-foot-diameter stator vane stages fell out of the engine as it was under repair. The incident was later recalled by some of the team as memorable, as it hit one of them in the chest as it fell. Also, as the new replacement airfoil blades were inserted, at least two were inserted incorrectly, with one being inserted back-to-front or "inverted 180," a mistake that was not noticed at the time.

Following the repair, the engine was inspected and tested on several occasions, finally being logged as spare and available on 7 September 2011.

The engine remained in storage at Osan for six months, until, on 17 February 2012, it was installed into the jet that suffered a catastrophic engine failure during a training exercise on 21 March 2012.

The destroyed jet was later valued at $21.6 million. Reparations and compensation paid by the USAF to farmland owners was $187,419.

16 Communications mast

Location: near Al Dhafra Air Base, UAE
Date: 28 March 2012
Aircraft type: F-15
Fatalities: 1
Cost of damage: $47.1 million

The role of the F-15 "Strike Eagle" in warfare is to fly into hostile airspace—over enemy territory—at supersonic speed towards a given target for an air-to-ground attack. Once the target is reached, the F-15 will launch-release its weapons ("the F-15 can carry most weapons in the Air Force inventory"). The capability of the F-15 is distinguishable from a conventional bomber in that the F-15 can "fight its way to a target ... and fight its way out."

The crew of an F-15 comprises two persons sitting one behind the other, the pilot at the front and behind him the WSO, or weapons systems officer. This second-seat role includes numerous navigation responsibilities beyond the obvious duty of launching bombs and missiles (including Sidewinder air-to-air intercept-attack missiles). The WSO specializes in navigation but is perfectly competent to fly the jet.

Al Dhafra Air Base (on the outskirts of Abu Dhabi in the United Arab Emirates or UAE) and Camp Lemonnier (in Djibouti, a small country in Africa with a total population of 800,000) are two "forward" U.S. military bases, from which missions into Somalia, Syria, Yemen, Iraq, Iran, or Afghanistan may be launched.

Part of the strike-ready force at Al Dhafra is at least one squadron of F-15 Strike Eagle fighter jets. U.S. activities at both of the bases are rarely publicized and are often designated as secret.

On the night of Wednesday, 28 March 2012, a group ("package") of

Ground view of the communications mast near Al Dhafra Air Base in the UAE, which was struck by a low-flying F-15 during a training mission in 2012.

thirty-five warplanes were flying an air interdiction night training mission out of Al Dhafra (the specific location is redacted from the official Accident Report, but is cited in various other sources including the reliable Aviation-safety online resource).

The thirty-five jets were divided in initially into two groups: twenty-seven flying as "Blue Air" would seek to gain access to specific targets, while a group of eight flying as "Red Air" would attempt to block them and counterattack. (The color-coding of the two groups is not intended to carry any particular meaning, but of course the color red is symbolic in that it is the color associated with communism—and the communist enemy of the Cold War, the Soviet Union.)

This particular training mission was taking place out over the million-square-mile wilderness of the Arabian Desert during darkness. Even with their NVGs (night-vision goggles) on, the pilots had been briefed that it was going to be "pretty dark." In terms of visual references on the ground—cultural references—there was not going be much around, and when flying at altitude it was likely that for the pilot there would be no visually discernable horizon. This more-extreme-than-usual darkness factor had been repeated several times during different aspects of the pre-flight commentaries and briefings. The crews had also been briefed to expect further

16 Communications mast

limitations to visibility below 10,000 feet caused by wind-blown sand and particles.

One of the crews that evening was two unnamed airmen flying an F-15 with a tail-number ending with the sequence 2035. During the early evening their mission got off to an annoying start: the first jet they made their way to ("stepped" to) was not crew-ready when the airmen arrived. Then, when a second jet was designated, that F-15 had technical problems around the oil gauge. So it was the third tail-number—2035—that they actually boarded and got underway with the training mission.

The basic plan for the mission was for the jets to depart Al Dhafra and gather as group (a "strike package") in a holding pattern before commencing a formidable coordinated attack. For such a mission, the key timing given to crews is the "time on target," the time at which the jet should be directly over its intended target.

On the way out, both men were wearing night vision goggles but even with these infrared imaging devices there was not much to see: it was just dark desert below. Later, when interviewed about the mission, some others in other jets remembered that with NVGs on, they could discern the stars in the night sky, but that was all.

The main mission that evening progressed uneventfully until just before eight o'clock during the return to base (RTB) portion of the mission.

The RTB for such a large number of planes is the job of the air-traffic controller. The controller is in regular contact with each plane seeking to land. The jets on this evening were flying in various holding positions out over desert at 1000-foot intervals with descent into base being achieved by dropping down a number of 1000-foot steps upon the instruction of air-traffic.

Aircraft 2035 had already descended down to 4,000 feet and was cleared to descend to 3,000 feet ahead of final runway approach at three minutes past eight o'clock.

All progressed unremarkably up until the pilot passed through 3,100 feet. As he did so, "the pilot pulsed the control stick backwards and forwards. This caused a quick pitch up and then a pitch down of the aircraft. The pilot simultaneously pushed the throttles forward from less than full power to full afterburner for two seconds." Following this unexpected maneuvering, "the pilot then aggressively pushed the control stick forward inducing a [substantial] negative-2.6 gravitational force on the aircraft." Next, "the pilot expressed verbal concern about what was going on around him, pulled the throttles back to less than full power and rolled the aircraft left." From there the pilot continued to express frustrations about his positioning and rolled the jet again several times.

The WSO, sitting immediately behind the pilot, was dumbfounded at what he was witnessing. When discussing it later, he recalled being afraid that any comment from him might make he unfolding situation worse. Sensing the jet roll for a third time, the WSO adjudged that the pilot "did not know which way was up" and grabbed his mirror controls.

The WSO took control of the jet and began to draw the jet towards a wings-level position. As he was leveling the wings, the automatic alert systems of the jet—both visual and audible—entered emergency ground-collision warning, with the visual displays suddenly taken over by a large pointing arrow indicating the fastest way to pull up to the horizon. The WSO used his control stick, following the guidance of the arrow in a maneuver that pulled the jet through 11-G force. As the WSO checked back to the cockpit visual displays, his altimeter reading was 88 feet. He instantly recognized that ground impact was inevitable and pulled hard on his emergency ejection handle. Both crew were automatically blasted up and away from the jet. Exactly 0.8 of one second later, the jet smashed into a communications tower on the ground and was destroyed.

Sadly, and unfortunately, during an automatic dual-seat ejection the front seat departs the aircraft a half-second after the rear one. The jet was already crashing as the second (front) seat departed, and the blast was not enough for the pilot's seat to clear the comms tower. The pilot's seat was catapulted away from the jet with explosive force; he was carried up and away from his aircraft, but also up and into one of the tall rigid steel structures within a group of radio masts on the ground and was killed.

The WSO's quick action had saved his life with less than a second to spare—he was thrown clear and parachuted down to the ground about fifty feet from the crash site. The total time from the pilot's first unexpected pitch-up-pitch-down maneuver to impact was eleven seconds.

The horrifying events of the evening were compounded further when a first-response search-and-rescue helicopter—a UAE Air Force helicopter—crash-landed at the site (suffered a "hard landing") and could not take off again. Eventually the WSO was flown to a military hospital and was later discharged with minor injuries.

The Accident Investigation sought reasons for the pilot's becoming spatially disorientated and noted that he was flying without the aid of several on-board visual display systems that would have made total disorientation very unlikely. The main one of these was the Electronic Attitude Director-Indicator, or EADI, "the primary source of aircraft attitude." As far as could be ascertained later, the pilot of 2035 was flying without his EADI on, and was (it seems) using only his head-up display to fly the plane.

In addition to his unconventional use of—or disdain for—several of the in-cockpit information streams, it was also surmised that the pilot had seen before him at some moment the largest of the comms towers, and its physical architecture had possibly functioned as an optical illusion. Its pronounced "Y" shape possibly appearing, confusingly to an onrushing jet pilot, as an upside-down or inverted conventional steel pylon.

The lost plane was later valued at $47.1 million.

17 Titanium fire

Location: 65 miles south of Al Dhafra Air Base
Date: 3 May 2012
Aircraft type: F-15
Fatalities: none
Cost of damage: $45.5 million

Al Dhafra Air Base in the UAE, twenty miles to the southwest of Abu Dhabi, is a USAF "forward base."

The 380th Air Expeditionary Wing is stationed at Al Dhafra. One of the jets that the 380th flies is the F-15 Strike Eagle. Like the F-16, the F-15 is one of the basic USAF attack aircraft. The F-15 "can penetrate enemy defense and outperform and outfight any current enemy aircraft." Fully laden for a combat mission, the F-15 can carry eleven tons of bombs. The F-15 has a crew of two: the pilot and the weapons systems operator, or WSO, who is responsible for target selection and navigation.

On 3 May 2012, one of the activities out of the base was a significant training sortie. The mission was a simulated attack-defend exercise with six simulated hostile F-15s or "Red Air" jets attempting to drop bombs overhead of certain agreed spots, with a substantial number ("package") of friendly fighter jets seeking to thwart their advance—eight F-15s flying as "Blue Air."

One of the Red Air simulated bogeys was an F-15 with callsign DALLAS22.

The DALLAS22 crew "showed," or reported ready for work, at 7:20 a.m. After the various briefings and preflight activities, the airmen made their way to the aircraft with takeoff from base at 10:29. The surface

Ground view of the crash site of a destroyed F-15 that crashed 70 degrees nose-low and inverted into an area of barren uninhabited land in the Arabian Desert, around 65 miles south of Abu Dhabi.

temperature at the time of takeoff was 97 degrees Fahrenheit (36 degrees Celsius) with dust and haze over the desert at low altitudes—a typically hot and dry morning in the Emirates.

At 10:50 a.m., the simulated air battle began with DALLAS22 repeatedly attempting to gain access to their designated notional spot.

At one moment during the training, the Red Air jet that DALLAS22 was paired with for the day was simulated shot down, and this left DALLAS22 somewhat exposed. Soon after the simulated shoot-down of his "wingman," the pilot of DALLAS22 maneuvered and began a full afterburner ascent from 2,400 feet up to around 10,000 feet—to gain thinking space and a chance to consider attack options. The jet was flying at close to supersonic speed, so the climb was expected to take just a few seconds.

The pilot pulled firmly back on his control stick to lift the jet's nose 25 degrees and placed both jet engine throttles to full or AB—afterburner. At around 5,500 feet in the midst of the afterburner climb, both the pilot and WSO "heard a loud bang." Immediately after the loud bang, the jet's nose began "shaking up and down," and the plane, uncommanded, began rolling and yawing to the right.

Moments after the initial loud bang, the pilot consulted his right engine temperature gauge. It was winding up precipitously: 2,400 Fahren-

17 Titanium fire

heit and rising. DALLAS22's pilot first brought his right-side engine throttle to idle position, and then, shortly after, to shut-off position. The F-15 is airworthy with one engine turned off or lost due to damage or mechanical failure; it can be flown "engine out" or "one out."

The pilot began to fly full-left-stick, full-left-rudder in an effort to retain level flight. Then, at 7,000 feet and around 400 m.p.h., DALLAS22 suddenly rolled violently to the right, at which the Pilot called: "Bailout! Bailout! Bailout!" to the WSO. Then, moments later, he had second thoughts and commanded, "Hang on!"

The pilot was concerned to get the jet as near to wings-level as possible before ejection, so he continued for a few moments to struggle with the aircraft: he was determined to get an attitude and speed that it would be advantageous for ejection.

Immediately after the pilot's "Hang on!" both crew began to be inundated with warning and caution messages and alerts, the most apparent and insistent of which was the audible in-cockpit voice message: "Warning, warning: engine-fire right.... Warning, warning: engine fire-right.... Warning, warning: burn-through right.... Warning, warning: accessory drive fire." In the same few moments, both crew turned to see through the canopy: smoke was pouring out of the right side intake vent. At this, the pilot instantly deployed his right-side fire extinguisher system.

As both the pilot and WSO looked back across to their display screens, the cautions confronting them began to increase to the point of becoming overwhelming. Both occupants were aware of "an excessive number of" warnings and cautions being issued, to the extent that these were "too numerous to be individually addressed."

Seconds later, both the pilot and WSO looked over to see an intense fire burning on the right wing with bright flames shooting from the right-side Pratt & Whitney F100: the fire-extinguisher system had had little or no effect.

In these moments—during the command "Hang on"—the jet suddenly suffered a complete on-board electrical failure, including all in-flight radio communications systems.

With the fire on the wing raging and all electrical power gone, the pilot recognized that further efforts to gain controlled flight were futile. Without any intercom, he turned in his seat to perform the "bailout" hand signal. The jet was near-level at 7,000 feet at a speed of 460 m.p.h. The pilot pulled hard on his ejection lever, rapidly catapulting the two up and away from the stricken plane.

Fifteen seconds later, the aircraft—70 degrees nose-low and upside down—crashed into an area of barren uninhabited land in the Arabian Desert around sixty-five miles south of Abu Dhabi.

Both crew members had a "good chute," and both landed unharmed shortly before midday.

A few minutes later, the two walked towards and entered an abandoned outbuilding in the desert in order to gain shade from the harsh and intense heat of the noon sun. At 12:20 p.m. a UAE search-and-rescue helicopter landed close to the outbuilding and took the two aboard.

During the Accident Investigation, any initial cause of the catastrophic jet-engine fire could not be determined conclusively.

It was, however, determined that at some moment during the fire, certain titanium-metal-based components ignited ("a rare ignition of the titanium components within the engine resulting in an extremely destructive fire"). Titanium burns extremely fiercely, reaching temperatures of 6,000 degrees Fahrenheit. The burning mass of molten titanium was soon "burning through the engine casing and into the fuselage." The molten mass at such temperatures could not be contained by any safety design or feature, including the on-board fire extinguishers, and the fire soon began to cause "catastrophic ... thermal damage, leading to associated failure of critical hydraulic and electrical systems."

The final conclusion reached by the Investigation Panel was that "an unidentified component failed for an unknown reason during normal engine operation."

The lost F-15 was later valued at $45.5 million.

18 Belly flop

Location: Tyndall Air Force Base, Florida
Date: 31 May 2012
Aircraft type: F-22 Raptor
Fatalities: none
Cost of damage: $35 million

The USAF describes the F-22 Raptor as "the Air Force's newest fighter aircraft ... its combination of stealth, supercruise, maneuverability, and integrated avionics, coupled with improved supportability, represents an exponential leap in warfighting capabilities ... the F-22—a critical component of the Global Strike Task Force—is designed to project air

18 Belly flop

A $140 million F-22 Raptor on the runway at Tyndall Air Force Base. The trainee pilot forgot to increase jet engine thrust from IDLE to MIL setting shortly after takeoff, causing the jet to "settle" back onto the runway and slide on its belly for several thousand feet before coming to a standstill. The oversight caused at least $30 million of damage.

dominance, rapidly and at great distances, and defeat threats attempting to deny access to U.S. Air Force, Army, Navy and Marine Corps. The F-22 cannot be matched by any known or projected fighter aircraft." One of the myriad valuable components of an F-22 is its "stealth" non-reflective radar-absorbing outer skin.

The unit cost of an F-22 is stated as $143 million, but this is an understatement: that is the figure to manufacture and fit out an F-22, and does not take into consideration the research and development costs, which have been estimated as between $50 and $100 billion. There are not that many planes in the USAF inventory that are equally or more valuable. The B-1B is stated at $317 million, and the B-2 at $1.1 billion. It therefore follows that only the most competent and trusted USAF pilots get to fly Raptors.

One of the activities ongoing at Tyndall Air Force Base in Florida is the training-up of Raptor pilots. The pilots are selected from the overall pool of current F-15 and F-16 pilots—in other words, the trainees arriving at Tyndall are already brilliant pilots in their own right.

On 31 May 2012, one such trainee Raptor pilot was on his second day of flight training, flying as RAGE12. The first day had been really nothing more than a general familiarization sortie with ninety minutes' flying time. The second day was very focused on landing practice, with time to be given to instrument landings; surveillance radar approach; overhead patterns; and visual straight-in landings.

On the morning of May 31, before commencing training, RAGE12 had a Fiber One bar, a coffee, and also a Rock Star energy drink before proceeding to his F-22. For the sortie in the morning, he flew a range of different types of landings, each time with his instructor flying behind him, correcting him and giving notes from the "chase" position.

Over the lunch period, the pilot had wanted to get a hot meal. He had requested a "container lunch," but it had not arrived by the time that he proceeded ("stepped") out to his jet for his afternoon sortie. So he had only what he could find on the "pilot bus"—a mobile trolley-bar—a Nutri-Grain bar augmented with a couple of Slim Jims and a Gatorade.

The late-afternoon second sortie was again—as the morning session had been—organized around practice landings. One way to maximize the opportunities for landing practices is to fly touch-and-go: the pilot makes his final approach and lands normally, then, rather than slowing the plane, the pilot raises the nose and within a few seconds brings up the throttles and takes off again. The use of the touch-and-go gets a trainee in particular straight back up in the air, ready to approach again.

At 16:45 p.m., RAGE12 flew in towards the Tyndall runway on his eighth touch-and-go of the day. This was to be one of his last practices towards the end of the second of two sorties. His instructor was in "chase" and was observing him closely.

As RAGE12 made his approach, he was about 10 m.p.h. fast over the by-the-book stated-as-preferred approach speed (nothing unusual for pilots transitioning from F-15s, as RAGE12 was), and he was also talking to the Tyndall Control Tower up until about six seconds before touchdown. Apart from being very slightly fast, the landing was really quite unremarkable, meaning that it was competent, even excellent.

Upon landing safely, RAGE12 immediately shifted the emphasis to takeoff. A few seconds after the successful touchdown, the pilot raised his nose ten degrees and became airborne again. One second later (very promptly indeed after takeoff) the pilot went "gear up," meaning he retracted the wheels into their hidden aerodynamic stowed position.

Then, for a reason that cannot be fully explained, the pilot simply forgot to increase his main throttle power, in a moment when, of course, main throttle power is absolutely required in order to climb smartly up and away from the runway. What the pilot did was an omission: he did

18 Belly flop

not bring up his main throttle control from IDLE setting to MILITARY POWER, or MIL.

For one to two seconds the pilot noticed nothing unusual, then he became aware of the jet sinking back down to the ground. Instantly recognizing his error, he immediately turned his throttles to full-performance afterburner power (70,000 pounds of forward thrust) and attempted to lower the landing gear. He later recalled, "In my brain I have pushed the power up and lowered the gear all at the same time. Whether that ended up happening before or after the belly was fully on the ground, I don't know."

Unfortunately, RAGE12 was already settling down onto the surface of the runway: the full blast on the throttles came too late to get the Raptor airborne, nor was there space or time available for the pilot to get his wheels back down.

The result was a catastrophic comedy: the plane, perfectly aligned in the center of the runway, sank back to the ground on its (super-valuable and fragile) underside and began to skid, careering noisily along at hundred and fifty mile an hour. The jet had "settled" down onto the runway—the impact was very gentle, almost controlled, and could not really be described as a crash. As the pilot later recalled: "I've gone to AB and I've tried to throw the gear back down [unsuccessfully] and then somewhere in there I've obviously settled … it [the Raptor] basically sort of belly slaps."

The jet's momentum on the smooth surface carried it sliding along the entire length of the Tyndall runway in a straight line with the pilot sitting in place absolutely helpless to do anything more than shut down his engines and watch the sparks fly. He later recalled that he was "dropping the occasional f-bomb" as he went, no more than a passenger on a hazardous and embarrassing three-thousand-foot free ride across the base. "It's very stable, probably more stable than when it's on its actual struts [wheels]."

The F-22 eventually slid to halt, still resting on its underside, still in the middle of the runway lane. The pilot, completely unharmed, unlocked his canopy and climbed out of his jet to safety.

The scraping of the belly of the aircraft was quite destructive to numerous systems, including, of course, the super-expensive stealth cladding as well as the main weapons-bay doors; the nose landing-gear doors; the outboard main landing-gear doors (and internal components); the lower missile launch detector; and the edges of the horizontal stabilizers.

The required repairs to the precious Raptor were later calculated to be $35 million.

19 Cut-up wake

Location: Alpha 78 "gunnery range" within the
Eglin Range Complex, near Eglin Air Force Base, Florida
Date: 13 June 2012
Aircraft type: CV-22
Fatalities: none
Cost of damage: $78.5 million

The USAF CV-22 Osprey is a tilt-rotor or prop-rotor—an aircraft that can take off and land as a helicopter and then, once airborne, convert its overhead rotor wings into forward-facing propellers. The entire engine blocks ("nacelles") with the propeller-rotors still in place can twist through 90 degrees in midair—controlled from the cockpit.

Visually, when set up as a plane, the CV-22's two enormous propellers

Aerial view of the crash site at Alpha 78 "gunnery range" within the Eglin Range Complex, near Eglin Air Force Base, Florida, in which a tilt-rotor CV-22 was destroyed. The lost aircraft was valued at $78 million.

19 Cut-up wake

appear as oversized and rather out of proportion. Equally, when set up as a helicopter, the twin rotor-blades appear much stubbier and fatter than the rotors on a conventional helicopter.

The premise and purpose ("mission") for the development of the CV-22 was in response to the requirements of modern warfare, in particular the need to infiltrate and later exfiltrate small groups of Special Ops forces (on counterterrorism missions, for example) deep inside hostile territory. The helicopter or "helo" is a basic option—like, say, the two HH-60s that flew into Pakistan on a mission to locate and execute Osama bin Laden. The issue with the helicopter option from a Special Ops' point of view is that it will tend to approach a set-down point slow and low, which is not the case for a CV-22. The typical cruising altitude of an HH-60 is around 10,000 feet, whereas the CV-22 can climb to 25,000 feet. Furthermore, once converted, a CV-22 can fly at around 270 m.p.h., as compared to an HH-60's top speed of 170 m.p.h.

When the CV-22 was first commissioned there were few other tilt-rotors out there—novelties only—so much of the research and development at Bell-Boeing was primary and pioneering. Thousands of man-hour days were accrued testing prototypes in purpose-built wind tunnels. When the first CV-22s were finally delivered in 2007, all the research costs were attached to the overall bill—which was around $40 billion.

Perhaps precisely because of its quality of being neither one thing nor the other, the CV-22 has repeatedly been targeted by bureaucrats, politicians, journalists and others who have claimed variously that it is unsafe, a waste of money, a white elephant, etc. Even within the USAF, the helicopter and fixed-wing "cultures" are definitely distinctive and separated, so that the CV-22 tends to retain a somewhat vexed status.

The 8th Special Operations Wing—based at Hurlburt Field, within Eglin Air Force Base, Florida—flies, among other aircraft, a number of CV-22s.

Eglin is not on the main peninsula of Florida, but on the western panhandle of the state—facing onto the coast of the Gulf of Mexico.

Around Eglin, mainly to the north of the base, there are several Department of Defense restricted sites, including a number of live-fire ranges where military training missions can be carried on using live ammunition and ordnance.

On 13 June 2012, two CV-22 crews based at Hurlburt were handed a multi-component live-fire training mission. They were to start with "single-ship proficiency maneuvers at Hurlburt, followed by day gunnery practice at Alpha 78 and single-ship low visibility approach work at helicopter landing zones inside Eglin." Then, after refueling at Hurlburt, they would "return to Alpha 78 for night gunnery practice, followed by night low visibility approach work."

The two CV-22s in helicopter mode were to depart Hurlburt and fly in close formation out over the coast of the Gulf of Mexico and head west for a few miles before turning back inland toward a designated live-fire range. After turning inland, they were to descend, flying in slow and low towards their simulated targets. The CV-22 has various armaments, including a .50 caliber machine gun that mounts directly onto the aft ramp when open and is operated by the flight engineer.

The two CV-22s took off from Hurlburt at 6:30 p.m. on a clear and fine early evening—a light breeze, seven miles visibility; the hottest part of the day had seen temperatures of 87 degrees Fahrenheit.

At the controls of one of the two tilt-rotors training that day was Captain Brett Cassidy—he was the pilot at the controls, officially copilot—and sitting next to him was the pilot or aircraft commander, Major Brian Luce.

The six or seven minutes of the mission progressed uneventfully, including takeoff and the flight down the coast.

The two turbo-props began to head towards Alpha 78 live-fire range, descending as they went, and in close formation.

This inbound leg of the route was a wide left-hand arc followed by a tight 180-degree turn just before crossing into Alpha 78—with both helicopters descending to around 300 feet for the first simulated attack. The two flew the arc, with Cassidy and Luce's helicopter flying subordinate to the lead—they were a little behind it and off its left side.

As they both turned, Cassidy cut very slightly across the flight path of his lead, and momentarily entered the hazardous stream of turbulence or "wake" caused by the thundering rotor blades of the aircraft up ahead.

As its left side tilt-rotor entered the turbulent air, Luce's helicopter was violently buffeted and bumped around: it rolled perilously to its left side and began to suddenly lose altitude. "Once the helicopter's left proprotor entered the lead's wake the helicopter immediately began an uncommanded roll to the left, reaching a maximum of 63 degrees of left bank, 23 degrees nose-low and 2,880 feet per minute descent."

As the left-side rotor entered the choppy air, it entered a vortex-ring-like state, or began settling with power; that is, its rotor was rotating as expected but was not achieving lift due to the disturbed quality of the air. (In a true vortex-ring event, a helicopter ceases to obtain lift due to becoming embroiled in *its own* wake.)

In the midst of the violent uncommanded rolls, Luce grabbed his set of controls and fought to level the helicopter. Working together, the two pilots were able to level out, but the momentum of their descent could not be arrested. The helicopter's twin rotors were churning through air with maximum lift applied, but without effect.

Within ten seconds of first crossing into the turbulent airstream, Luce and Cassidy's Osprey had descended from about five hundred feet to just above the line of the treetops of the pine forest below them. At 6:40 p.m., around ten minutes after takeoff, Luce's Osprey came crunching down to the ground through the tall trees in a heavy crash landing.

Upon impact with sandy soil, the CV-22 burst into flames—a thick plume of black smoke immediately visible to the lead still in the sky above.

The two pilots and three further crew scrambled—or were dragged—to safety (there were two flight engineers aboard, plus an instructor flight engineer).

Moments later, the CV-22 was engulfed in a post-crash fire that completely destroyed the aircraft.

All on board were injured in the crash impact, but there were no serious injuries or fatalities. Impact-absorbing seats in the cockpit and cabin had deployed during the crash landing.

Within five minutes the lead CV-22 landed near to the crash site and began to evacuate Luce and his crew.

The value of the lost aircraft was later estimated at $78.5 million.

The Accident Panel reporting on the loss noted that the effects of air turbulence as regards the wake of another aircraft is not available to train on the USAFs CV-22 simulator setup. Vortex-ring state is available on such simulators and this is the closest that can be trained virtually.

20 Fuel-line shutoff

Location: Pacific Ocean
Date: 3 July 2012
Aircraft type: F-16
Fatalities: none
Cost of damage: $32.6 million

The U.S. military's "primary mission" is to "promote stability; dissuade/deter aggression, and swiftly defeat enemies." Its given role is essentially that of a global security service, with the Earth's surface divided into several designated "areas of responsibility." One such "area of responsibility" (as regards the USAF) is PACAF—Pacific Air Forces. The area "extends from the west coast of the United States to the east coast of Africa and from the Arctic to the Antarctic, covering more than 100 million square miles. The area is home to 50 percent of the world's population in 36 nations and over one third of the global economic output."

U.S. operations in the Pacific depend on bases on the sovereign territory islands of Hawaii and Guam, but also many host nation bases: autonomous U.S. Air Bases on other friendly countries—such as South Korea and Japan.

Misawa Air Base in Japan—four hundred miles and a seven-hour drive north of Tokyo—is a U.S. "forward" base with a particular value to the U.S. military: a USAF jet departing Misawa headed back to the U.S., to Eilson or JBER, or any other U.S. Air Base in Alaska, will have a natural, logical, and obvious route that will cause it to fly all the way up the eastern coast of Russia—all three thousand miles of it, up-to-and-including the Bering Strait (the fifty-to-sixty-mile-wide channel that separates the U.S. from Russia).

Keeping in mind that USA and Russia are the two most extreme nuclear powers on Earth—7,000 nuclear weapons each—this segment of the Pacific Ocean between the two countries is under continuous scrutiny and surveillance. Misawa is also a key SIGINT intelligence "listening station" tuned in to Russian military comms at all times.

If Russia were intent on delivering a nuclear bomb to the U.S., a fighter-protected heavy bomber would likely depart one of the most easterly air bases of the Voyenno-Vozdushnye Sily Rossii (Russian Air Force) such as Ukrainka or Zavitinsk in Amur Oblast, for example. Such a bomber could fly a route either over Siberia in Russian airspace before heading south towards the U.S. or it could fly due east from base out across the Pacific. Either route would cause the bomber to cross the Misawa-to-Eilson diagonal.

The 35th Fighter Wing is based at Misawa. The 35th flies many—perhaps daily—cross-country flights to and from Eilson Air Base in Alaska.

The flights are not a provocation to action by anyone; they are simply jets on cross-country missions which just happen to be flying all the way along the east coast of Russia—a convenient and direct route. Such flights are often connected with maintenance and are in no way recognized or listed as "patrols."

On 3 July 2012, an Air Force F-16 fighter pilot callsign JEST73 was

20 Fuel-line shutoff

handed just such a "cross-country" mission: he was to fly his jet in a group with three others cruising at 25,000 feet from Misawa to Eilson, Alaska. JEST23 taxied towards the Misawa runway at 8:35 a.m. with takeoff at 9:00 a.m.

The F-16 is capable of flying at 1,700 mph at 50,000 feet, but on this flight JEST23 was cruising at 25,000 feet and at around 900 m.p.h.

As the flight progressed, it was punctuated by a series of midair or air-to-air refuels, with fuel supplied by an Air Refueling Wing jet—a KC-135 Stratotanker. In addition to his main internal fuel tank, JEST23 was also taking on fuel into three externally mounted fuel tanks—three large bomb-shaped containers attached to the underside of his wings and fuselage.

Immediately after JEST23 got a fourth refill tankful of jet fuel, the lone pilot noticed by way of his engine RPM gauge that his sole jet engine was losing power—it was down to about 70 percent power.

At 11:09 a.m. JEST23 alerted the other jets on the sortie to his situation by radio and continued on his route ("loss of thrust.... RPMS rolling back"). There was no way he could make an emergency landing: he was way out over the Pacific, far from the coast of Alaska; he was in the middle of nowhere.

After flying on reduced power for around three minutes, JEST23 looked up to the instrument panel and saw that his engine's RPM gauge was now winding down towards zero. All power from the jet was gone; he had flamed out; he was engine out over the Pacific.

F-16 pilots are trained to go through a number of steps in such a situation. The Airstart Checklist includes first flame-out restart (restart the engine using the cockpit controls); then, windmill restart; then, consider engine-out glide-in landing (if the available glide distance allows for a reachable airfield in range—thirty miles is an average glide-in striking distance available to an F-16 without power); then, as a last resort, the pilot should level the aircraft, preferably to below 15,000 feet, reduce speed to below 280 m.p.h., and eject, leaving his jet to its fate.

Four times the pilot attempted a flame-out restart, restarting his jet engine while in mid-air, each time with no effect. A glide-in engine-out landing was impossible: there was no land whatsoever in sight. With the restart efforts, JEST23 had already descended from his original 25,000 feet into the safe-to-eject "envelope."

Recognizing that his flight was doomed, the pilot pulled back slightly on his control stick to bring the F-16's nose level, and then pulled down hard on his ejection handle. The explosive charge under his seat detonated instantly, catapulting him up and away from his plane.

Seconds later the F-16 crashed into the Pacific. "Upon impact the aircraft disintegrated and sank." Many fragments of the wrecked plane were later recovered from the ocean floor—two miles down—by U.S. Navy salvage teams. The value of the lost jet was later estimated to be $33 million.

The pilot was unharmed and gained "a good chute." As he splashed down into the Pacific, his one-man life raft automatically inflated.

The pilots of the KC-135 refueling aircraft were well aware of the developing situation and continued to overfly the area of the pilot's position, relaying many details of the crash situation to the search-and- rescue coordinator. The critical element in the rescue was not locating the pilot but getting a ship—any ship—to rescue him. The pilot was marooned in a floating life raft in the middle of the Pacific—hundreds of miles from dry land in the midst of the largest and deepest ocean on Earth. Rescue coordinators put out a request for help from any ship in the area of the crash—naval, commercial, pleasure craft, it didn't matter.

One ship that responded was *Manukai*, a 700-foot, U.S.-registered, fully laden commercial container ship, carrying a cargo of 30,000 tons. The *Manukai*'s captain agreed to divert to the rescue zone, and within five hours the large container vessel entered the locale of the floating survivor.

The problem with *Manukai* was that the presence of such a large vessel—creating a twenty-foot-high wake and back-wash behind her as she went—would be extremely hazardous if encountered by the now-dehydrated survivor in a flimsy non-steerable life raft. Fortunately, at around 5:30 p.m., over six hours from the moment of ejection, a much smaller (and safer) Japanese research ship, the *Hokko Maru*, a Japanese fishery scientific research vessel, also diverting to the crash site, arrived into the locale of the crash.

At 5:44 p.m. the survivor was brought aboard the *Hokku Maru*. This was welcomed, but the USAF search-and-rescue coordinator wanted the pilot deposited into U.S. hands as soon as possible, and so requested that the airman be immediately transferred to the *Manukai* container ship.

At 6:00 p.m. the pilot was taken aboard *Manukai*.

From its diverted position, the container ship set course as instructed to the U.S. Naval Base at Dutch Harbor on the remote U.S.-territorial island of Unalaska—an Aleutian Island one thousand miles from the mainland. At Dutch Harbor, the survivor was transferred to a U.S. coastguard aircraft and flown to Joint Base Elmendorf–Richardson—JBER—near Anchorage, Alaska.

It was later established that soon after the fourth refueling, the jet's main fuel-line shutoff valve had closed "uncommanded," causing the jet engine to become starved of fuel. At first it had partially closed (for three minutes), and then closed completely.

The Accident Investigation team analyzed the maintenance regimens pertaining to the lost jet and interviewed all engineers and mechanics who were logged as having done work on it. After the accident (but before the investigation began) some of the maintenance data-history stored on the USAF's centralized Integrated Maintenance Data System computer database was deleted for unexplained reasons.

It was eventually established that the jet had been out of USAF hands prior to the accident for "extensive maintenance" by Lockheed Martin (the manufacturer). The civilian Lockheed technicians were working on the jet at Misawa from May 15 to June 7 (just a few weeks before the accident). During this maintenance the mechanics would have been maintaining and inspecting the fuel shutoff valve.

The paperwork showed that it was a certain "Mechanic 58" who had worked on this particular aircraft component during the Lockheed service. When interviewed and asked to go over his procedures, Mechanic 58 "fell short" of the expected proficiency standard.

Among a number of shortcomings in his approach to maintaining the valve in question was the operative's choice of maintenance substances. Rather than using the USAF-procedure-specified product Con-Tac Corrosion Preventative Compound (a lubricant and corrosion prevention spray for metal surfaces), the operative was using instead Electron 22 (a solvent-degreaser), a product that was no reasonable substitute for Con-Tac.

When the Investigation team looked into this further, they found that not only had Mechanic 58 not checked out a bottle of the spray for his work order, but that, in fact, there was no Con-Tac anywhere within the Lockheed facility—and none had been ordered for at least two years.

21 Flaps gone

Location: Tinker AFB, Oklahoma
Date: 1 November 2012
Aircraft type: B-52

Fatalities: none
Cost of damage: $1.1 million

In the eastern suburbs of Oklahoma City (pop.: 600,000), after Smith Village and Del City, there is one of the USAF's main aircraft repair and maintenance complexes. The Air Logistics Complex is something of a suburb in its own right: eight million square feet of industrial floor space spread out over sixty-three separate buildings where just under ten thousand mechanics, engineers, and technicians work each day on USAF aircraft.

Much of the work carried out is scheduled overhauls. Just as any auto requires an annual full service, so too USAF jets require a complete overhaul at certain intervals. The designated interval between major services for the B-52—the iconic eight-engine heavy bomber in service continuously since 1955—is four years. B-52s arriving for service at the Air Logistics Complex arrive by way of Tinker Air Base, and this is the base from which maintainers' test flights or functional-check flights (FCFs) depart.

The once-every-four-years service of a B-52 requires the near-complete dismantling of the plane. The service order requires the relevant engineers and mechanics to "disassemble, refurbish, reassemble, paint, and flight-test each B-52." The strip-down and reassemble is achieved by the use of many itemized checklists—one for almost each component assembly or mechanism.

The B-52 is a very large and powerful jet plane with a wingspan of a hundred and eighty-six feet. Along the non-leading edge of each wing (each wing is eighty-five feet long), there are "flaps" in two sets: the inner flaps, and the outer flaps. These are smooth flat metal surfaces that emerge from the rear of the wing to give the plane more lift when it is so required. They increase the surface area of the wings and are used mainly during takeoff and landing.

As objects, the flaps of a B-52 are substantial: each one is a low, flat cuboid thirty-two feet long, nine feet wide, weighing two tons. The machinery for moving these flaps naturally gets serviced as part of a B-52 major service.

The machine assembly for moving a flap backwards and forwards on a B-52 is not high-tech. The B-52 is an intentionally rugged plane with an emphasis on mechanical rather than electronic controls. All the flight-control surfaces, including the flaps, are designed to be usable with all power gone by the manipulation of power-out pulley-and-cable systems.

21 Flaps gone

The movement of a flap (extend-retract) is made by the movement of a simple drive-screw. This is a thin steel eight-foot-long pole with a continuous diagonal groove in it which turns forwards or reverse (clockwise or counterclockwise) through a gearbox. There are two drive-screws for each flap on a B-52, so there are a total of eight flap drive-screws.

For each of these drive-screws there is a cap or retainer plug fixed to the end of it, which has the function of stopping the extend operation. Without any such cap, the flap could just unwind through the gearbox and keep on winding, so that the entire flap could just fall off the back of the wing. These end-caps are made of steel and screw into the long drive-screw pole, giving a definite end limit for flap extension. The cap is a screw-in flange, nothing more than that—and not more than three inches across.

On 1 November 2012, a certain B-52 had recently completed a full service at Tinker and was all set for a functional-check flight. The purpose of such a flight is for the pilots to go rigorously through a series of functionality checklists making sure the refreshed jet is fully ready to be returned to its usual squadron. The crew that day was from the 10th Flight Test Squadron. There were four airmen in total, including an instructor instructing one of the three ordinary crew towards his functional-flight check qualification.

In the late-morning of 1 November, the four made their way "stepped" the B-52 and departed Runway 18 at Tinker at 12:35 p.m. on a bright and clear early afternoon. "Winds at take-off were calm and the sky was clear, with unrestricted visibility."

It was the copilot who was at the controls for takeoff and climb-out—he was the one under instruction that afternoon. For takeoff the copilot had opted to make full use of his flaps—100 percent or fully extended, as is quite usual.

During the climb-out from Tinker, at around 1,000 feet altitude, just as the copilot was retracting the flaps from their extended-out-for-takeoff position, at 12:37 p.m.—less than two minutes after takeoff—all three airmen aboard heard a loud "bang, boom, thud." At which their jet began to roll and bank violently to the left.

The copilot was momentarily flummoxed, and the pilot instantly returned the plane to his command and took the controls. His main objective was to counter the uncommanded and perilous left roll and bank, and he began by applying full-right-rudder and full-right-yoke. Even with the flight controls at full-right, the highly experienced pilot was finding it impossible to control his jet.

As the emergency situation continued, with the pilot grappling with the controls, around twenty-five seconds after the first banging noise, there came a second alarming "bang, boom, thud." Then, immediately after the noise, the aircraft ceased to roll and bank and became controllable again. Whatever had happened second seemed to have corrected the first problem, as now the jet was definitely responding as expected to flight control inputs.

The crew of the B-52 discussed the situation with the control tower at Tinker: something fairly drastic had happened, but they were not sure what. The tower called upon a training flight that was underway close to base: a student fighter-pilot in a Talon T-38 with his instructor. The tower requested that the Talon close in on the B-52 and do a visual external inspection. (The B-52 cockpit has very limited aft visibility and few windows.)

As the T-38 intercepted, the Talon's pilot saw immediately what the problem was: the B-52 had lost both its inner wing flaps. They were gone—completely missing from the back of each wing. At this news there was both relief and consternation in the B-52 cockpit. The jet was airworthy and there was no developing emergency, but for an ordinary landing the missing flaps would usually be required. All that remained was to decide what would be the safest way to land the bomber with two flaps vanished.

Fortunately, a highly experienced B-52 crew of the 93rd Bomb Squadron was at this time in the 10th Squadron main building at Tinker, having recently arrived on temporary duty from Barksdale Air Force Base, Louisiana. The 93rd crew were immediately briefed on the airborne B-52's plight and there was some discussion as to the best format for landing. In addition, a call was placed to the technical center of Boeing—the manufacturer—as regards the best plan for landing.

In the end it was agreed that the lighter the jet, the better: at its lightest, completely unladen and with little fuel, the jet could more easily be landed from a slow no-flap approach. With the plan established, it remained only for the crew to fly a holding pattern—circling—in the vicinity of the base for two hours to "burn-down fuel," and so decrease the weight of the plane.

At 14:30 p.m. that afternoon, the crew successfully landed the jet back at Tinker with no casualties and no further damage to the jet.

While the fuel "burn down" go-around circuits were still ongoing, back on the ground, reports had started coming in by phone to the base from members of the public and law enforcement: several witnesses had just seen "large parts falling from an aircraft."

21 Flaps gone

Before the B-52 had even landed, a law enforcement helicopter began a search for the objects as reported to them by members of the public and located them in woodland around Stanley Draper Lake, about three miles south of Tinker.

Once they were located, it was Tinker Air Base personnel who recovered the two B-52 two inner flaps. Both two-ton flaps had fallen over 1,000 feet through the air and had impacted the ground—fortunately—in unpopulated woodland.

Astonishingly, the two flaps that had become detached were symmetrical: it was the same flap portion from each wing that had detached. Once the first had gone, the plane had become uncontrollable, with level flight becoming possible again when the second (the same position flap on the other wing) had also fallen out. It was just chance that both had fallen from two corresponding points.

For no immediately apparent reason beyond perhaps convenience of transportation, the personnel recovering the two flaps decided to cut each one into a number of smaller (and so more manageable) pieces before transporting them back to base—and thereby destroying them.

The later Accident Investigation found that the two flaps under scrutiny had been installed onto the B-52 without any drive-screw end-caps in place. As they were extended, they moved through the length of the threaded drive-screw poles, and with nothing to stop the motor's unwinding motion, the two flaps separated from the plane. They just continued unwinding through the drive screw until they fell off the back of the wings.

The documentation pertaining to the overhaul of the two flaps—the WCDs, or Work Control Documents—showed that the flap mechanisms had been worked on in the Wheel and Gearbox Shop.

The paperwork revealed that shoddy work had been carried out by two certain mechanics, "MX1" and "MX4," with fitting back onto the jet being done by "MX6" and "MX7." The vital mistake was in the reassembly of the flaps: the all-important retainer end-caps at the end of the each of the drive screw poles had simply not been installed.

The estimated repair cost of replacing the flaps on the B-52 was $1.1 million.

22 Roll off the top

Location: near Owens Dry Lake, Eastern Sierra, California
Date: 27 December 2012
Aircraft type: F-16
Fatalities: none
Cost of damage: $21.4 million

USAF fighter jets such as the F-16 Fighting Falcon are super-agile and highly maneuverable through the air. One basic reference point for maneuverability is a plane's capability during air-to-air close quarters combat, in which two adversary jets, flying well within visual range, maneuver one against the other, with the intention getting a clear shot with a missile, or an air-to-air armor-piercing gun. This activity known as "dogfighting."

The objective during a dogfight is to destroy the opposing aircraft outright or else cause to it crash because of its being rendered uncontrollable due to battle damage. Dogfighting is an arena in which a fighter jet's mobility, and the pilot's quick thinking, are challenged and tested to the maximum.

Within military aviation, the continuing relevance of the dogfight is much debated and contested. Many modern fighter jets can positively identify a hostile jet at thirty miles, and the emergence of heat-seeking and laser-guided missiles often removes the requirement for a clear and clean shot at an adversary. However, an entrenched perception tends to linger: when two fighting forces come into conflict, the fastest, most maneuverable, and most lethal jets of each adversary will inevitably come into direct conflict with each other at some point. And this being so, discussions around the status of the air-to-air dogfight are nothing but barroom chatter or a fair subject for discussion in a warfighting committee. The operational reality is that all USAF fighter pilots rehearse and practice dogfight maneuvers on a weekly basis. Close-quarters aggressive maneuvering is an ordinary part of every fighter pilot's regular flying sorties.

If nothing else, basic fighter maneuvers, or BFM, enable the pilot to gain and practice extreme control of his machine—the tightest possible turning circle; the most rapid climb; the neatest roll; and so on.

Such training sorties are flown above all to "maintain pilot proficiency," meaning that whenever an airman is called upon—even at short notice—he will be absolutely ready to fly and fight. At the most extreme,

22 Roll off the top

an on-alert F-16 pilot "scrambling" can be airborne and *en route* towards a hostile midair target at a speed of 1,700 m.p.h. within five to six minutes.

Fighter pilots of the 144th Fighter Wing based at Fresno Air National Guard Base in California very often fly training sorties based around dogfight-type maneuvers and simulated attacks.

On 27 December 2012, a very experienced F-16 fighter pilot—originally trained at Edwards—was flying (together with a second F-16 pilot) a training mission incorporating some dogfight or BFM profiles. The first was flying as callsign DOGS41 and the second, the partner or "wingman," was flying as DOGS42.

The two jets departed Fresno Yosemite International Airport at 14:24 p.m. Fresno is in the middle of California equidistant from Los Angeles and San Francisco (both cities are two hundred miles away), with the Sierra Nevada Mountains and the peak of Mount Whitney (14,000 feet) rising dramatically only twenty miles east of the base.

There was something rather reckless or actually gung-ho ("unthinkingly enthusiastic and eager, especially about taking part in fighting or warfare") about DOGS41's frame of mind that afternoon. As he taxied out to the runway at Fresno, DOGS41 realized that his main computerized in-flight GPS navigation system was showing inaccurate data and needed a reset. He decided to let it go and take off anyway, even though the GPS was actually displaying inaccurate data by at least 100 miles so.

After takeoff and climb-out, the two jets flew into an area of restricted military airspace over California known as R2508. As per the agreed sortie directives, DOGS41 and DOGS42 were to first perform a basic G-force-awareness exercise in order to acclimatize and check readiness for high-G-force maneuvers: both pilot readiness and jet readiness. This part of the mission both pilots decided to scrap and pass over, preferring to go straight into the adversary-based performance maneuvering.

Then, during the flying maneuvers, DOGS41 varied wildly from the basic maneuvers profiles—to such an extent that he was several times on the radio instructing DOGS42 for starting positions; his attacks that afternoon were tending to improvisation and even free reign. No substantive learning outcomes for the session had been discussed with DOGS42 prior to the flight's departure.

Several times through the one-versus-one simulated attack, DOGS41 flew the Immelmann turn or roll-off-the-top maneuver: pulling back hard aft on his stick so that from level flight the jet pitched up dramatically. The fuselage suddenly turned vertical—space rocket–like—as it climbed at full force with the afterburner making the tailpipe glow red-hot. At the top of each such climb, after about 2,000 feet gained, DOGS41 would let momentum loss and gravity alone slow the plane and pull it "over the top," inverting it as it fell backwards, until it was level but upside down. At this he would roll 180 degrees and accelerate away—a prime and classic defensive maneuver. But the way DOGS41 was performing roll-off-the-tops that day was more like air acrobatics than anything with definite strategic purpose.

Each time he did the maneuver to go "over the top," DOGS41 was slowing his jet's speed down so dramatically that the aircraft's on-board sensors were forewarning of an impending air stall. Each time his jet slowed at the top of the climb, the in-cockpit oral warning alert was sounding: the soothing digitized voice of "Betty" would begin to call out the caution each time twice in quick succession: Warning-Warning.... Warning-Warning.... Warning-Warning," together with a continuous low-pitch tone and a visual-display caution light flashing up on the instrument panel.

With the cockpit warning sounding, DOGS41 was allowing the jet to continue to slow as far as he could push it before finally rolling 180 and accelerating away. There was no definite reason why DOGS41 was doing these maneuvers so slowly except perhaps the thrill-seeking pleasure of flying the jet to the edge of its "flight envelope."

The first time that he did the maneuver that day (15:22 p.m.), he had the air-stall audible warning come on in the cockpit for eight seconds. The second time he did the maneuver the air-stall warning was on for twelve seconds. Correct procedure requires the F-16 pilot to react to any such stall warning within one to two seconds.

At 15:31 DOGS41 applied full aft stick for the third time, taking the jet straight up—vertically—from 13,800 feet to 15,800 feet within seconds. As he let the jet slow to go over-the-top, his airspeed was only 190 m.p.h.—where 300–400 m.p.h. would be an ordinary range for required and desirable speed. With the jet upside down and flat on its back coming out of the climb, DOGS41 entered a deep, unrecoverable air stall. The jet's speed was not sufficient to keep it airborne and it began to fall, still flat on its back, as a deadweight from the sky.

The F-16 was falling from the sky at 12,000 feet per minute from a starting altitude of only 15,000 feet and with mountains reaching to over 14,000 feet within the immediate vicinity.

The jet began spinning and bumping around wildly as it went—twirling around (or yawing) like a Christmas tree decoration caught in a breeze.

22 Roll off the top

First thing the pilot did was inform his wingman of the situation, calling "Ballistic" over the radio intercom. Moments later he called again, this time: "out-of-control."

With no more than thirty seconds available in which to complete recovery, the pilot began his emergency CAPS procedure—flight controls to neutral settings; jet engine to idle.

As he passed through 7,000 feet, upside down and still spinning around wildly, Betty was becoming insistent: "Warning-Warning. PULL UP ... Warning-Warning. CHECK ALTITUDE ... Warning-Warning.... TERRAIN." And behind the female voice were the low-tone air-stall warning and bong-bong-bong-bong pull-up chime. Visual alerts were flashing on the instrument panel and blinking in the HUD.

The pilot now focused on his jet's pitch: he pulled-pushed repeatedly on his control stick, causing the nose to pitch up then down, up then down. He wanted to get the horizon level, and to do that he was raising and lowering the nose—"pitch rocking." The problem was that these pitch-altering inputs were having no effect.

The pilot craned his neck back and looked down on the Sierra Nevada mountaintops, and beyond to the smooth, flat stretch of Owens Valley.

At 7,000 feet the pilot recognized that his recovery effort had failed and that he had just a few seconds until impact with the ground. At 6,200 feet the pilot reached down, grasped the ejection lever, and pulled hard. At 15:33, the explosive under-seat charge catapulted him out of the jet and up and away to safety.

Seconds later the doomed F-16—still spinning around; still inverted—crashed to the ground and exploded in open scrubland in Owens Valley near the flat dry-lakebed expanse of Owens Lake in Inyo County, just east of the Sierra Nevada Mountains, ten miles south of the small town of Lone Pine.

The pilot had a "good chute"—his emergency parachute opened correctly—and he floated down to land within clear view of the post-crash fireball engulfing his jet.

Shortly after landing, he walked to the nearest main road, and at 15:45—thirteen minutes after ejection—the pilot made contact with the California Highway Patrol.

Later, at a hospital in Lone Pine, the pilot was examined and found to have only minor injuries. He was returned back to base by helicopter by 23:10 p.m.

The lost jet was later valued at $21.4 million.

23 Spatial D

Location: Adriatic Sea off the coast of Ravenna, Italy
Date: 28 January 2013
Aircraft type: F-16
Fatalities: 1
Cost of damage: $28.4 million

In the north of Italy, about sixty miles inland from Venice—the famous city built on a network of charming canals and waterways—is the small town of Aviano.

Close to the town is Aviano Air Base, one of at least seven USAF bases in Italy. Since the USAF was evicted from France in 1967, the active bases in Italy and the UK have become vital strategic locations, and the base is kept in a state of constant high alert.

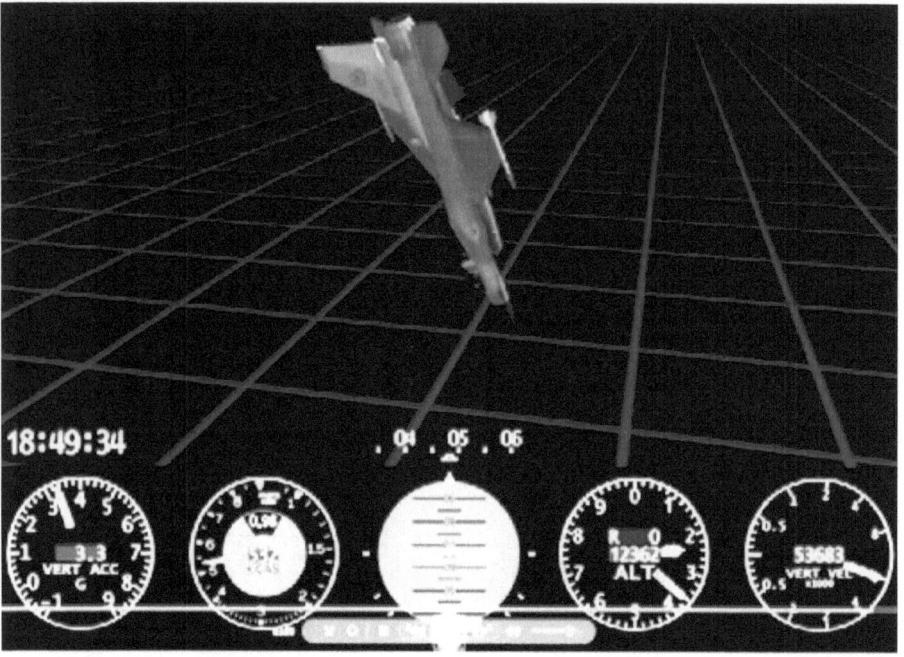

A still from the official USAF computer model animation of the crash—showing the in-air position or attitude of an F-16 moments before its impact with the surface of the Adriatic Sea.

23 Spatial D

One of the squadrons based at Aviano is the 555th Fighter Squadron, which flies F-16 to "perform air-and-space control-and-force application roles of counter-air, strategic attack and counter-land, including interdiction and close-air-support."

The F-16 is the backbone of the USAF fighter-jet inventory with at least one thousand in service. Since its introduction in 1979, the F-16 has become entrenched as one of the basic warfighting machines of the modern age. At least twenty-eight other countries rely on the F-16 in a key defense role.

One of the scenarios that F-16 pilots at Aviano train for is attacks during darkness. Many training missions are set at night, and for these the pilots wear NVGs—infrared-based night-vision "goggles" mounted onto their helmets.

On the evening of 28 January 2013, such a training mission was taking place at Aviano. The sortie of that evening required six F-16s to fly out over the Adriatic Sea: four would be flying as friendly, and two would be flying as simulated hostiles—a night opposed surface attack mission.

The arrangement was a classic 4V2, in this instance pitting CLAW flight (the friendly jets) against VENOM flight (the simulated hostiles). CLAW's mission "was to act as four friendly aircraft attacking enemy ground targets; two enemy aircraft simulated by VENOM flight were to protect those targets." The sortie for CLAW jets was set to include "takeoff, navigation to the airspace, air-to-air engagement with VENOM, surface attacks against ground targets and threat reactions against simulated surface-to-air missiles (SAMs)."

Having completed all necessary preparations and planning, the six jets departed Aviano just after seven o'clock in the evening. Once the jets had made their way into restricted NATO/USAF airspace (two areas designated SARA and SPEEDY), each pilot carried out a G-awareness maneuver, as is required in advance of high-G-force maneuvering. The awareness maneuvers, at least two sudden ninety-degree turns in midair, are a chance to check that both pilot and jet are "good to go" as regards the high-G-force maneuvering to come.

As the flight lead flew through the SPEEDY airspace, it became clear that cloud all around would make air-to-air attack and defend too risky. Visibility was too poor, unfortunately, and the two VENOM jets were instructed to RTB (return to base). Then the leader of the mission split the remaining four jets into two twos and assigned them different altitudes to practice certain possible warfare scenarios.

CLAW23 and CLAW24 were indicated to set their radio frequency to a unique setting and then descend and train in the altitude range of 15–19,000 feet, while CLAW21 (32-year-old pilot Major Lucas Gruenther) and CLAW22 would work in the altitude range of 20–24,000 feet.

CLAW21 and CLAW22 practiced a number of simulated attack-and-defend situations, one of which was defending against a surface-to-air missile, or SAM avoidance.

A SAM is a flying bomb intended to detonate on impact with an enemy aircraft. One of the ways that F-16s defend themselves against any such missile is to dive out of its path at the last possible moment, so causing the missile to overshoot. As such missiles travel at speeds from 1,000 to 3,000 m.p.h., once the missile has passed its target, it needs time to turn around and relocate the target jet.

Such maneuvers are a last resort, really, and are known as "last ditch." In a "last ditch" effort, a pilot will usually raise or lower the nose of the aircraft 90 degrees and accelerate to a higher or lower altitude using full afterburner.

At 19:48 on the evening of 28 January, CLAW22 called a simulated incoming SAM to his partner CLAW21: "Missiles to your right three o'clock, six miles." That is, the pilot calling out the imagined attack asked the other to react to missiles on course to impact his right side within a few seconds.

At this, CLAW21 performed a classic "last ditch" maneuver: he rolled inverted to the right and then dived down 40 degrees nose-low at 460 m.p.h. continuing the descent for ten seconds. CLAW22 called over the radio, "Missile overshoot"—a successful maneuver.

At this moment (19:49:13), rather than come back on the radio with an OK confirmation, CLAW21 responded unexpectedly with: "Knock it off, I'm spatial D." The diving pilot was announcing that he had completely lost his bearings (spatial disorientation, or spatial D for brevity), and was asking for all training to cease.

The situation for the disoriented pilot was immediately critical: he was flying on a course down towards the sea below, accelerating towards five hundred miles per hour from an altitude of less than 18,000 feet. He had no more than few seconds to recover his awareness and pull up.

At hearing of his wingman's predicament, CLAW22 called over the radio his own words of advice: "Look at the round dials," meaning forget all else and recover with reference only to the fundamental basic aviation gauges—airspeed; altitude; attitude, or position in space.

Confronted with this life-or-death situation, CLAW21 began to maneuver. He rolled his jet 180 degrees (to fully inverted) and increased the angle of descent from 40 degrees nose-low to 70 degrees nose-low. The maneuvers had made the perilous situation worse, with the jet now arrowing straight down toward the sea below with airspeed of over six hundred miles per hour and still accelerating.

As the tormented jet passed through 7,900 feet, the pilot brought the nose up towards the horizon with a 9-G-force pull-up—the aircraft was beginning to level and was on course for a successful recovery. But in his disoriented or semi-disoriented state, the pilot remained absolutely uncertain of his position, and three seconds after the pull-up he made the decision that his situation was unrecoverable and ejected. (Alex Gruenther, Lucas's brother, later stated: "You just have to put yourself in the cockpit—you're going down 1,000 feet a second, pulling eight-Gs, warning lights and audible alarms are going off.")

As the pilot's canopy detached and ejection commenced, the pilot was catapulted from the F-16, which was traveling through the dark night sky at speed of at least five hundred miles an hour. As the pilot departed the aircraft, intense windrush ripped his helmet from his head. Then, one second later, a drogue parachute detonated and instantly slowed his forward movement, causing a "lateral snapback" with a force on the pilot's neck of at least 40-G—absolutely unsurvivable. The pilot suffered massive head and neck trauma during the ejection sequence and was killed.

At the moment of ejection for any standard USAF ejector seat—the ACES system—an emergency broadcast beacon should begin to transmit. For some reason, CLAW21's beacon was not working. There was no trace or signal; the jet in peril simply disappeared from U.S. radars and the cockpit radio was dead.

CLAW22 radioed to the supervisor of flying back at base that he had lost radio contact with his wingman. He then requested air traffic control at Padova for clearance to descend and began to search for his partner, but on the bleak, rainy and cloudy night, without any transmissions or information to guide him, his search was futile.

The arrangements for USAF sorties flown in Italy is that responsibility for search-and-rescue support is intentionally retained by the host nation. Within ten minutes of the alarm being raised, an Italian search-and-rescue helicopter had departed Cervia Air Base and was en route to the suspected crash zone. Within one hour, the Italian helicopter was forced to return to base due to poor visibility and deteriorating weather conditions.

The following day, the civilian Coast Guard station at Ravenna took control of the search-and-rescue mission, with the Italian helicopter going out on two further sorties scanning out over the Adriatic.

For the following three days, the Italian search effort was ongoing, but was continuously hampered by limited resources and poor weather. It was not until 31 January at around three o'clock in the afternoon that the pilot's body was recovered from the sea.

From 31 January to 7 February, the Italian state took custody of the pilot's remains, with the U.S. involvement frustratingly limited. An autopsy of the pilot's body was deemed to be desirable, and the USAF was offered the opportunity to send along a surgeon representative to be present.

On 8 February the pilot's remains were taken aboard a USAF C-17 at Aviano and flown to the USA.

The destroyed F-16 was later valued at $28.4 million.

24 Dutch roll

Location: south of Chaldovar, Kyrgyzstan
Date: 3 May 2013
Aircraft type: KC-135
Fatalities: 3
Cost of damage: $66.3 million

From 2001 through 2014, the small Central Asian country Kyrgyzstan (population: six million) was a USAF host nation.

The USAF base known as Transit Center at Manas, near the Kyrgyzstan town of Bishkek, was one of main U.S. supply-line bases during the early stages of the War in Afghanistan. In 2014 the base was closed after the Kyrgyzstan parliament-assembly voted to cease leasing bases to the USA. The base was only eight hundred miles from the Russian border, and Russia lobbied Kyrgyzstan to end the lease.

Through 2013, a number of KC-135s were flying from the Transit Center, carrying on refueling missions over Afghanistan. The KC-135 jet is the main USAF aircraft for midair refueling. Planes in need of jet fuel, or "JF" as many airmen refer to it, dock with its long aft boom-nozzle. A typical KC-135 mission will require the jet to take off with its storage tanks full of fuel and make its way to any number of midair rendezvous points.

On 13 February 2013, one particular KC-135 at Manas was impounded as unsafe due to unexplained "rudder hunting," causing unwanted, annoying, and potentially dangerous in-flight oscillations. The crew of the flight

24 *Dutch roll*

The crash site area a few miles south of Chaldovar in the Kyrgyz Republic. The plane disintegrated in midair following a violent explosion, spreading wreckage debris over a radius of several miles.

reporting the issue had disengaged their on-board automatic yaw-damper and returned to base.

The technicians charged with the repair inspected the jet and determined that it was actually the rudder control unit that was defective and so replaced it. After that the jet had had no more reported problems with the rudder or yaw-damper through fourteen sorties.

On 3 May 2013, a KC-135 crew was handed a workaday refueling sortie. Their plane that day was the one that had been repaired some months back.

The two flying the jet that day were both recently qualified in their roles; they were both twenty-seven years old too. Captain Mark Voss, the pilot and aircraft commander, was flying only his eleventh flight as senior leader. His copilot was Captain Victoria "Tory" Pinckney, known as extremely rigorous and determined, but also inexperienced. She had crewed in Stratotankers for six months in winter 2011 and had only recently requalified after a period of not flying.

Together with the two flying the plane was Sgt. Tre Mackey, the fuel boom operator. He was the most experienced on-board that day, with ten years' service.

During preflight checks, the two pilots became aware that the on-board GPS-based weather radar was turning off and restarting periodically for no apparent reason ("a fault that would cause the [radar] power to cycle on and off throughout the flight"). As they taxied out to their runway, Voss was still troubleshooting it.

The jet departed Manas at 14:38 p.m. with a route heading due west over Kyrgyzstan at first, then south towards Afghanistan.

As soon as the two pilots completed their takeoff and initial climb-out, they became aware of a definite oscillation of the plane: the nose kept on repeatedly repositioning one to two degrees from side to side as she went. This continuous slight yawing is known as "rudder hunting." As Captain Voss noted: "It's kind of waffling." It was, at this time, Pinckney at the controls. At first Voss dismissed the issue with a terse instruction: "Use the auto-pilot if you don't think you can handle it."

Voss then wondered if the rolling-and-yawing was being caused by a one-off external factor: perhaps a bird issue or a foreign object on one wing. He thought there might be "something hanging off our jet." He sent Mackey (the boom op) to go and do a visual inspection of the wings using the small inspection window in back. Mackey came up negative. There was nothing unusual, unexpected, or suspicious in view at all.

This being so, as far as Voss could figure it, the yaw-damper had gone; like the radar, it was malfunctioning and working only intermittently. "I think the yaw-damper is inoperative.... Sorry, guys, let's turn it off." At this point, Voss perhaps inadvertently turned off the auto-pilot but left the probably faulty yaw-damper on.

The rudder hunting was a nuisance; nothing more than that. Then, as the plane was still proceeding towards its first operational rendezvous, in addition to the rudder hunting effect, there came a second unwanted effect: a slight roll from one side to the other every few seconds.

With the jet still en route to its first rendezvous, Voss and Pinckney both tried, at different moments, using well-timed manual rudder inputs to apply equal-opposite counter-rudder, in order to cancel out the oscillations—both the yawing (rudder hunting) and the rolling (Dutch roll).

The problem with manually counteracting such oscillations using rudder inputs is that these efforts can very easily exacerbate the problem. Such efforts are discouraged and actually contrary to standard procedure: "Pilots should not attempt to damp Dutch roll manually with the rudder ... improper excitation and recovery techniques cause higher than normal cumulative stress in the vertical stabilizer."

In terms of training, Dutch roll is a tricky phenomenon to teach and

24 Dutch roll

prepare pilots for because USAF flight simulators cannot simulate the effect at all. Furthermore, inducing it in airborne plane is actually forbidden because it can develop quickly into an out-of-control situation if not handled successfully, and so too will put excessive stress through the fuselage. Given the lack of experience of the two pilots and their absence of general training on the topic, neither noted the issue of the oscillations as Dutch roll specifically, but rather as just an annoying playing-up of one of several state-of-the-art automatic on-board systems or an unknown factor.

The general atmosphere in the cockpit was to just get on with the job. Both the yawing and the rolling were treated as irritants, rather like the malfunctioning weather radar; defects that had to be tolerated. Voss might have realized the seriousness of the unwanted yawing-rolling and thought about returning to base. But he didn't. Instead he decided to carry on the flight hoping to hold the yaw-roll annoyance to an acceptable level.

At around nine minutes into the flight, Voss was at the controls, and with the rolling-and-yawing oscillations still continuing, he began a wide left-hand turn, in keeping with the flight-path agreed with air traffic control. Voss made the turn using the jet's rudder rather than—given the yawing—go for the turn relying only on the wing ailerons.

Choosing this method to turn his jet had an immediate and serious consequence. The jet began to shudder and roll as if caught in a hurricane-force turbulence, rocking and shaking in a series of out-of-control midair spasms. The rolling and yawing suddenly increased to at least 30 degrees each sway.

As the jet continued through the left turn still in this wild rolling state, the force on the jet's tail-rudder was just too strong, and it suddenly snapped cleanly away from the plane at the hinges. The sudden change to the aerodynamics was catastrophic, with the down force on the vertical stabilizers overstressing them so that seconds later the entire tail section of the jet broke off and fell away. The jet was no longer controllable or capable of remaining in the air.

The doomed plane was suddenly plunging down from 20,000 feet up in an eighty-degree nose dive towards an area of hilly cattle-grazing land not far from the village of Chaldovar, in Kyrgyzstan, in the western foothills of the Himalayas near the border with Kazakhstan. No pilot, regardless of experience, would be able to pull up from this near-vertical dive.

In many USAF planes in such an emergency, the crew can be removed from a stricken plane within one to two seconds using ejection catapults under the seats—the emergency egress systems. Unfortunately, the KC-135 is not fitted with an ejection system or any form of last-resort emergency escape possibility—such as, say, strapping on a parachute and clambering out of an escape hatch.

As the plane continued to dive, it was breaking apart as it went. The fuselage broke into three main sections, and as this mid air disintegration was happening—a few seconds after the tail was lost—at around 10,000 feet, an electrical spark ignited the jet's cargo of highly flammable and highly explosive jet fuel. The plane was transformed into a sickening exploding fireball as the three burning fuselage sections crashed back down to earth at hundreds of miles per hour.

The three crew members were killed in the crash. The search-and-rescue operation was initially hampered by a number of factors.

The USAF personnel who initially set out towards the crash site ninety miles from base were not in appropriate vehicles to successfully approach such a remote and hilly location. It was also raining hard all that afternoon and evening. Then, once Air Force personnel arrived at the crash scene (after about four hours), they found that the Kyrgyzstan Army had already sealed the area off and had no immediate inclination to turn the site over to U.S. forces. Kyrgyzstan, a sovereign nation, had its own emergency units and a major emergency could not be simply handed over to an external visiting force. It was not clear if civilians had been killed, or even that the fireball was in fact a plane crash. Eyewitness reports by villagers described a series of massive midair explosions rather than a plane crash.

The standoff continued for some hours until eventually the U.S. ambassador resolved the impasse. It was not until after eleven o'clock that night—nine hours after the crash—that U.S. personnel finally gained access to the site and the search for the missing air crew began.

The lost jet was later valued at $66.3 million.

25 Stockton impromptu

Location: over Stockton Lake, Missouri
Date: 22 May 2013
Aircraft type: A-10
Fatalities: none
Cost of damage: $700,000

25 Stockton impromptu

Hangar photograph of the ripped and torn tail section of the A-10, which was climbing as it struck a span of electricity cables.

Stockton Lake is a large V-shaped man-made lake in Missouri. The lake was formed by constructing a dam over the Sac River in 1969. The lake extends over forty square miles of water surface. The woodland surrounding the lake is protected from development and the entire area is set aside for leisure and enjoyment. The amenities provided include facilities for sailing, swimming, fishing, hunting, camping, and picnics.

A hundred miles north of Stockton Lake—about halfway between Stockton and Kansas City—is Whiteman Air Force Base. Whiteman is perhaps best-known as the main home base of the B-2 Spirit stealth bomber. But there is more to Whiteman than the B-2. One of the units based at Whiteman is the 442nd Fighter Wing whose overall mission is to "operate, maintain and support the A-10 Thunderbolt at the highest level of combat readiness."

The A-10 is the only USAF fighter jet designed to fly slow-and-low over a battlefield ("long-loiter") in order to provide close air support for ground troops. Given the 442nd's purpose, it follows that many of the peacetime sorties flown by A-10 pilots in and out of Whiteman are intended to simulate low-altitude air-to-ground attacks.

On 22 May 2013, two very experienced A-10 pilots were scheduled to fly a training-practice mission. The leader, DEUCE1, had 1660 flight-hours in A10s logged; DEUCE2 had 2359 flight-hours in A10s logged.

The training mission had several segments. Initially the two would make their way to an area of restricted military-owned land for simulated air-to-ground attacks using practice-only non-live Maverick missiles. The live version carries a hundred and twenty pounds of explosive as a precision-guided bomb. As well as the low-altitude attacks, the two jets were also due to practice midair refueling with a rendezvous with a KC-135 fuel-tanker jet scheduled in. Then finally the two would practice low-altitude navigation before returning to base.

Following the mission briefing (during which both airmen were focused and attentive) and ground checks to their planes, DEUCE1 and DEUCE2 departed Whiteman during the midafternoon, at 3:07 p.m. For various reasons the practice segments were rearranged as the mission unfolded so that the air-to-air refuel practice came first, followed by the Maverick training in Truman "C" Military Operating Area, a gravel pit complex south of the base.

The two then departed the Truman range en route to another Military Operating Area. At around 3:40 p.m. (a half-hour after takeoff) the two jets began to fly towards Stockton Lake.

By USAF convention, five hundred feet is generally the lowest altitude that a U.S. warplane will fly during ordinary training. Training at lower altitudes, such as for aircraft on low-altitude attack practice, is supposed to be only in short, pre-defined segments and will generally take place over restricted military land. ("Do not operate aircraft over non-congested areas at an altitude of less than 500 feet except over open water ... under such exceptions [e.g., open water] pilots must not operate aircraft closer than 500 feet to any person, vessel, vehicle, or structure.")

As DEUCE1 and DEUCE2 proceeded in the direction of Stockton, DEUCE2 descended in order to come in fast-and-low over the lake—a rather dramatic venture that was not a scheduled part of the training.

DEUCE2 headed in toward the lake at an altitude of only a hundred and forty feet, and he was well aware of this because he was receiving repeated in-cockpit warnings from the audible warning system. A computerized female voice ("Betty") was repeating: "Altitude! Altitude! ... Altitude! Altitude! ... Altitude! Altitude!" Fifty-two times the repeated low-altitude warning sounded through seven minutes as DEUCE2 flew towards

25 Stockton impromptu

the lake, crossed the Stockton shoreline, and continued out over the expanse of water at three hundred and fifty miles per hour.

As he flew, DEUCE2 was studiously ignoring the low-altitude warnings. He did not react to any one of them; he was disregarding the warnings completely, and in fact he was whistling a happy tune as he went.

On the lake that day there were several civilian sailing boats—pleasure boats. Two of these boats in particular were of interest to DEUCE2; their presence on the lake that day might have been known in advance to the pilot.

Upon sighting the two boats, DEUCE2 banked aggressively (80 degrees of bank) and turned towards the first one. In response to this maneuver, the jet's on-board computer issued an urgent "Break-X" imminent-ground-impact audible warning: "Pull up! Pull up!" DEUCE2 took no notice of the warning and continued on his way, flying in directly over the first boat at a height of only a hundred and thirty feet above the water—a dramatic impromptu fly-by. Then DEUCE2 headed on towards the next boat that he had spotted for a second impromptu low-altitude fly-by.

As these unscheduled and prohibited maneuvers were ongoing, DEUCE1—the leader of the two jets—radioed in to DEUCE2 a notification of an approaching hazard. On such two-jet or "two ship" formations, when flying at extreme low altitude, all looming obstacles are declared and noted by both pilots as they go.

In this instance, DEUCE1 called electricity cables two miles away: a set of four unmarked electricity supply cables ("a major power transmission line") spanning the lake, held above the water by two tall concrete towers, one on each side just south of the Highway 245 Bridge. By coincidence, the four thick twenty-core tensioned steel cables spanned the lake at an elevation of a hundred and forty feet above the water.

To the radio-intercom hazard warning, DEUCE2 responded with a standard acknowledgment: "Two," meaning that he had heard the message but had not yet seen the obstacle for himself (at which time by Air Force convention he would declare "contact"). In these moments, DEUCE2 had his attention focused on completing his second surprising and unscheduled impromptu fly-by.

At one moment (3:48 p.m.), with his jet still crossing the water at three hundred and fifty miles per hour, DEUCE2 looked up ahead and suddenly became aware of the electricity cables that DEUCE1 had noted: the four bundles of wire cable were looming immediately ahead. In reaction, the pilot pulled up sharply, almost instinctively—with his control stick maximum aft (pulled backwards toward the pilot).

The A-10 pitched up spectacularly and began to climb with the nose easily clearing the hurdle. But even with maximum stick, DEUCE2's rate of climb was not quite enough to stop the right side tail elevator-stabilizer from catching on the uppermost cable. Fortunately the upper run of the cross-lake cabling was a tensioner and static disperser and was not carrying electrical charge.

The cable caught the A-10's tail, slicing like a wire cheese-cutter through the body-work, shearing off a section and cutting cleanly through various internal systems—including electrical wiring and the main right-side hydraulics. Various fragments of the A-10's tail section fell into the water, as well as several components of the practice munitions mounted below the jet. Hydraulic fluid began to leak from the damaged area.

The A-10 was explicitly designed to withstand just such midair damage, which was not unlike battle damage. DEUCE2 was not fazed: "[I just] hit those power lines," he radioed to DEUCE1. And then: "Knock it off," a notification that he could no longer continue the remainder of the practice mission as planned.

Leaking hydraulic fluid and with part of his stabilizer missing, DEUCE2 made his way back to Whiteman, where he requested an emergency landing as a precaution. The plane was without right-side hydraulics but was still airworthy. The A-10 was immediately impounded and parked in a restricted-access hangar pending a full investigation.

The cost of repairs to the damaged A-10 was estimated at $700,000.

The official USAF investigation into the incident concluded that the pilot "maneuvered his aircraft for a low pass over a boat on Stockton Lake in violation of published flight rules and operating procedures." A complete picture of the motivation for the impromptu was not established by the Investigation Panel as the pilot declined to be interviewed, per independent legal advice he had received.

26 Okinawa corkscrew

Location: the Pacific Ocean, sixty miles east of Okinawa
Date: 28 May 2013
Aircraft type: F-15

26 Okinawa corkscrew

Fatalities: none
Cost of damage: $31.9 million

Okinawa is one of a group of Pacific islands known as the Ryukyu Islands. The population of 1.3 million is majority indigenous Ryukyuan people. Among many other significant achievements, the Okinawan Ryukyuan first codified and practiced a form of hand-to-hand combat known as karate-do, "the way of the empty hand."

The Islands have a vexed history of invasion and subjugation by China and Japan. Okinawa is formally a Japanese territory, but the island is extremely remote from the mainland, which is 1,200 miles away. The Ryukyuan people are not recognized as a separate indigenous culture by the Japanese state; to the Japanese government, Okinawans are regular Japanese citizens.

After World War II, following the Japanese surrender to the Allied forces, the U.S. established a large number of permanent military "forward bases" on Okinawa. The arrival of U.S. forces taking control of the island followed centuries of annexation and occupation by various imperial powers.

The U.S. military sites cover around 30 percent of Okinawa Island: thirty-two restricted sites that appear on local maps only as jagged plain gray shapes with all topographical details subject to redaction. Encountering unexpectedly a run of razor wire marking the perimeter of one or another U.S. military site is an unavoidable aspect of life on Okinawa, with several of the restricted areas limiting access to some of the most appealing areas of natural beauty.

At least twenty-five thousand U.S. service personnel are billeted on Okinawa at Camp Schwab, Camp Hansen, Camp Courtney, Camp McTureous, Camp Kuwae, and Camp Zukeran. Then there are a number of training grounds: Northern Training Area; Kin Blue Beach Training Area; Ukibaru Jima Training Area; Tsuken Jima Training Area. Numerous further sites are given over to communications, ammunition storage and oil storage.

For the majority of Okinawans, the presence of U.S. forces is unwelcome and unacceptable. Seventy to 80 percent of Okinawans are unhappy with the present arrangements. Okinawan residents resent the impact of the U.S. military presence on their quality of life. Beyond the dehumanizing psychological impact of being surrounded by a war-ready military, the residents resent the air pollution, noise pollution, and soil pollution created by the military presence. Equally, residents fear being actually caught up in a military accident—such as a plane or helicopter crash. In short, the presence of the U.S. military places a pall over the island.

The USAF has a primary mission in the Asia-Pacific region: "promote stability, dissuade/deter aggression, and swiftly defeat enemies." The largest USAF base in the Asia-Pacific region is Kadena, on Okinawa Island. One of many squadrons based at Kadena is the 44th Fighter Squadron of F-15 jets. The squadron's raison d'être is the provision of "unmatched air superiority on demand."

The F-15 fighter jet first entered service in 1978. The fighter has been in continuous service for forty years. As it has aged, its reputation as a dazzling and effective fighter has been tempered somewhat by its apparent susceptibility to bizarre and catastrophic midair mechanical breakdowns.

On 27 May 2013, two F-15 pilots of the 44th were handed a straightforward training mission to take place the following day. The mission that day was "dogfighting" practice—known technically basic fighter maneuvers, or BFM. The two jets were to head out over an area of open sea around sixty miles east of Okinawa in the Pacific Ocean—an airspace designated as USAF Training Area W-173—and carry on a range of simulated attack-defend tactical maneuvers.

The main aim during a dogfight is for the attacking jet to maneuver into a position where a clear shot can be taken at the enemy jet. Equally, the one defending moves to evade and prevent the attacker from being able to sight up a clear shot. Dogfighting uses the full extent of a fighter jet's thrust and maneuverability in a range of highly acrobatic and aggressive twists, rolls, dives, climbs and turns.

The two jets departed from Kadena at 8:20 a.m. on 28 May, flying under the callsigns KNIFE1 and KNIFE2. KNIFE1 was the lead that day with KNIFE2 the subordinate.

Once established at around 20,000 feet in the W-173 airspace, the two began by performing a G-force awareness maneuver—180-degree turns at increasing speeds intended to check the readiness of jet and pilot for the high-G-force dogfighting to come. Then the two set up for the first hostile encounter.

For the first dogfight simulation, KNIFE1 was defending against a simulated attack from KNIFE2. Typical BFM encounters have a format comparable to a judo or wrestling bout: the attacker has around two minutes to achieve a kill shot, or else that round has been won (as it were) by the defender.

The way that the parameters were set up that day was that the attacker

26 Okinawa corkscrew

would roll and accelerate some distance away from the one defending. Then he would turn back towards his quarry. As he was zooming in on target, the attacker was bound to announce his imminent arrival with the radio-intercom statement: "Six thousand," meaning he was six thousand feet away; this was the signal for the dogfight to commence with intensity.

After two minutes of dramatic maneuvering in the first bout of the morning, KNIFE1 called for a cessation: "Knock it off! Knock it off." Then it was the turn of KNIFE2 to defend against an onslaught from KNIFE1.

At one moment during the jockeying and vying, KNIFE2 executed a dramatic nose-down corkscrew dive—achieved by placing one of his jet engines to full afterburner and the other to a lesser thrust setting, causing the jet to spin wildly as it was descending. The tactic was a success, and KNIFE1 called "Knock it off" without having achieved a shot at KNIFE2.

As the call came through, KNIFE2 was still tumbling through around 14,000 feet in his defensive maneuver. Upon the call, KNIFE2 began to make efforts to pull up to level flight. But as he did so the pilot "noticed that the plane did not respond to flight control inputs."

KNIFE2 set his twin jet engines to idle and began in earnest efforts to arrest his out-of-control dive. Every technique that he tried in order to level out had no effect on the corkscrew motion. The pilot's overall perception was that the entire range of controls were suddenly non-functional: his varied inputs were not getting translated through to actual alterations of the rudder, ailerons, etc.

As KNIFE2 was spinning out of control with his jet seemingly unresponsive, he looked to the cockpit dashboard and saw several warning lights illuminated on the caution panel.

As he continued to struggle with his flight controls, KNIFE2 spoke coolly over the radio intercom to the flight lead: "I think we've seen this before.... I don't think this one's recovering." This comment was a pointed reference to the fact that two of his close colleagues—other F-15 pilots at Kadena—had been involved in similar emergencies in which the planes they were flying had become suddenly uncontrollable.

Within twenty seconds of the first signs of a malfunction, KNIFE2 had descended from 14,000 feet down to 6,000 feet—the lowest safe altitude for emergency ejection. As KNIFE2 called "six thousand," KNIFE1 instructed the out-of-control pilot to eject. At this command, KNIFE2 reached for his ejection lever and was catapulted out of his jet.

The F-15 continued to spin wildly nose-low, accelerating as it went, until at about five hundred feet above water the spinning ceased. Seconds later, the jet nose-dived into open sea at an estimated speed of 345 m.p.h. The wrecked jet sank to the ocean floor—unrecoverable at a depth of at least one mile below the surface.

The pilot's ejection parachute opened correctly and his auto-inflate life raft deployed on a lanyard below him. Immediately after he splashed down, the vulnerable pilot hauled himself into his life raft and turned on his emergency transmitters. He was exposed and unprotected, floating alone in the ocean, but KNIFE1 had seen everything and was in discussions with the Supervisor of Flying at Kadena.

The first rescue aircraft to respond to the emergency signals were a Japanese Coast Guard helicopter and a Japanese Air Self Defense Force helicopter. Both arrived overhead of the marooned pilot within fifteen minutes of his transmitter beacon's being turned on.

The Japanese Air Self Defense Force helicopter efficiently hoisted the unharmed pilot to safety, flying him to Camp Foster medical facilities on Okinawa. Upon evaluation at the hospital, unit the pilot was found to have suffered only bruising to his arms around the biceps. A comprehensive series of X-rays revealed no significant injuries, and KNIFE2 was discharged within hours.

Navy surveyors later pronounced the wreckage of the crashed F-15 unrecoverable. The value of the crashed jet was estimated at $31.9 million.

27 Birdstrike Luke

Location: close to Luke Air Force Base, Arizona
Date: 26 June 2013
Aircraft type: F-16D
Fatalities: none
Cost of damage: $22.7 million

The correct procedure in the event of experiencing a severe engine problem soon after takeoff in an F-16 might register as counterintuitive to the layman: the pilot should proceed to climb at full power straight ahead gaining speed and altitude as quickly as possible—with the aim of seeking to obtain the maximum time-altitude possible in which to evaluate and resolve the issue. Higher altitude equates to increased time available to work a problem out, and in the case of an engine problem, the jet's

27 Birdstrike Luke

The destroyed F-16D was almost completely buried in the crash. All that remained visible was the aircraft's splintered tailpipe.

automatic systems need time to react and adjust as much as the human commander.

Luke Air Force Base is located in Arizona in the western suburbs of the city of Phoenix. There are two main runways; the ground level footprint of the base is around four square miles. Much of the USAF aviation activity in and out of Luke is concerned with training pilots, an overall task defined as a mission "to develop America's Airman today for tomorrow ... to deliver unrivaled air, space and cyberspace education and training."

One squadron based at Luke is the 309th Fighter Squadron. The 309 FS has a primary responsibility "for training the world's finest fighter pilots and maintenance technicians."

One of the jets that the 309th flies is the F-16 D, a variation of the classic single-engine supersonic fighter. The variation provides two cockpit seats—one set directly behind the other—enabling an instructor pilot to sit behind an F-16 student pilot. The cockpit is set up so that each pilot position has full access to the flight controls: the plane can be flown from the back seat or the front seat.

Some of the student pilots allocated to the base are green recruits transitioning from trainer jets like the T-38 Talon, while others are experienced pilots who are regaining their F-16 pilot certification. An F-16 pilot, once qualified, must continue to fly sorties regularly, or else his certification will expire.

In June 2013, one student pilot arrived at Luke with a requirement to regain full F-16 pilot status following a three and a half years in a non-flying role. The pilot in question was really only a "student" for designated administrative purposes, since he actually had at least two thousand flight hours piloting F-16s logged. He usually had more F-16 hours than his designated instructor on any given day's training. And so it was on 26 June: the student had at least one thousand F-16 hours more than his instructor for that day's flying.

The plan was for the student pilot, sitting up front, to perform a series of training profiles with the instructor pilot sitting behind him in the rear seat. It was only the student's second training flight back in in an F-16 following his three years in a non-flying role, so he was maybe a little rusty.

The two began their sortie late in the afternoon and were airborne by approximately 6:20 p.m., flying as callsign RADON11. The main training segment of the sortie progressed as planned, rather uneventfully, with syllabus activities including aircraft handling; straight-in visual-flight-rules landings; and formation flying practice.

Towards the end of the session the instructor took the controls as he needed to perform a rear-seat takeoff-landing—purely for the purposes of keeping his activity log current. It was a tick-box exercise which was expected to take only a few minutes. The plan was to do the landing-takeoff as efficiently as possible by doing a touch-and-go: he would land the jet and then, within a few seconds, still moving at speed along the runway, he would gain clearance for an immediate takeoff.

At 6:53 p.m., the instructor began his takeoff. Just after he had retracted his wheels ("gear up") and begun his climb away from the runway, the student in the front observed three small dark flashes pass off his right side, together with an abnormal engine noise, a "low grade buzzing," followed by a "light buzz, pop, bang," accompanied by an unpleasant "acrid smell" coming though his oxygen mask.

It was apparent to both pilots that their jet engine had sucked in ("ingested") a number of small birds—sparrows, perhaps, or a similar species. For USAF pilots as much as commercial jet pilots, a bird strike

27 Birdstrike Luke

is an extremely undesirable and potentially catastrophic occurrence, and engine recovery is by no means guaranteed.

As the incinerating objects were passing through the jet, it was banging and popping and losing-then-gaining power every few seconds, giving the instructor pilot at the controls the feeling that it could seize or fail completely any second.

Another UASF pilot flying nearby—callsign HONKER11—came over the radio to report "an orange flame and sparks" shooting spectacularly from out of the F-16's tailpipe.

The correct procedure for a low-altitude bird strike is for the pilot to climb smartly away—in a straight line, preferably—in order to gain enough altitude to troubleshoot. In the case of this particular strike, the reaction of the instructor pilot was different from accepted and trained-for procedure: rather than proceed to climb straight and well up into the air at speed, he made instead first tight right-hand one-eighty turn, followed by a wide left-hand loop.

The pilot felt like the engine was going to go unrecoverable at any moment, and he wanted to *turn back towards a landing runway* at Luke just as soon as he could. He did not like the sound of what he was hearing, and the intermittent loss of thrust seemed to him to be intensifying. He felt like he could lose his engine at any moment; he was not confident in it.

In these thirty or thirty-five seconds since the first pops and bangs, neither pilot had really put any focus on reviewing their instrument panel gauges. The situation was simply unfolding in the moment with the instructor pilot flying "by the seat of his pants," that is, using only visual observation and instinct.

The problem was that in making his turn back to base, as opposed to climbing straight up and away, the pilot was all the while sapping his jet's airspeed, and he was not gaining altitude very quickly either. As he came out of the wide turn, the consequences of his decision were becoming obvious: the jet was climbing nose-high but with an airspeed of only 130 m.p.h. The F-16 was close to its sink-speed, too slow to fly (around 160 m.p.h. is the basic minimum airspeed for an F-16, and much faster than that is usual in a climb-out).

The instructor had got himself caught in a no-man's land of being neither set for an emergency forced landing nor high enough up to consider options. Very often following a bird ingestion, after a few horrifying belches, a Pratt and Whitney jet will recover and function as normal (there are several anti-bird recovery systems onboard).

In losing speed as he had by making the turn, the instructor was now so slow that the stall warnings were sounding in the cockpit: "Warning! Warning! ... Warning! Warning! ... Warning! Warning!" The instructor pilot assessed his situation: his jet was about to enter a midair stall and begin dropping out of the sky.

The student in the front seat was looking on aghast: he "was just not ready" for such an in-flight emergency. He was unprepared and in any case was not at the controls. He knew well enough that a high-speed straight-up climb-out was their best option in the circumstances but did not feel comfortable *instructing his instructor* so.

Then, in these slow-airspeed moments, there came again, now louder and more violent, a bang followed by shudders behind ("aft"). In the midst of the clanking bangs and the air-stall warnings, the instructor tipped his intercom mic and commanded: "Bail! Bail! Bail!" At 18:54 both pilots pulled on their ejection handles and were blasted clear of the F-16. Both pilots suffered only minor injuries during the ejection sequence and parachute landings.

Their jet flew for eight miles before eventually crashing close to the perimeter fence of Luke Air Force Base. The jet's impact speed—350 m.p.h.—was such that it was severely compressed and almost completely buried in the impact. What was left to see at the surface looked like a six-feet-across stainless steel modern art sculpture resembling a clump of grossly enlarged giant pencil-shavings.

The crashed jet was beyond repair—the value of the lost plane estimated at $22.7 million.

---

28 Lights-out intercept

Location: Restricted airspace area 386—
over the Atlantic Ocean off the coast of Maryland
Date: 1 August 2013
Aircraft type: F-16
Fatalities: none
Cost of damage: $22.9 million

One of the ways that U.S. airspace is protected—an unceasing and continuous watch—is through the Aerospace Control Alert mission, "a national network of fully loaded aircraft ready to protect the country on

28 Lights-out intercept

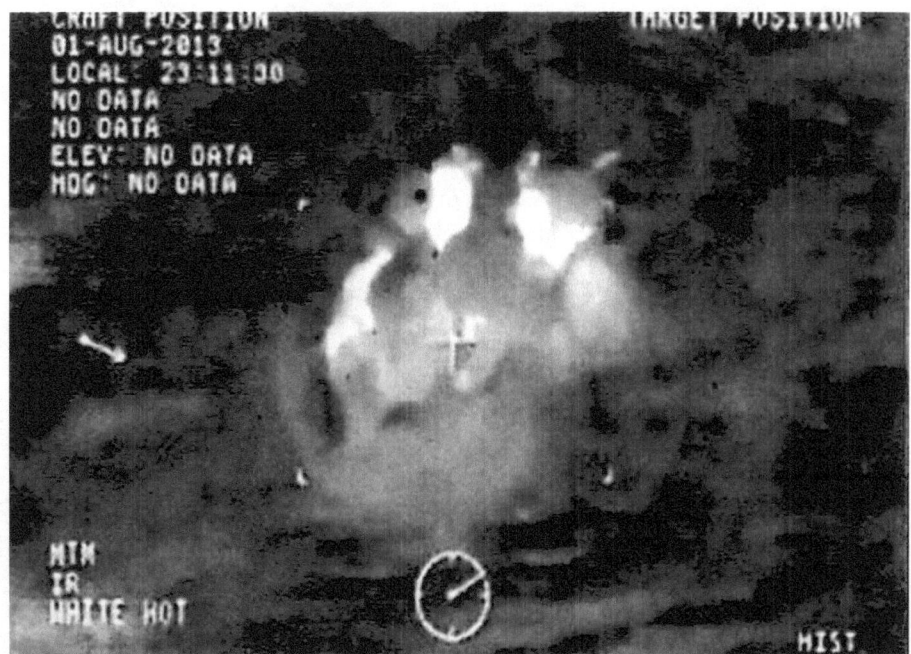

Video grab of the view from the rescue helicopter depicting the ejected F-16 pilot and a medic preparing to be winched from the water.

a moment's notice ... aircraft, aircrew and launch personnel diligently ensure the immediate capability to intercept, inspect, influence and, if necessary, defeat [i.e., shoot down] a potential airborne threat."

A control-alert sortie will begin with an unknown and therefore unwelcome aircraft flying directly towards or actually entering U.S. airspace. Such an aircraft may be one from a military air force of another country or it may be a civilian aircraft of unknown origin; the only initial criterion is that it is a plane that is not identifying itself.

Immediately upon such a potential threat emerging, F-16s will be "scrambled"—pilots on standby will rush to their jets with the intention of becoming airborne within less than five minutes. Once airborne the U.S. jets will proceed immediately towards the unknown aircraft at supersonic speeds.

Upon reaching the vicinity of the unidentified aircraft, the control-alert jets will perform a midair interception. First they will fly up close to the unknown aircraft and visually observe the activity in the cockpit; such an inspection may reveal the rogue pilot to be incapacitated or disoriented, for example. The U.S. jets will typically signal to the hostile by repeatedly rocking wings or flashing their lights in order to communicate: "follow me." At this, the alien aircraft must comply with the clear instruction to be escorted away from U.S. airspace. In some circumstances, depending on the communications, the rogue-hostile may be shot down by the interceptors, but only once clearance has been given from higher command.

The Aerospace Control Alert mission has developed into a grid of airspace areas of responsibility. So, for example, Colorado Air National Guard jets are tasked with "protecting anything west of the Mississippi River as far north as the Canadian border and as far south as the Mexican border." Another example is the District of Columbia Air National Guard—the control-alert force that protects the airspace over Washington, D.C., and so the U.S. Congress (the seat of democracy) and the president's workplace and residence, the White House.

The District of Columbia Air National Guard is thus tasked with a key component of the overall control-alert picture. The principal squadron fulfilling this task for the District of Columbia is the 121st Fighter Squadron based at Andrews Air Force Base—or Joint Base Andrews, as it has been recently renamed—the U.S. air base that forms one of the eastern suburbs of Washington. Only fifteen miles from the Capitol Building, Andrews is well-known as the place where the president's VC-25 or *Air Force One* is stationed.

The 121st Squadron flies F-16s for their control-alert tasking. On any ordinary day, apart from readiness to perform an Aerospace Control-Alert, the pilots will also fly various practice sorties in order to be fully prepared for any emergent security threat.

For the evening of 1 August 2013, five of the F-16 pilots of the 121st had been handed a night-intercept practice mission. The arrangement for the sortie was that two of the jets would fly as simulated hostiles while three others would perform various interceptions. One of the three was actually in training and was under instruction from the leader of the three, whose callsign was MA1.

The five jets departed Andrews shortly before ten o'clock in the evening, with all involved wearing night-vision goggles (NVGs), infrared-based light amplification devices that enable the user to see operate in near complete darkness. They proceeded from Maryland out over the Atlantic to a segment of restricted U.S. military airspace known as 386 or Warning Area 386.

The early stages of the mission passed off uneventfully: the simulated bogeys flew a set course at around 10,000 feet with the three others performing a number of interceptions.

28 Lights-out intercept

Well into the mission, MA1 directed the simulated hostiles to go lights-out—they were to turn off all external lights. (Any authentic emergent airborne threat launched at night towards the U.S. would be very unlikely to keep their external lights on.)

The three friendly jets set about practicing lights-out night interceptions. The emphasis at this stage of the mission was on the one of the three who was in training. The trainee under instruction from MA1 kept making a complete hash of his intercept and was well-short of passing the certification he was seeking. At one moment—at around 10:20 p.m.—MA1, perhaps slightly frustrated at the lack of ability in his student, directed the trainee to fly chase position (following directly behind) while he performed a lights-out intercept as a demonstration.

However, at this moment, rather than fly a by-the-book perfect intercept, MA1 began to close in on the sim-hostiles using an unconventional and extraordinary technique. Essentially his method was to forego the in-cockpit information feeds appearing on his head-up display and on his radar display screen and instead gain visually the hostile's jet-engine exhaust plume—the vapor trail pouring out from behind the jet he was closing on. MA1 used only this as reference as he flew in towards the target intercept approaching from behind.

Also, apart from the unexpected tracking technique, MA1 approached extremely fast—he was flying towards the target at around four hundred and fifty miles per hour. His closing speed was at least a hundred miles per hour faster than a target jet proceeding through the night sky at around three hundred and fifty miles per hour. A typical by-the-book final-closing approach speed would be five to ten miles per hour faster.

As he closed in on his object of interest, MA1 was advancing at great speed and without reference to his on-board displays. At ten twenty-thee and fifty-three seconds, the urgent warning "Break-X" displayed in front of him—an alert informing the pilot to urgently change course. At ten twenty-thee and fifty-six seconds (three seconds after the Break-X), MA1 smashed into the simulated bogey he had been chasing, ripping off its left tail stabilizer—the horizontal tail section.

Immediately upon impact, the simulated jet became uncontrollable and began to spin wildly. The unfortunate pilot was suddenly cast into a grim situation: lights out on a moonless night at only ten thousand feet over the Atlantic in an uncontrollable nose-down jet flying at around three hundred miles per hour.

The pilot flying as hostile was in a catastrophic situation. He waited for the next moment that his plane rolled wings level to the horizon and pulled his ejection handle. As he was blasted clear of the jet and his parachute opened, the pilot suffered considerable "flailing" injuries, meaning his legs and arms were not fully strapped or secured at the moment of ejection. He was, in the pilot's own words, "thrown around like a rag doll."

The F-16 crashed into the Atlantic and disintegrated on impact.

The pilot's parachute opened normally with a life raft hanging from a lanyard below him as he splashed down into the Atlantic less than a minute after the collision. As he hit the water and sought to come aboard his life raft, the pilot realized that he could not move his legs. He had sustained ligament tearing to his knee and ankle joints and was unable to swing his legs up into the raft.

The pilot drifted, marooned at sea, struggling repeatedly to clamber into his life raft with the absolutely real and pressing prospect of death by hypothermia before being rescued. Eventually, after about forty minutes, the pilot finally scrambled inside his raft and turned on his survival kit radio. Around one hour later a USAF HH-60 helicopter hovered above him and a Navy diver began to strap him into a floating stretcher.

The pilot was then airlifted to a USAF hospital facility. His injuries were serious but not life-threatening. Over some months the pilot's leg injuries were operated on, and following a period of rehabilitation he was returned to full flying-duty status.

The midair collision did not cause any significant damage to MA1 and he returned to Andrews uneventfully without the need to declare any emergency or to make a forced landing. The pilot of MA1 was later found to have been flying recklessly and the final Accident Report was not equivocal in blaming his action for the loss of a F-16 valued at $21.9 million and around $1 million of repairs to the surviving jet.

29 Racetrack gun pattern

Location: Okinawa Island, Japan
Date: 5 August 2013
Aircraft type: HH-60 Pave Hawk
Fatalities: 1
Cost of damage: $38 million

Kadena Air Base on Okinawa Island, a Japanese territory, is the USAF's main hub in the Pacific-Asia region with around twenty thousand

29 Racetrack gun pattern

Air Force personnel present. In addition to the actual base, there are many other restricted U.S.-military-only sites on the small island. Overall the U.S. military has taken over about 20 percent of all the land on the island.

Many Okinawans are dissatisfied with the present arrangement. Many see Japan as an invading and colonizing imperial force on the island, and for that reason the Japanese had no reasonable right to hand so much of the island over to the U.S. military at the cessation of World War II.

In terms of everyday life, Okinawans bemoan the presence of such massive ongoing military activity as unsettling. Others decry the toxic chemicals and substances—oil and jet fuel, for example—that regularly pollute some of the most spectacular areas of natural beauty on the island. There are those who fear being caught up in a military accident or mishap—air crashes are frequent.

"You Fuck Up, We Pick Up" is how the 33rd Rescue Squadron's main activity is sometimes humorously and informally described. Their primary activity: search and rescue flying the HH-60 helicopter. "The primary mission of the HH-60G Pave Hawk helicopter is to conduct day or night personnel recovery operations into hostile environments to recover isolated personnel during war." The Pave Hawk is the USAF version of the fast and highly maneuverable Army Black Hawk helicopter—recognizable through the air by its wide vertical stabilizer below the tail rotor and its prominent refueling boom-nozzle jutting out under the right-hand side of the nose cone.

The Pave is designed and fitted to fly into hostile territory and urgently extract military personnel on the ground. Often a search-and-rescue mission will require first locating the persons to be exfiltrated, and for this reason the USAF Paves are fitted with high-tech search-and-rescue equipment such as forward-looking infrared imaging and color weather radar. A fully fitted-out Pave Hawk costs the Air Force $40 million.

In 2013, certain helicopter crews of the 33rd were in training based at Kadena on Okinawa. The Pave has a crew of four. In addition to a pilot and copilot there will be—sitting in two rear seat positions—a flight engineer and an aerial gunner.

Simulated missions or training sorties are a basic component of much Air Force activity. To ensure combat readiness, pilots and crews are very often involved in flying missions with artificial targets, artificial enemy positions, and in the case of the 33rd, artificial crash survivors—wounded and vulnerable U.S. personnel in artificial hostile territory.

During August 2013, some Pave Hawk crews of the 33rd were flying training missions using the U.S. military Central Training Area on Okinawa. On 5 August, one such simulated mission was given to two Pave crews. Working together as a two-helicopter or "two-ship" formation, the teams were required to respond under scramble conditions to a call to find and rescue a survivor of a downed helicopter in enemy territory—where there would be the likelihood of hostile small-arms fire in and around the rescue site.

A crucial component of the mission that day was rapid response under "scramble" conditions: the crews were to be given only the grid coordinates of the survivor and some basic information about the hostile presence. It would then be for the crew, led by the pilot and aircraft commander, to formulate a rescue plan ("gameplan") and, proceeding as quickly as possible, make their way by air to the crash site with the intention of picking up all survivors and transporting them back to friendly medical facilities.

The mission began with the scramble call at 15:15. Within twenty minutes—at 15:35—the two helicopters took off. The two helicopters quickly navigated successfully to the simulated crash site (only about fourteen miles northeast of the air base). Both aircraft had onboard two Air Force paramedics, known as pararescuemen or PJs.

The first Pave Hawk (the lead, and superior of the two) landed and let out its two PJs while the second Pave Hawk covered them with the aerial gunner training his lethal .50 caliber mounted belt-feed gun on the crash site area. Then, when the lead took off, the second Pave landed and also let out two more PJs.

Once this was done, and both helicopters were airborne again, they began to fly in a prearranged "gun patrol" pattern overhead of the crash site at around a hundred and fifty feet up. The pattern agreed was a classic "racetrack" circuit in a figure-eight shape—with the crash site at the midpoint.

Pretty much as soon as they were both airborne again, the two Paves came under hostile fire—small-arms fire incoming towards the crash site and into the air towards the rescue teams. The Pave Hawks returned fire (the enemy was soon simulated killed) and then continued to patrol from above.

In the case of engaging an enemy (or many other reasons), it may be the copilot who takes the flight controls, and so it was that afternoon in Okinawa aboard the second helicopter.

The two helicopters had flown around seven of their racetrack loops when, at one moment—at ten past four in the afternoon—the copilot of the second noticed that his circuits had been progressively drifting slightly each time and decided unilaterally to correct the westward drift by performing a right-hand turn rather than a left-hand turn away from the crash site. (It was definitely the most efficient way of getting back over the crash site.) Turning this way brought the second helicopter rather close to the other one, but not so close as for there to be any immediate danger of a collision.

Of the four crew on board, three were fine with the copilot's action, but the pilot and aircraft commander was not. As the unexpected turn occurred, he happened to be peering through his helicopter's greenhouse window—a window in the roof looking up to the sky above—when the other Pave came looming into view above them. He perceived its presence as being extremely close and an imminent collision threat.

The pilot's reaction to his perception of the other helicopter's being much too close was to seek to move to a lower altitude as quickly as possible. With the copilot's full performance left-hand turn still in progress and the helicopter banking sharply to around 50 degrees, the pilot leaped up and seized the controls. This move immediately decreased the collective control, causing his aircraft to bank even more steeply and then lose altitude.

Within a few seconds (these maneuvers had begun at only a hundred and fifty feet up), the helicopter began to descend towards the tree line of the forest below—an undulating and verdurous area of subtropical forest with trees rising over forty feet.

Now it was the descent into the trees that became the pilot's focus. He increased the collective control dramatically in an attempt to regain altitude, but the sudden change was too abrupt; the rotors were only "mushing through" the air without any significant lift being achieved.

As their helicopter contacted the treetops, the Pave crew of four immediately recognized that the situation was unrecoverable: they were going down. The pilot reconciled himself to a hard landing or crash-landing coming down through trees, and reduced power to idle.

An abrupt but non-catastrophic hard landing might have been possible from a height of forty feet if the helicopter were impacting soft level terrain, but in this case the ground below was not level, or even near level. It was in fact a steep and rocky hillside.

At 16:05 the Pave Hawk crashed into the forest. As it hit the ground, the fuselage rolled part way down the hillside, came to a stop on its side, and burst into flames.

With the wreck ablaze, surrounded by clouds of dense toxic black smoke and .50 caliber ammunition detonating in the heat, three of the four airmen clambered out to safety. The gunner was trapped for a time and had to use a medic's stretcher as a ladder to climb out. The simulated mission had been horrifyingly and ironically reversed: a real helicopter was downed with survivors in peril and a real crew member missing—the flight engineer.

The lead Pave was immediately on the scene and successfully rescued three of the crew as the post-crash blaze took hold, issuing profuse thick black smoke that soon rendered the crash site completely inaccessible. It was not until twenty-four hours later, with the fire out, that the remains of the engineer were located, still strapped into his seat in the burnt-out wreck of the downed HH-60G.

It is such incidents that terrify Okinawans—and also anger them. The USAF does not offer transparency with such incidents as they unfold. The only detail will be such a document as the official Accident Report issued months or years later. This particular crash was close to several small villages, including Ginoza. The residents saw the rising plume of smoke but were offered no particular reassurance from the USAF. Of course, the local authorities also had no information on the event either. Fear and anger about such incidents prompted a local protest march about the continuing U.S. military presence on the island.

30 Fuel-line leak

Location: near Broadus, Montana
Date: 19 August 2013
Aircraft type: B-1B
Fatalities: none
Cost of damage: $317 million

The B-1B is a USAF heavy bomber that sits—or flies—alongside the B-2 and B-52. (The designation "B" is for bomber.)

The B-1B is a terrifying and impressive machine. One of the most lethal machines ever devised and produced by humans, "it carries the largest payload of both guided and unguided weapons [i.e., bombs] in the Air Force inventory. It can rapidly deliver massive quantities of precision and non-precision weapons against any adversary, anywhere in the world."

30 Fuel-line leak

An aerial view of crash site of a destroyed B-1B near Broadus, Montana.

The B-1B heavy bomber can carry forty-two tons of bombs ("84 500-pound Mk-82 or 24 2,000-pound Mk-84 general purpose bombs; up to 84 500-pound Mk-62 or 8 2,000-pound Mk-65 Quick Strike naval mines; 30 cluster munitions—CBU-87, -89, -97—or 30 Wind-Corrected Munitions Dispensers—CBU-103, -104, -105; up to 24 2,000-pound GBU-31 or 15 500-pound GBU-38 Joint Direct Attack Munitions; up to 24 AGM-158A Joint Air-to-Surface Standoff Missiles; 15 GBU-54 Laser Joint Direct Attack Munitions"). If fitted to carry nuclear weapons, the B-1B could carry fourteen atomic bombs on one mission.

In delivering—dropping—these bombs, a B-1B will typically descend from its cruising altitude, swooping down to below 1,000 feet, screaming over its target zone at around 900 m.p.h.

The B-1B's physical shape transcends aerodynamic streamlining; there is a very definite quality of styling, too—a sense that the designers also *aestheticized*. The jet has smooth organic-homogenous curves, an oily gray skin and a noticeably lighter beak-like nose cone that can put one in mind of a long-necked seabird in flight.

This sleekness is redoubled when, after takeoff and climb-out, the B-2 pilot, at the flick of a certain switch, is able to alter the angle of the wings from straight out and perpendicular the fuselage to sharply swept back—

which brings them in much tighter to the fuselage at 67 degrees swept back.

As the wings pivot—they are each sixty feet long and weigh many tons—a portion of the wing on each side slides through a narrow slot and enters a cavity in the fuselage. When the wings are in their forward straight-out position, the opening of this cavity is hidden, covered by a flap of thin metal that echoes precisely the shape of the wing in profile—a tapering curved shape. Whenever the wing sweeps back, it pushes this cover or "fold-down baffle" down flat and actually slides over the top of it.

The B-1Bs are all assigned to either the 7th Bomb Wing at Dyess Air Force Base in Texas or the 28th Bomb Wing at Ellsworth Air Force Base in South Dakota. Ellsworth Air Force Base is just east of Rapid City. Its geographic position is intrinsically strategic: starting from any compass point, an advancing ground attack against the aircraft stationed at Ellsworth would have to successfully proceed over at least a thousand miles of hostile and defended terrain (U.S. airspace) in order to arrive over the target. As a further precaution, all the aircraft at Ellsworth are housed in bomb-proof hangars.

One of the bomb squadrons based at Ellsworth is the 34th Bomb Squadron ("Thunderbirds"). The overall mission of the 34th has been formulated efficiently: "to employ the B-1B to defeat America's enemies across the globe at a moment's notice."

On the morning of 19 August 2013 at Ellsworth, a four-man B-1B crew was handed a training mission. There was the pilot, Major Frank Biancardi; his copilot, Captain Curtis Michael; and sitting behind them were two weapons systems officers, Brandon Packard and Chad Nishizuka. The mission that morning for the four included training for a low-altitude bomb-drop: advancing towards a given target zone at around 900 m.p.h. at an altitude of 1,000 feet and dropping simulated bombs on a simulated target.

At nine o'clock in the morning, the B-1 departed Ellsworth with a full-performance afterburner takeoff and climbed to 20,000 feet en route to the locale of the target zone. The target that morning was within the Powder River Training Complex, a rectangular-shaped block of restricted (closed to civilians) Department of Defense land. The area of around 30,000 square miles (about the size of Switzerland) extended—controversially—over the prairie grasslands of North Dakota, South Dakota, Montana and Wyoming.

After climb-out and reaching cruising altitude, Biancardi reduced thrust and moved the wings of his jet into their swept-back position. (The swept-back position is the ordinary position outside of takeoff and landing.) With the wings into their maximum aerodynamic setting, the B-1 began to advance towards the simulated bomb-drop, first descending to 10,000 feet.

Eight minutes later, the pilots took the jet down to 1,000 feet (the required low-altitude starting position for the attack) and began to fly in towards their target setting at full afterburner thrust—maximum speed.

At 9:14 a.m., just after four-afterburner full-performance had been selected and all aboard were focused on the final approach to the attack site, an alarming noise was heard by those in the cockpit, coming, it seemed to some, from the left rear side of the jet: a "bang," "pop," "violent," and "loud explosion."

The jet twisted and recoiled in the air, banking wildly left, and then became controllable again. There had been an on-board explosion of some kind, but the jet was still airworthy and the atmosphere in the cabin remained calm.

The B-1B is covered with sensors and data-monitoring status gauges so that almost every system can be monitored in real time—hydraulics, thrust, fuel supply, etc. But in this instance there had been no warnings or alerts illuminated in the cockpit before the explosion. Immediately after the loud bang, several cautions illuminated, including "Engine 1 Fire" and "Engine 2 Fire."

The crew deployed the engine-fire-suppressant systems, which are not comparable to any ordinary civilian fire extinguisher. A chosen internal sector of the jet is sealed off air-tight automatically as an oxygen-defeating chemical such as heptafluoropropane is released into the sealed chamber. The typical time for all oxygen to be removed from such a chamber upon deployment is about one second.

Biancardi climbed urgently back up to 10,000 feet—in any such situation the general aviation guidance is to climb in order to gain time and space to troubleshoot. As well as gaining altitude, the pilot also began to set course for an immediate emergency return to base—with one of the four crew setting the grid coordinates for Ellsworth into the navigation system.

With the "Engine Fire" panels still flashing, Biancardi and Michael began to shut down the two left-side engines (the B-1B can fly this way if so required).

Around one minute after the first distressing explosion was heard, there came a second volley (almost simultaneous in rapid succession) of loud explosions. The B-1B reeled, pitching down nose-low, and again rolled left. In the moment of the second blast, all electrical power in the cockpit was lost.

The pilot immediately commanded: "Bail! Bail! Bail!" And the four airmen reached for their ejection handles. All crew members ejected safely.

The B-1B crashed to earth at 9:16. "Debris from the aircraft spread over a seventeen-mile area of privately-owned, grass covered pastureland within the Military Operating Area, approximately twenty-four miles east of Broadus, Montana."

The most likely sequence of events of the disaster were later set out by an investigation team. As the jet had entered the Powder River airspace, the pilot had activated the wings into swept-back position. As the left wing was pivoting back, rather than slide over the fold-down baffle, the wing had instead forced the baffle back into the cavity area as it went, shunting the section of flat metal into a four-inch-wide flexible hose carrying jet fuel—the main fuel-line.

The leading edge of the baffle crushed and cut into the thick flexible hose with a deep V-shaped gouge as it was forced into contact by the sweeping wing. The movement of the wing caused the baffle to tear through the fuel pipe, creating a leak. For eight minutes, the pipe was leaking jet fuel, which was pumping from the torn pipe at around a hundred gallons a minute. Over a thousand gallons leaked out of the punctured hose in total.

As the jet fuel flowed freely into the left wing and left side of the fuselage, it was undetected and in fact undetectable by the aircraft's sensors and pressure gauges. At one moment—as Biancardi placed his controls to full afterburner at 1,000 feet—some of the fuel came into contact with certain "hot components" of one of the left-side jet engines, causing an explosion that blew away parts of the left wing. This blast began a chain-reaction of explosion events ("a cascade of catastrophic explosions") that ripped through the main fuel tanks. The force of the explosions also severed all electrical supply cables to the cockpit.

The lost jet was valued at $317 million.

---

31 Cley goose strike

Location: North Norfolk coast near Cley
Date: 7 January 2014

31 Cley goose strike

Aircraft type: HH-60
Fatalities: 4
Cost of damage: $40.3 million

Many thousands of wild geese winter in Great Britain, flocking together in large gaggles around coastal marshlands. Wild geese are migratory and groups of the wildfowl assemble hundreds at a time flying *en masse* in definite V-shaped formations away from their breeding grounds to warmer land each winter. (A large gaggle on the wing is an impressive sight: a single shimmering shape that swoops and rises as one.) Many such flocks of geese arrive to the coasts of North Norfolk, in England, each year from their breeding grounds in Norway, Iceland and Greenland.

Given that a wild goose weighs around eight to twelve pounds, it is obvious that a large or small gaggle on the wing is an explicit hazard to low-flying aircraft. Due to the dangers posed by low-flying birds, certain areas known to be replete with birds—such as Blakeney Point Nature Reserve, "host to large flocks of migratory birds"—are formally designated as restricted sites by the MOD (the British Ministry of Defence) and air traffic must avoid "by 500 feet or 2 nautical miles for flying operations." Migratory birds gather in many places all along the North Norfolk coastline, and their presence is not limited only to Blakeney Point Nature Reserve.

RAF (Royal Air Force) Lakenheath, in Suffolk, England, is, despite the prefix, a U.S. air base—the main base of the USAF 48th Fighter Wing. This attack force of fighter jets is supported by other aircraft such as the HH-60 search-and-rescue helicopters of the 56th Rescue Squadron.

U.S. forces stationed at Lakenheath form part of USAFE—United States Air Forces in Europe. The overall mission of USAFE is "to achieve the objectives of the United States and the North Atlantic Treaty Organization. Its assets stand ready to perform close air support, air interdiction, air defense, in-flight refueling, long-range transport, and support of maritime operations."

Many of the daily training missions for the fighter-jet pilots of the 48th Wing take place out over the open sea—the North Sea off the east coast of the British mainland. For search-and-rescue teams, the areas close to the North Norfolk coastline, about forty miles north of the base, are often utilized for training sorties.

The search-and-rescue crews of the 56th fly HH-60 Pave Hawk helicopters—a modified and upgraded version of the U.S. army Black Hawk. The Pave Hawk is fitted with numerous on-board electronic systems that make the search for a man down on the ground more efficient, including a 3-D real-time infrared-based video feed and low-altitude real-time terrain mapping. The Pave can proceed towards a rescue at a hundred and eighty miles an hour, gaining altitude up to 10,000 feet.

The search and rescue crews also use night-vision devices fitted directly onto their helmets. These binocular-like vision enhancers amplify infrared light, enabling airmen to see quite adequately during darkness.

A Pave crew consists of four airmen: pilot, copilot, aerial gunner and flight engineer. A typical training mission for the crews of the 56th is the requirement to locate and rescue simulated downed airmen from a simulated crash site.

On 7 January 2014, two HH-60 crews were handed an NVG (night-vision goggles to be worn) night-training mission, the narrative of which was the requirement to rescue a simulated downed F-15 pilot. The location of the simulated rescue was close to the North Norfolk coastline, around fifty miles north-northeast of the air base, about two miles inland from Blakeney Point Nature Reserve.

The second of the two crews, "Chalk 2," comprised Captain Christopher Stover; Captain Sean Ruane; Technical Sergeant Dale Mathews; and Staff Sergeant Afton Ponce. On that night they were the subordinate crew; the other helicopter was the flight lead.

The mission commenced on schedule at 17:33 p.m. with some strong gusting winds observed as the two HH-60s flew north up to the Norfolk coastal area at an altitude of five hundred feet. The two arrived at a pre-arranged Initial Point to the south of the village of Blakeney.

As the two helicopters made preparations for their low-altitude (one hundred feet) run-in towards the survivor pickup zone, the flight lead was aware that the wind—which was gusting to thirty-five miles per hour—was dragging the two aircraft in a northerly direction directly over Wiveton and Blakeney. The flight lead was not satisfied with this, as overflying inhabited areas at night is not allowed by MOD restriction due to causing unnecessary disturbance. With the requirement not to unsettle and disrupt civilians on the ground, Chalk 1 called for both helicopters to move the IP north of Blakeney village, right up on the coastline.

Soon after arriving and orbiting in the new IP position—just after six o'clock in the evening—the two set off at low altitude heading east down the shoreline to the landing zone near the village of Salthouse; Chalk 1, the lead, was flying about one half mile ahead of Chalk 2. The new route took the helicopters over several marshland areas including Cley Marshes, near the village of Cley.

Chalk one passed over Cley Marshes without incident. As Chalk 2

31 Cley goose strike

passed, with Chris Stover at the controls, the noise of the approaching helicopter only one hundred feet overhead (or possibly in delayed reaction to the first aircraft's noise) caused a group of startled geese to take flight. Very quickly the group of around ten large birds ascended entering the helicopter's flight-path. ("At some point during the helicopter's approach to the landing zone a flock of birds took flight from Cley Marshes. The sound of the approaching helicopter likely startled the geese. The geese took approximately one minute to reach one hundred and ten feet—the altitude of the helicopter.")

As the birds rose, Chalk 2 caught the full force of a group of geese in formation soaring towards it. The HH-60 was suddenly in the midst of an onslaught, a barrage of soft but lethal missiles smashing into the helicopter. Pilot Stover was thundering through the night air at around 120 m.p.h., chopping through a hail of frightened, flapping wildfowl.

It is probable that more than one goose smashed through the helicopter's plexi-windshield. In those moments it is likely that both the pilot and the copilot were knocked unconscious—each bird had the impact force of "fifty-three times the kinetic energy of a baseball moving at a hundred miles per hour." It is probable that birds penetrating the cockpit also smashed into the flight controls, such as the roll trim actuator, causing all kinds of uncommanded movement.

Chalk 2 banked and rolled steeply, passing through a bank of 90 degrees (and thus losing all potential for vertical lift), causing it to crash to the ground uncontrolled, killing the four crew on impact.

Within ten seconds the flight lead was circling back, visual scanning for its partner. There was no evidence of their partner aircraft whatsoever, but there was a fire burning on the ground below just inland from the shoreline at Cley.

Within three and a half minutes, Chalk 1 landed on the beach and the airmen made their way towards the fire. Very soon after landing the fire was established as a crash site with no survivors. Beyond the mangled wreck of twisted metal on the beach at Cley, a trail of bloody goose remains were spread along the beach.

The remains of the four airmen were eventually returned to Dover Air Force Base, Delaware, with full military honors.

The goose remains were collected and shipped to the research laboratories of the Smithsonian Institution, where scientists evaluated them. The species was pink-footed goose, one of the most profuse winter presences at Cley Marshes.

The value of the lost helicopter was later estimated at $40.3 million.

Unusually, a poignant eulogy to the four lost airmen was included in the official USAF report into the accident: "On 7 January 2014, four airmen from the 56th Rescue Squadron took flight on a training exercise in an HH-60 Pave Hawk. As the moon lit the English countryside, tragedy claimed their lives ... although their lives ended in an unexpected instant, their sacrifice did not spark in that moment—it crescendoed over lifetimes of dedication to serving their country and those they loved ... their dedication shall forever be in our memories through the Rescue Motto: *these things that we do that others may live.*"

32 Domestic object

Location: Eglin Air Force Base, Florida
Date: 23 June 2014
Aircraft type: F-35
Fatalities: none
Cost of damage: at least $50 million

The F-35 USAF fighter jet—the Lockheed Martin F-35 Lightning II—is the direct replacement for the F-16 fighter jet, which has been in service since 1979. ("There exists an aging fleet of tactical aircraft worldwide. The F-35 is intended to solve that problem.") The F-35's mission during warfare remains similar to the F-16: gain and sustain air superiority over any given geographical region or territory as required.

Eventually there will be at least 2,600 of the F-35s in active service in the USAF. "With stealth and a host of next-generation technologies the F-35 will be far and away the world's most advanced multi-role fighter." The F-35 "will bring an enhanced capability to survive in the advanced threat environment in which it was designed to operate." With such a large number in service, the F-35 will eventually become one of the most profuse aircraft types—whether military or civilian.

The development, production, testing and entry into service of the supersonic F-35 fighter jet was one of the most vexed, scrutinized—and some say chaotic—procurement processes in the history of the USAF. The government allocated budget for the F-35 is $1.5 trillion through 2050. As defense journalist Adam Ciralsky argued in 2013, "The aircraft is at least seven years behind schedule and plagued by a risky development

32 Domestic object

The fire-damaged F-35 on the ground at Eglin Air Force Base. Damage to the jet was estimated to be at least $50 million.

strategy, shoddy management, laissez-faire oversight, countless design flaws, and skyrocketing costs."

Eglin Air Base is one of the largest USAF bases. Located midway between Jacksonville and New Orleans, Eglin is a self-contained village with its own on-base shops and streets besides the many hangars and facilities. There are around ten thousand personnel living on-base.

During 2014, one of the activities ongoing at Eglin was the training of pilots to fly the new F-35 fighter. The training of pilots had been going very slowly, causing an atmosphere of consternation and frustration to build up. There was pressure to get the F-35 program back on track, but so far too few jets had actually been delivered. And with the ones that had, the schedule was stop-start, with any number of temporary groundings and delays. The F-35 was still under evaluation by test pilots, and many of the absolute limits of the "flight envelope" were subject to revision, so that pilots flying training and instruction sorties could not expect to push the jet too hard. In addition, the avionics systems were hampered by "immature software"; the cockpit digital display systems were being calibrated and updated all the while as pilot training was ongoing.

Usually consecutive, these things were going on in parallel because the F-35 schedule for delivery and entry into active service had fallen so far behind the original timetable that it had been deemed necessary to start training pilots even with such limitations.

The 58th Fighter Squadron at Eglin—nicknamed somewhat zealously the Mighty Gorillas—is tasked with training air pilots for the F-35. In the spring of 2014, the 58th gained access to some of the first F-35s off the production line: twenty-four were assigned to them with a responsibility to begin urgently training pilots.

On 23 June 2014, one F-35 instructor pilot at Eglin was to depart base for a "continuation training" flight—a general sortie that would give him much-needed flying time in the new plane. Although he was an experienced instructor pilot, he had only flown thirty-three hours in total in F-35s.

At a little before nine o'clock in the morning the pilot proceeded ("stepped") to his waiting aircraft.

Every USAF jet is checked over thoroughly and serviced as required after every sortie flight, and that Monday morning the more-or-less brand-new $150 million jet had no known issues.

The pilot taxied out to the Eglin runway awaiting his clearance to takeoff.

The sequence of events for a jet takeoff is as follows: arrive in position on runway; brakes on; wait for permission to take off; increase jet engine power; brakes off; takeoff "roll" commences; at a given speed, raise nose around 15 degrees in anticipation of takeoff; become airborne; landing gear up; climb smartly away to a designated altitude.

At nine minutes past nine, the pilot received his clearance to take off from the Eglin tower. He turned his throttle from IDLE to MIL (the main power setting short of full-performance afterburner setting) and began his "roll" down the runway.

In order to take off, the pilot must gain a pre-calibrated speed (around 140 m.p.h. for an F-35) on the runway, and once at that speed, he will gently pull back on his control stick—"unstick" or "rotate"—to raise the nose of his jet, and as he does so he will start to become airborne.

As the pilot was just reaching his rotate speed he heard a "loud bang." He saw on his main display screen a caution warning: ENG STALL ("engine stall") and noticed that he had lost all thrust. As he continued down the runway, decelerating as he went, an audible in-cockpit warning—a digitized female voice known to some pilots as Betty—began to sound: "Fire, fire … fire, fire … fire, fire."

The pilot glanced back at his main display screen, where further cautions were flashing on: FIRE GEAR ("fire alight in the wheel-well") and HYD FLUID ("hydraulic fluid level very low"). With the jet's speed still declining, more cautions flashed on: BLD LEAK ENG ("hot engine exhaust detected

32 Domestic object

outside of the engine"), IPP FAIL ("main electrical power supply failure") and HYD FAIL ("hydraulic power system failure").

The pilot continued to check his speed, bringing the plane to a standstill on the main runway and shutting down before he clambered out, following his emergency exit or "emergency egress" procedure. As he jogged away from the jet—as required under emergency egress—he looked back to see the rear of his jet consumed by a fiercely burning fireball, throwing off thick black smoke. Flames were shooting through an obvious hole in the top of the fuselage.

Within less than one minute, an Eglin fire crew was on the scene. The blaze was declared extinguished seven minutes and twenty-two seconds later. Soon after the fire was put out, Air Force personnel recovered a number of engine fragments in a trail behind the jet, including a three-inch-wide steel strip at least five feet long: the jet's forward integral arm.

An official investigation eventually established the course of events.

At some time before the sortie of 23 June, the aircraft's jet engine had been subject to a "hard tip-rub event" in the engine's fan section—the front of the engine, which sucks in air. At some undefined and unknown moment, two of the spinning components involved with forcing air into the jet system had contacted each other at high temperature, causing invisible fractures to the forward integral arm. With the integral arm in this damaged condition, the jet had remained in use for an unknown amount of time.

During the takeoff roll on 23 June, the fractures in the forward integral arm caused it to "catastrophically fail" and collapse into the main jet cavity. The long piece of steel then became subject to the jet's thrust, which launched it with great force towards the rear of the jet. The strip of metal was not moving through the engine as a clean length of metal, but rather an unpredictably flailing and spinning fragment. Soon after liberation—during the "roll"—the arm whipped across the engine casing side wall and burst straight through it, puncturing the casing and piercing the fuselage. It emerged and exited at speed—now javelin-like—as a projectile from the jet.

As the metal strip cut through the engine wall, it also sliced through various pipes and hoses, including a main hydraulic system hose and a main jet-fuel supply hose. Jet fuel entering a jet engine such as the F-35 is fed in under pressure, and once the hose had been slashed through by the red-hot long sliver of metal, fuel pumped freely into the disintegrating engine, igniting and spreading fire into several rear areas of the plane.

The fire damage to the mid-and-rear of the aircraft was later estimated at a minimum of $50 million in repairs, with the jet to be out of service for years.

The investigation team was unable to establish the specifics of the "hard tip-rub event," other than that it had taken place "at an undetermined time prior to the mishap." There was no evidence that the mechanics or engineers had acted improperly, as the damage—micro cracks—was not evident to the naked eye and could only be observed under a microscope.

33 Down to Louisiana

Location: George Washington National Forest, Virginia
Date: 27 August 2014
Aircraft type: F-15
Fatalities: 1
Cost of damage: $45.2 million

F-15 pilot Lieutenant Colonel Morris "Moose" Fontenot graduated the Air Force Academy in 1996. During his years of active service, he flew with the Wild Boars (390th Fighter Squadron); the Gorillas (58th Fighter Squadron); the Gamecocks (19th Fighter Squadron); and the Fighting Cocks (67th Fighting Squadron). Fontenot had accumulated 2,100 F-15 flight-hours. Fellow airmen have described the pilot as "a pretty intense guy," a "brilliant aviator," and "very respected in the [F-15] Eagle community."

At the end of 2013, Fontenot retired from active service and joined the 104th Fighter Squadron of the Air Force Reserve—based at Barnes Air National Guard Base in Massachusetts, a hundred miles west of Boston.

On 26 August 2014, Fontenot was feeling unwell and excused himself from a professional briefing at Barnes due to symptoms he described to other airmen variously as a "head cold" or a "sinus infection."

On 27 August 2014, Fontenot was up and active by six o'clock in the morning around Barnes, looking and sounding fine. No one he saw that morning later recalled him behaving strangely or seeming unwell or appearing stressed in any way.

On that particular Wednesday, Fontenot had been handed the task of delivering a certain F-15 jet to engineers who were required to install

33 Down to Louisiana

Aerial view of the crash site of an F-15 in the George Washington Forest, Virginia.

a new on-board radar system. The upgrade would be taking place at the Naval Air Station Joint Reserve Base New Orleans, near Belle Chasse, in Louisiana. Fontenot was scheduled to arrive there around mid-morning.

By road, a trip from Barnes to New Orleans will take twenty-four hours nonstop. For Fontenot, the fourteen-hundred-mile journey could be comfortably completed in a couple of hours: the single-seat supersonic F-15 has a max speed of 1875 m.p.h.—thrust supplied by two Pratt & Whitney F100s.

Fontenot's agreed route that morning for the routine point-to-point sortie was to fly due southwest all the way down to the Deep South with the Eastern Seaboard Atlantic coastline on the left (or port) side at all times.

It was a bright, clear morning with excellent visibility and calm winds. Fontenot departed Barnes as planned, taking off at 8:06 a.m. with the callsign HAWK11. The pilot soon climbed to the agreed cruise altitude of forty-three thousand feet. He was flying high-subsonic or low-supersonic, around seven hundred to eight hundred miles per hour.

The trip was progressing smoothly, unremarkable in every way up to one moment at 8:55 a.m. Fifty minutes into the journey, not yet halfway to his destination, Fontenot's F-15 began to rapidly descend from its cruising altitude. Soon after the descent was initiated, Fontenot declared an in-flight emergency to Virginia Air Traffic Control—"HAWK11 declaring emergency." An air traffic control operator appealed to HAWK11 for more information on the nature of the emergency and received a terse and basically valueless reply: "Affirm. Standby," as the jet passed through 36,000 feet.

The jet was pitched nose-low inverted, descending steadily at twelve thousand feet per minute. There were no stick inputs during this time except the initial one to point the jet towards the ground. There was no sense that the pilot wrestled with the jet in any way due to some emergent malfunction. "Radar data showed no evidence that the pilot maneuvered to recover the aircraft between the final call to Washington [air traffic control] Center and impact."

The only warning that did come on in the cockpit at some undetermined point was the Environmental Control System warning light, indicating "higher than normal temperature in the avionics bay." Such lights come on often in an F-15 and this alone would not usually be a reason to declare an emergency; the ECS high would have been uncomfortable and irritating at most.

Through the next minute and a half, the plane's course remained unwavering, nose-down, with an airspeed steady to increasing—eventually rising to over nine hundred miles per hour. During the descent there were several moments at which the pilot could have safely ejected. Equally, the pilot could have brought the F-15's nose up to pull out of the dive from as low an altitude as only three thousand feet.

For a reason that will never be known with any certainty, the pilot made no effort to eject or any attempt to recover from the dive. At 8:58 a.m., Fontenot was killed as his F-15 crashed nose-first at supersonic speed into dense mountainous woodland within the George Washington National Forest in Virginia. Emergency services at Augusta County Sheriff's Department in Deerfield were soon alerted to the disaster by phone calls from several members of the public describing a plume of dense black smoke rising up from amid the forest.

Due to the remote location ("rugged terrain") of the crash site, it took first responders one hour and forty minutes to pinpoint and gain access to the burning wreckage. "Initial responders arrived at the crash site at 10:41 a.m. and observed pieces of debris within a 300-to-450 foot radius from the point of impact. Although several pieces of debris appeared to be smoldering, the fire was contained to the impact crater."

Civilian first responders incorrectly presumed that the pilot had ejected and did not search for human remains; their focus was on getting the fire out. It was the following day, 28 August, that a USAF search-and-rescue team recovered Fontenot's remains.

The destroyed plane was later officially valued at $45.2 million.

A later investigation and "tear down" of the wreckage revealed that all the main systems of the F-15 were functioning normally during the descent and up to the moment of impact.

The precise circumstances of the moments leading up to the accident will never be known with any certainty since there was no crash-survivable data recorder ("black box") installed on the plane. In addition, there were no eyewitness accounts; no survivors; and limited data from the post-crash tear-down.

The Accident Investigation team that was convened came to the conclusion that Fontenot became *incapacitated* sometime after his final "Affirm. Standby," radio message was made to air traffic control.

34 Ghostrider

Location: near Eglin Air Force Base, Florida
Date: 21 April 2015
Aircraft type: AC-130J
Fatalities: none
Cost of damage: $115.6

The USAF test-pilot teams at Edwards, Arnold, and Eglin undertake the precise evaluation of any aircraft placed under their scrutiny, interrogating and documenting the flight performance and handling of any plane they are tasked to review.

Whenever a new aircraft or an upgraded aircraft is being delivered to the USAF from the manufacturer, the first example will undergo a relentless series of tests. Only when these are signed off and agreed will the USAF take delivery of the air vehicle.

The test teams flying such missions will usually have an active role in planning the format of the testing—writing the Test Directive test cards by selecting certain sets of flight parameters, combinations that will be

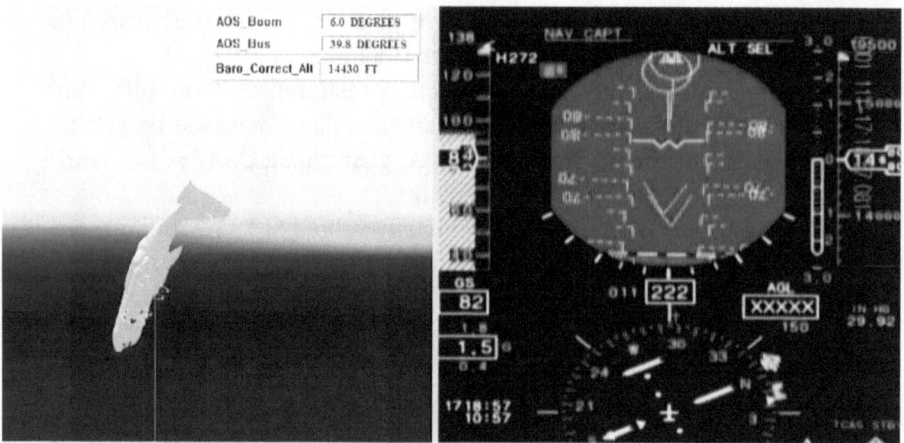

Still from USAF computer modeling of the stricken AC-130J moments before ground impact.

repeated with slightly altering increments or decrements each pass. The work can be very exacting and requires perhaps just a little obsessiveness; exactingness and meticulousness are crucial qualities that any test pilot should possess, far more so than seat-of-the-pants bravery and fearlessness that is so essential to the Hollywood-civilian stereotype.

During 2014–15 at Eglin, one of the aircraft under test was the AC-130J Ghostrider. The AC-130J is a highly modified C-130 Hercules utility-transportation and heavy-airlift workhorse.

The Ghostrider modifications set up the turbo-prop aircraft for close air support and air attack; that is, the modifications make it a "gunship" fitted with a Gatling-type cannon and a trainable 105 millimeter cannon, among other weapons systems. ("The AC-130J Ghostrider's primary missions are close air support, air interdiction and armed reconnaissance. Close air support missions include troops-in-contact, convoy escort, and point air-defense. Air interdiction missions are conducted against pre-planned targets or targets of opportunity and include strike coordination and reconnaissance and over-watch mission sets. The AC-130J will provide ground forces an expeditionary, direct-fire platform that is persistent, ideally suited for urban operations and delivers precision low-yield munitions against ground targets.") The Ghostrider is designed to fly in at night, attacking ground targets in support of Special Operations personnel.

The C-130 has been in continuous service for forty years with air forces around the world, so its aerodynamic handling characteristics are very well understood. But there are definite differences between the C-

130 and the Ghostrider. The modification has two rounded humps added to the exterior sides of the fuselage to provide required clearance for the 30mm cannon, for example. Its interior weight distribution is unique also. This being the case, the Ghostrider needed to be tested extensively. One of the key outcomes of test flights is the accurate setting up of the in-cockpit warnings that flash up and are heard by crew if an aircraft enters a hazardous flight attitude. Each aircraft is unique in this way, with a specific individual maximum pitch-up angle of attack, maximum rudder deflection, or minimum speed through the air ("stall speed"). For all such parameters, the in-cockpit automatic warning system (ICAWS) will be programmed so that the pilot will be aware of dangerous maneuvering.

When it first arrived at Eglin, the Ghostrider went through a very exhaustive examination of its flight parameters or flight "envelope." All of the main testing of the Ghostrider was done under an extensive program of test flights known as Test Directive 17 JON. The 17 JON team had repeatedly scrutinized just about every imaginable flight parameter of the Ghostrider through much of 2014. By the end of 17 JON, the technical director of the 413th Test Flight Squadron had all but signed off the Ghostrider as a fully tested product.

In early December of 2014 the test team—the pilots and engineers who had actually flown the test flights—raised some qualms. For them the testing that had been carried out was not extensive enough. In particular they were concerned about the plane's performance and handling as regards sideslip—the aircraft's handling when drifting left or right as it goes. The team was adamant that more testing was needed, mainly around sideslip. This was rationalized by a major recovery-required incident during 17 JON when a Ghostrider departed controlled flight and was recovered after descending out of control through five thousand feet—from a starting altitude of ten thousand feet up.

The squadron commander was not convinced that further tests were essential, nor was the technical director. As the technical director had made clear: any package of tests flown is not absolutely exhaustive, and cannot be; but the package will be robust and as good as it can be given inevitable time and cost constraints.

During December 2014 there was something of a standoff between the Ghostrider testers and the 413th senior management, with the test pilots finally winning out. As one of the senior management team commented: "It was one of those kinds of deals where you may have disagreed with it and you may have not completely understood exactly why, or if it made sense at all but it became more of those ones, as a function of being able to—to execute and get further testing done, we needed to play nice with—with the folks who were making the recommendations, even if we didn't necessarily believe one hundred per cent in." In the spring of 2015 a new package of tests focusing very much on sideslip parameters was agreed: Test Directive 23 JON.

On 21 April 2015, at Eglin, the fourth flight of 23 JON was scheduled. The team that "stepped" or proceeded to the aircraft in the late morning was a group of eight airmen—pilot; copilot; test conductor; two loadmasters, and three flight engineers.

On the first three flights of the 23 JON directive, the team had tested certain sideslip parameters in many increments and decrements through a hundred and eighty-three slightly different set-ups—each of which had been recorded and tabulated. For the flight of 21 April, the emphasis was on pressure applied to the rudder—increments of ten pounds per square inch on each run, working ever closer to edge of the safe flight characteristics, or "nibbling the envelope."

The Ghostrider test pilots departed Eglin at 12:18 p.m. and climbed out from the Florida coast out over the Gulf of Mexico at 15,000 feet to an area of restricted airspace known as W-15.

A little over one hour into the test mission, at 13:24 p.m., one of the increments being flown extended past the limits of the Ghostrider's capability. The given left rudder pressure for the certain increment being tested caused the plane to suddenly become uncontrollable; the near-fully-deflected rudder had locked out. The plane suddenly pitched violently down into an alarming inverted nose dive.

At this, the test conductor onboard calmly called: "Recover." Departure from controlled flight is a trained-for aspect of test pilot work, and this command is a call for all crew to focus on regaining controlled flight as soon as possible.

The unexpected ninety-degree inverted nose dive caused chaos in the unpressurized cabin with many objects flying though the air and bouncing around—from clipboards to an untethered fire extinguisher.

During the moments after the "Recover" call, the pilot at the controls was distracted: "I was disoriented.... It was almost like the aircraft was doing something that I couldn't figure out why it was doing it ... at one point I remember looking at the water—it was very difficult to make a reference of which way was what because of the water [the Gulf of Mexico]." The pilot was applying certain control-stick inputs, but they just were not decisive enough to get the plane out of its startling dive.

Recognizing his pilot's temporary malaise, the copilot called out clearly: "Nose down.... Power out.... Let go, let go," but these suggestions were not acted upon quickly enough. At "some undetermined point" about twenty seconds after the nose dive had begun, the copilot grabbed the controls and pulled up hard, dragging the jet through a rough but vital four-G-force wings-level-to-horizon maneuver, recovering successfully and level at just under 10,000 feet.

Just as the copilot regained the horizon, the smoke detector warning flashed on in the cockpit, and the already febrile atmosphere was further complicated by the requirement for all in the cabin to immediately put on respirators ("gas masks"). The copilot continued to fly the plane, declaring an in-flight emergency to the tower at Eglin.

Moments later, one of the loadmasters returned from the cargo hold. It was not smoke, but fine powder issuing from a burst fire extinguisher that had smashed open during the roll-and-invert that had set the cargo-bay smoke detectors off.

With the copilot still at the controls, the Ghostrider passed back over the Florida coastline and began its descent into Eglin. The test team landed back at Eglin without further incident.

The critical recovery maneuver had saved the crew's lives, but was later understood to have overstressed the main fuselage beyond its maximum stress tolerances. The plane—although appearing visually intact and in perfect-new condition—was written off as no longer airworthy. The value of the lost plane was estimated at $115.6 million.

35 Fire by the microwave

Location: Offutt Air Force Base, Nebraska
Date: 30 April 2015
Aircraft type: RC-135V
Fatalities: none
Cost of damage: $62.4 million

The USAF's Boeing RC-135V is not a warplane within a conventional framework of physical weapons of attack—such as bombs, missiles and cannons.

The RC-135V is a reconnaissance plane fitted with many surveillance devices—$100–200 million dollars' worth of eavesdropping, comms-interception, radar and imaging devices. "The RC-135V contains an on-board

The interior of the RC-135V following a fire that broke out in the aft galley area.

sensor suite which allows the mission crew to detect, identify and geolocate signals throughout the electromagnetic spectrum."

The RC-135V, or "Rivet Joint" as the V-iteration had been named, is instantly recognizable by its imposing jutting nose cone ("big chin") and the many irregular protruding spines—aerials, radio dishes, sensors—dotted along the roof of its fuselage.

Unlike, say, the U-2 "spy plane," which gathers reconnaissance data in advance of warfare, the Rivet Joint is set up for on-scene real-time reconnaissance: directly overflying enemy positions in a theater of operations in order to tune in and listen to battlefield communications in the moment that they occur. This type of communications intelligence is known as signals intelligence, or SIGINT.

During a combat operation the RC-135 will overfly a battle-space and effectively monitor, track, map and define the enemy positions, comms structures, and much else. Carrying on this in-flight task are the RC-135V's intel operatives, often known as Ravens. The Ravens are not only intercepting enemy communications; they are also actively scrutinizing, pro-

35 Fire by the microwave

cessing, and interpreting them. Unlike the air crew flying the jet, all Ravens are required to have full Top Secret security clearance.

The main cabin area of an RC-135V has approximately the same floor space as a mid-size commercial jet. The majority of this is given over to Raven workstations—twenty seats in a long row all down the windowless left side of the compartment. There is just enough space behind the row of standard Air Force office chairs to squeeze past down towards the lavatory and rest area-galley at the back of the plane.

From a Raven point of view, the RC-135V cabin is only a flying computer room. Work carries on much as if the workstations were lined up in a crowded stuffy workspace in an air base building on the ground.

The overall look of the Raven corridor is really very different from movie representations of the same. The Raven workstations on an RC-135V are reminiscent of a provincial customer-care call center, with tatty beige keyboards, drab gray chairs, one tiny unisex lavatory way in back (often out of order), and a small break-time galley and rest area next to it with two chairs and a microwave oven stacked up on top of a fridge.

The overall mission of the 343rd Reconnaissance Squadron is to "provide worldwide reconnaissance for national command authorities, Combat Commands, the intelligence community, and war fighters." The 343rd is based at Offutt Air Force Base, two hundred miles from Kansas City on the Nebraska-Iowa border. Offutt Base is an important strategic command center of the U.S. military. For example, on September 11, 2001, President George W. Bush was flown to Offutt, where he was briefed at a secure underground command room on the ongoing terror attacks.

On 30 April 2015, an ordinary RC-135V training mission sortie was scheduled at Offutt for an RC-135V crew. There were five flying the plane—pilot, copilot, navigator, electronic-warfare officer and mission supervisor—and a group of Ravens. The eight-hour mission required the jet to overfly a simulated enemy located somewhere in the Southern states of the U.S. The mission was planned to get started at 6 o'clock in the evening with a full eight-hour shift of intelligence gathering work for the twenty-two intel operatives.

As the Ravens came on board for their night mission, there was an unusually strong smell of chemical toilet fumes wafting out from the lavatory in back all through the main workstation corridor. As one of the Ravens later explained: "It smelled like the lavatory door had been open and it just ... like the whole jet had been closed the entire ... for a week or so. It smelled kinda nasty in there." As one who was on board later commented: "Multiple people ... individuals on the crew were mentioning it and reflecting on that, as I recall."

With all intel personnel in their seats and still busy booting into their systems, the pilot taxied out towards the Offutt runway by around 6:20 p.m., and at 6:24 p.m., permission to take off came through from the tower.

The pilot turned out onto the runway, set the throttles to takeoff thrust, and commenced his takeoff roll. Accelerating rapidly, he was moving at around sixty miles per hour, maybe ten seconds from takeoff, when his tactical coordinator began to urgently request his attention over the intercom.

The tactical coordinator was sitting behind the main flight crew and was in a unique position in that he was hearing both the flight-crew cockpit internal comms (coming through in the left ear of his headphones) and the intercom discussions—or chit-chat—of the intelligence personnel (coming through the right ear of his headphones) simultaneously. "I'm watching the [takeoff roll] speeds, and that's when I hear on private—the pilot doesn't have access to private. But I hear on private on my right ear (because I do dichotic) I hear all the radios going crazy, shouting 'Fire, fire ... there's smoke,' and it just got really chaotic ... people started shouting, you know, escalatory, and it's not like how they briefed like it's nice and orderly, no, everyone's freaking out. That's when they call over interphone and call, about fire, and that's when the pilot, he's like, 'What?' because— it was so much chaff [intercom chatter]—everyone's drowning each other, all you could hear was just the radios which is not normal, because everyone's [supposed to be complying with] sanitized comms. Almost I hear people screaming. And that's when I relayed to the pilot on his hot mic, I'm like: *there's a fire.*"

When the news came through, the pilot called abort to the tower and brought up his brake levers. As the jet was still slowing, the tactical coordinator and other flight crew members moved swiftly aft, where they were confronted by a scene of disorder and confusion.

A fire augmented (it was later confirmed) by a disconnected oxygen pipe was shooting out blowtorch-like from just above the microwave oven in the tiny aft galley. The intense fire had already melted away an area of internal paneling and was burning and melting through the many bundles of cabling held behind the panels. ("And when I say fire I mean a pressurized torch shooting out ... just above where the microwave sits and the containers. It wasn't, you know, your typical campfire, what you expect to see a fire where it was just kinda wafting—this fire was shooting out with force.") Thick white smoke was billowing through the cabin. ("The only thing that maybe struck me as a little odd was the smoke was all white.")

Some of the Ravens were moving away from the blaze down the narrow corridor towards the cockpit. Many were breaking out their personal oxygen supply bottles. ("I look back and see all the smoke, it's—the Tactical Co-ordinator was on oxygen, so were the Ravens, they were on oxygen…. It's just smoke, you can't see anything in the aft-galley area because it's completely white-out.")

With the jet slowing rapidly, the flight crew primed the emergency escape chute close to the cockpit and stood ready. As the plane came to a halt, the panicked Ravens began to bottleneck and bunch around the door, exiting hastily as soon as it was flung open. Apart from several cases of minor smoke inhalation, there were no injuries to those on board.

At 18:25 the alarm had been raised; at 18:29 a fire crew arrived and entered the burning jet as it stood on the Offutt runway, and soon put out the blaze. The fire had burned for no more than six minutes but caused at least $62 million of damage to the onboard tech systems and internal structures of the plane.

The official Accident Investigation panel later established that some of the joints in the pipework carrying oxygen had not been fully tightened—torqued—and had been left by mechanics on the ground only finger-tight. This caused an explosive leak of pressurized oxygen from the tubing, hence the blowtorch-like jet of flames shooting from above the microwave oven.

36 Unseen traffic

Location: near Berkeley County Airport, South Carolina
Date: 7 July 2015
Aircraft type: F-16
Fatalities: 2 civilians
Cost of damage: $29.1 million

The 55th Fighter Squadron of the USAF, "the Fighting Fifty-Fifth," maintains "a state of combat readiness," with the potential to meet "any challenge, anytime, anywhere." The 55th is based at Shaw Air Force Base in South Carolina and flies the F-16 fighter jet, "a high performance weapons system used by the United States and allied nations."

Ground view of the crash site of the USAF F-16 that was involved in a midair collision with a civilian Cessna.

Tuesday, 7 July 2015, the experienced F-16 pilot Major Aaron Johnson was flying a check-flight sortie, meaning that he was testing out a jet that had recently been repaired and maintained, a flight to "verify corrective maintenance."

The setup for that day's mission was for Johnson to depart Shaw and fly a number of instrument approach landings (the pilot relies on cockpit gauges rather than visual references in order to descend in towards the landing runway) at two small regional airports not far from Shaw. First, he would fly out a hundred miles east to perform practice landings at Myrtle Beach Airport, which is associated with vacationers arriving and departing on the Atlantic coast along the Grand Strand coastline.

Then, having completed a few instrument landings at Myrtle Beach, Johnson was intending to do another set of practices flying down the South Carolina coastline—directly above the sixty-mile-long stretch of the Grand Strand sandy-beach coastline—to Charleston Airport, where he would perform again a series of practice landings under instrument landing rules. There was not much cloud around that day, so there was no necessity to be landing using cockpit instruments at all—it was just that the recent repairs required him to assess the accuracy of his gauges.

Johnson departed Shaw at approximately 10:24 a.m. The F-16 pilot

36 Unseen traffic

completed his approaches at Myrtle Beach Airport—as had been planned—and then proceeded on his way high above the Atlantic coast heading southwest towards Charleston Airport with his second set of instrument landing approaches still to come.

Johnson first contacted the Charleston air traffic control approximately forty-five miles northeast of the airport at an altitude of six thousand feet. He requested heading and altitude directions ("vectors") for an instrument approach into the Charleston runway. Air traffic control directed Johnson to a 260-degree heading (west-southwest) at 10:52 a.m., instructing him to descend to sixteen hundred feet when approximately thirty-five miles northeast of Charleston.

As Johnson was making his way towards Charleston Airport, it so happened that a private pleasure flight was taking off from another local-regional airport at Berkeley County. The pleasure flight was a light aircraft, a tiny Cessna 150—a robust but slight aircraft type, used mainly as a trainer.

The Cessna was being piloted by a certain Joey Johnson (age thirty) who had one passenger on board: his father Michael Johnson (age sixty-eight). Joey Johnson was just out for a general low-altitude fly-around, and this being the case, he had no obligation to submit a flight plan to air traffic control. In fact, there is no control tower at Berkeley Airport.

The air traffic controller at Charleston could see the Cessna clearly on his radar screen and presumed that it would very likely stay well below 1000 feet. At one moment shortly after 11:00 a.m., the air traffic controller noticed that the Cessna was continuing to climb up and away from Berkeley. As the light aircraft broke through 1000 feet, the controller urgently noted the potential flight-path conflict to the F-16 pilot: "Traffic twelve o'clock, two miles, one thousand two hundred indicated type unknown." (In other words, another aircraft directly up ahead and heading straight towards you at a current altitude of one thousand two hundred feet.)

As he continued on his flight path in towards Charleston, the F-16 pilot's reaction to the message was first to presume that he had misheard it. In more than two thousand USAF flying hours he had never heard a controller call out a conflict of only two miles—twenty would be more standard.

The F-16 was descending in towards Charleston at close to two hundred miles per hour with the Cessna proceeding towards it at around ninety miles per hour—for an overall "closing speed" of around three hundred miles per hour.

The F-16 pilot's initial reaction was to continue on as he requested over his radio a confirmation of the position of the conflicting aircraft. In response—seventeen seconds after his initial request—the controller made his hazard warning more explicit: "If you don't have that traffic in sight, turn left heading one-eighty immediately."

The protocol in such potential conflict situations is that every aircraft pilot has a primary responsibility at all times to avoid midair collisions. Given the radar diagram that the controller was reviewing, the proximity of the light aircraft should have been such that it would be rather obvious to the F-16 pilot as he looked out of cockpit canopy. He was hoping that the F-16 pilot would soon see the hazard for himself and take his own avoidance action. If that were not the case, then the controller was recommending or in fact ordering the F-16 to turn around—either make visual contact and avoid, or turn around as a precaution. (The controller was not unduly worried about the close proximity, as he had a perception that an F-16 could "turn on a dime.")

Major Johnson was now worried and was scanning the airspace before him repeatedly ("aggressively"), but could see absolutely nothing like another plane. With no luck in getting a visual on the unknown conflicting aircraft, the F-16 pilot entered a smooth autopilot banking turn, as per his control tower instruction.

As the F-16 began its maneuver, the Cessna suddenly came dramatically into view: immediately ahead with no more than two or three seconds to impact. The fighter pilot pulled back hard aft on his control column, causing his F-16 to rise spectacularly into a sheer vertical climb. The last-ditch maneuver was sufficient to avoid a head-on collision between the two unequal aircraft, but not enough for the F-16 to completely clear the hazard. The fighter's blazing tailpipe clipped the Cessna.

The light aircraft immediately became uncontrollable, crashing to Earth seconds later, killing both on-board in the impact.

The F-16's tailpipe was ripped off in the collision and the fighter lost thrust.

With his airspeed decreasing and no means of improving it, Major Johnson made preparations for pilot ejection. He had determined that he could not make an engine-out landing. As his aircraft descended more-or-less uncontrollable through three hundred feet, Johnson ejected.

The doomed pilotless fighter jet continued to fly for at least two minutes in a gently descending arc until it crashed into woodland close to Lewisfield Plantation Road not far from Berkeley Country Club. The wrecked plane "broke apart as it tumbled across the forest floor," with the main fuselage beginning to burn in an intense post-crash fire that soon spread to a number of surrounding trees.

The entire incident was seen from the ground by numerous eyewitnesses, and several civilian reports of the crashes were made to the emergency services in the minutes after the disasters. County emergency vehicles were en route to both crash sites by 11:11 a.m.

Major Johnson ejected safely and parachuted to the ground, landing on open land within sight of the blazing wreck of his F-16.

37 Goggles case

Location: Jalalabad Airfield
Date: 2 October 2015
Aircraft type: C-130J
Fatalities: 14 (3 on the ground)
Cost of damage: $58.3 million

The C-130 Hercules is the U.S. Air Force's Daimler Freightliner semi-truck of the skies: a matte-gray hulking plane with four whining turbo-propeller engines. If you are in the U.S. military and you need to move some stuff somewhere, then there is a good chance it will be moved by a C-130 Hercules. The Air Force has more than four hundred on the books and in service.

The C-130 is a rugged plane, built for austere landings and takeoffs. A tarmac-and-concrete runway isn't required—any stretch of reasonably level dirt track, or just a flat open field, often will be adequate. Cargo is loaded and offloaded through a large aft door using a drive-straight-up loading ramp. Inside there are bays for standard U.S. military-sized pallets.

C-130s are a basic utility of U.S. operations in Afghanistan—with many of them based at Bagram Airfield when on operational deployment. Bagram, in the east of the country, thirty miles north of the capital Kabul, was controlled by the Taliban when the U.S. first invaded in 2001. Soon after the invasion commenced, the U.S. gained full control of the then-tiny airfield, after which it construction began. When completed, the base became a main U.S. military transport hub for freight ("materiel") into and out of Afghanistan.

The airfield is heavily fortified with thick concrete perimeter walls

The wreckage of the C-130J that crashed to Earth close to the perimeter of Jalalabad Airfield.

and is also notable for its visually imposing location. To the east of the base, the snow-covered mountains of the Hindu Kush rise up dramatically.

One early evening in late 2015, a certain C-130 "hard crew" on deployment at Bagram were handed their evening's schedule in the main operations building. Their schedule for the evening of 1 October involved a mission likely to complete in the early night hours of 2 October.

The C-130 has a standard crew of four. In the front seats there is the pilot (left seat) and copilot (right seat). Then there are two dedicated loadmasters who take charge of the on-load and off-load. The group was made up of the pilot, Capt. Jordan Pierson (28); copilot Capt. Jonathan "JJ" Golden (33); and two loadmasters: Staff Sgt. Ryan Hammond (26) and Senior Airman Quinn Johnson-Harris (21).

Added to the four standard crew there would also be two armed guards accompanying the flight: FAST ("Fly-Away Security Team"). Small groups of two or four are often allocated to airlift missions when the security conditions on the ground and on base cannot be guaranteed and the friendly status of ground staff is not absolute. FAST personnel are there to protect the U.S. materiel and the crew from a terror attack by, say, a lone suicide attacker armed with only a knife. On the evening of 1 October, two FAST officers were assigned: Senior Airman Nathan Sartain (29) and Airman 1st Class Kcey Ruiz (21).

It was a full schedule that the crew were given for that evening's work:

seven flights in all. To start with, the crew were to load up their C-130 and fly their cargo up to Jalalabad Airport—another U.S. military airport 100 miles to the northwest of Bagram, about fifteen minutes away by plane.

Once at Jalalabad, they were to off-load and pick up a second cargo, which was to come back to Bagram. Once they were back at Bagram, this round trip was to take place a second time with more freight to move.

Then, for the fifth leg of that evening's tasks, the crew were to fly out of Bagram once again to Kabul International Airport, with the requirement to on-load cargo and move it to Kandahar Airport. The seventh and last leg of that night's work would be the short flight back from Kandahar to home base at Bagram.

The C-130 crew initially gathered in the main operations building, where they checked out night-vision goggles—near-infrared-based, helmet-mounted vision devices that allow the wearer to see at night, in darkness. For the mission of 1 October, the requirement was for each of the four to wear night-vision goggles—or NVGs—throughout.

These goggles, which are shaped more like binoculars than goggles, are handed to airmen packed and ready to go in a hard case or flight case. The case for standard issue USAF night-vision goggles is made of tough plastic the size of a shoe box but slimmer with a plastic handle.

With pre-flight briefing over, the group made their way out to their plane at around twenty after eight o'clock. With on-load completed, the first flight leg to Jalalabad got underway on schedule at 21:36 p.m.

Soon after takeoff, during climb-out, the C-130 scored a bird strike—an unfortunate, annoying and messy collision with a bird in flight. No significant damage was thought to have been caused, but the decision was made to turn back to Bagram in order to have the affected engine checked over by mechanics on the ground. Ground inspection confirmed the crew's earlier view: the bird strike hadn't caused any damage to the plane, but it had put them back around an hour-and-a-half behind their original schedule.

It was not until 22:53 p.m. that the C-130 began again the first leg of the evening's cargo-moving tasks. Exactly twenty minutes later, at 23:13 p.m., pilot Pierson landed at Jalalabad, reporting some "fireworks" on the way in. It may have been actual fireworks he and the copilot saw as there was no hostile action anywhere around the vicinity of Jalalabad that night and the two did not take evasive action.

Upon landing, the off-loading soon got underway with the engines still running—a "hot" off-load and on-load. At one moment during the off-load, one of the loadmasters spoke by radio to the pilot: could he please raise up the tail-elevators to enable some tall cargo to come out the aft-door? (Loadmaster: "Hey, uh, do you mind raising up … the elevator in the back?" Pierson: "Yup, got it." Loadmaster: "Cool, thanks.") The elevators are the movable (they can be raised or lowered) rear sections on the tail stabilizer: the elevators droop down a little when they are inactive, and this being so, they block very slightly the top of the access door.

For some minutes, Pierson sat in his pilot's seat pulling back manually on his main control yoke, which is between the pilot's legs. It is the main mode of raising and lowering the altitude of the plane by means of affecting its pitch.

After about six minutes sitting this way waiting, Pierson had had enough and looked around for something to hold the yoke back (and so free up his hands for other things). He spotted his black plastic night-vision goggles case, which, as it happened, was just a perfect size for this piece of ad hoc improvisation, and he wedged it in between the yoke and the main instrument panel (partially obscuring part of the head-down primary flight display). As the loading continued, Pierson mentioned his trick to copilot Golden: "My NVG case is holding … the elevator."

Once the tall cargo was off the plane, the new load was brought aboard. This load was not tall, but it was heavy: five muddy-green Tri-Con metal shipping containers (the same type as used on civilian building construction sites as tool storage), each around four tons. The issue to be considered from a pilot's point of view in light of this cargo was maximum load weight capacity. The C-130 takes a maximum of twenty-one tons of military materiel in one load. The calculations were completed: it was a close call but O.K. The five shipping containers came up to twenty and one-half tons.

With all the discussion and calculating and scrutinizing inventory paperwork, neither Pierson nor Golden gave any thought to removing the hard case that was still wedged up between the yoke and instrument panel in the cockpit. The elevators were still propped-up in their artificially raised position.

Then, as the Tri-Con containers were going in, a group of five contractors (affiliates of the U.S. military) came by wanting to hitch a ride back to Bagram. Of course, a C-130 pilot has to accommodate if he can, and so the passenger request was signed off with the requirement to move one of the flat-green Tri-Cons from its place in the foremost pallet position in the cargo hold to another spot and then fold out two rows of passenger seats for the contractor group.

As the on-load was completing, the discussion between Pierson and

37 Goggles case

Golden turned to the near maxed-out load they were hauling on this second leg of the evening's itinerary. To Pierson, bearing in mind the five Tri-Cons, the pair of FAST security guards, the loadmasters and now the extra five contractor passengers, the load was give-or-take on maximum. The pilot made the decision to go for a full-performance takeoff—adjusted maximum effort, or AMAX.

In making his decision, Pierson also recalled that JJ Golden—next to him—was looking to upgrade from copilot to full C-130 pilot status. With this in mind, solely as an act of generosity, Pierson suggested that Golden take the flight controls for the full-performance takeoff.

At two minutes past midnight, the two had a brief conversation on this topic. Pierson: "The rest is your brief. When you log it, don't log it as a max effort takeoff, so I don't get ****** questions about it, because you're not ... copilots can't do max effort takeoffs. You know what I mean?" Golden: "Yeah, I mean, it's your call."

As they taxied back out to the Jalalabad runway, both pilot and copilot were using their night-vision goggles in an unlit cockpit. Johnson took the controls and increased thrust. Then, upon word from the control tower at Jalalabad, he released his brakes and commenced his takeoff roll—moving forward solely under power of his main engines.

Soon after brake release, Pierson called "Rotate," and Johnson pulled back on his yoke to ascend. A C-130 on a full-power takeoff pitches up sharply but smoothly and ascends rapidly.

Less than five seconds into takeoff, both Pierson and Johnson realized something was wrong. After the moments of initial dramatic ascent, the plane did not want to level out. It seemed to be possessed. Johnson called out to Pierson: "It's going off on its own!" The plane was continuing its alarming nose-up ascent, seemingly uncontrolled.

Pierson took the flight controls and attempted to level out, but as he did (eleven seconds after takeoff), an audible stall warning sounded in cockpit: they were pitched up too sharply and unsustainably at 35 degrees nose-high, then to 42 degrees nose-high. Both pilots assumed a trim malfunction and the copilot switched to emergency trim.

Pierson attempted to roll away, banking left out of the unsustainable nose-high climb. With the stall warnings sounding, there was no time to recover the aircraft—they were only 700 feet up.

Implausibly and unlikely as it may seem, the fact was that the black plastic hard-shell flight case for Pierson's night-vision goggles was still in place propping up the elevators, but neither of the two had noticed it. The case was stopping the yoke from moving fully forward, blocking the last couple of inches of movement. With the elevators jammed in a raised-up position, the plane wanted to continue climbing, but without a commensurate necessary airspeed.

The plane ceased its ascent and began an equally dramatic and sickening descent: uncontrolled, the plane was now falling back towards the runway nose-low at more than 100 feet per second. Pierson repeated three times over—spoken to the tower, to Johnson, and to himself in disbelief—an observation that was obvious to all of them: "We're going down. We're going down. We're going down."

Twenty-eight seconds after takeoff, the C-130 crashed back to earth, demolishing a section of perimeter wall and a guard tower at Jalalabad. The impact-force was later calculated as at least 70 G-force. Absolutely unsurvivable. All eleven on board were killed at the moment of impact, as well as three more in the demolished guard tower.

As the wrecked C-130 came to a halt, witnesses heard a loud explosion and then saw the flames of a ferocious post-crash fire bursting from the fuselage.

Jalalabad is not a full U.S. air base; it is only an airfield, and it has very limited emergency services. For reasons of "congestion and narrow access," it was thirty-eight minutes before firefighting crews arrived—too late to save the $50 million jet from total destruction.

The value of the lost aircraft was later calculated to be $58.3 million and the cargo $6.7 million.

38 Three-out takeoff

Location: Andersen Air Force Base, Guam
Date: 19 May 2016
Aircraft type: B-52
Fatalities: none
Cost of damage: $112 million

Andersen Air Force Base is a USAF "forward base" established on the Pacific island of Guam, six thousand miles from the coast of California. The island is literally a dot in the ocean (from its most northerly point to its most southerly is less than twenty miles), but its location is of supreme strategic importance to the U.S. military, allowing for a permanent local presence in the Asia-Pacific geographic region. The USAF retains CBP—

38 Three-out takeoff

Aerial view of the destroyed B-52 that careered off the end of the runway and burst into flames at Andersen Air Force Base on Guam.

"continuous bomber presence"—on the island, "in order to assure allies and deter adversaries ... a visible reminder that the United States is committed to the region and ready to act at a moment's notice. CBP missions from Guam offer persistent long-range strike capability through expanded loiter times while limiting stress on aircraft and aircrew."

Due to Guam's remote and isolated location (at least one thousand miles of clear sea in every direction), the USAF heavy bomb wings serving at Andersen operate with impunity. Hostile aerial reconnaissance is near impossible; the only means for an enemy to gain awareness of the jets flying in and out of Andersen is haphazard local monitoring or infiltration and espionage (spying).

The bomber squadrons on standby at Guam rotate, with deployments often lasting four to six months. Much of the time the bomber squadrons selected for service to Guam are those flying the B-52. The eight-jet-engine-powered B-52 has been operated continuously by the USAF since 1955; through sixty years the jet has become iconic—one of the most recognizable names and aircraft shapes in all military aviation.

Many of the missions out of Andersen are basically secret with the sortie details handed down as "Higher Headquarters-Directed." Knowledge of the details of such missions are limited to the designated members of the specific "mission cell." In the late spring of 2016, one such Higher Headquarters-Directed mission was handed to a B-52 "hard crew" of the 69th Expeditionary Bomb Squadron. The Squadron was on deployment from its home base, Minot Air Force Base, in North Dakota.

The mission was scheduled for 19 May and was to include a usual crew of five (pilot, copilot, radar navigator, navigator, electronic warfare officer) plus two extras (augment or spare pilot and a weapons system instructor).

The preflight work began around six o'clock in the morning. One of the details considered was the presence of birds. Birds getting sucked into a jet engine ("ingested") is a significant hazard for a military aircraft, particularly when the jet is vulnerable during the critical moments of takeoff. Bird-watch condition status on the morning of the mission was noted as low. (Prominent bird species often seen at Andersen include the Pacific golden plover, the yellow bittern, the island collared dove and the cattle egret.)

Although little is known about the details of the mission, it is known that the sortie required the B-52—callsign MACHO11—to be near fully-laden. Added to the heavy cargo, the B-52 was just under max fuel; around a hundred tons of jet fuel had been pumped into the B-52s tanks.

By ten after eight on the morning of 16 May, MACHO11 was on the runway at Andersen waiting to be cleared for takeoff—an tower status-instruction known as "line up and wait."

At 8:31 a.m. the Andersen air traffic control tower gave the jet permission to take off. The pilots set takeoff thrust on all eight engines and the plane began to move forward, commencing its "takeoff roll" along the runway. The takeoff roll progressed with the navigator calling the optimum moment for the pilot to "rotate" or pull back on the control stick, raising the nose in order to become airborne: "Coming up on s-one now."

As the pilot gained his decisive takeoff speed, he called this out to his crew: "Committed [to this takeoff]. Your [the crew's] throttles."

The thundering jet began to rise. Within two seconds—in the critical moments immediately after takeoff is called—the navigator observed in his nose-mounted forward-facing video feed (the "electro-optical viewing system") a small flock of birds passing by the jet and announced to all crew over the interphone-intercom: "Birds!" In the same moments, the copilot observed "a handful of birds" moving left-to-right in his window, and then immediately after heard "a couple of thuds," which he recognized as objects colliding with the aircraft.

Fearing bird ingestion into one or more of his jets, the pilot looked

38 Three-out takeoff

over to his engine stack dials and witnessed the thrust from three of his right-side engines (five, six and seven) dropping off rapidly. They were "spooling back towards zero"—meaning the thrust-indicator needle for each of the three was dropping back alarmingly. In the same moment, the pilot also noticed an abnormal reading on the oil-pressure gauge of the last remaining right-side engine—the needle was well past normal and rising.

Bird ingestion is unpredictable. Very often the incinerating bird will cause a few engine splutters known as compressor stalls, and then the engine will begin to function normally again—a Pratt and Whitney turbofan is robust and has systems to purge foreign objects. However, this is not guaranteed or assured: it does sometimes happen that a bird strike is catastrophic, causing the stricken engine to become unusable for flight— the engine is "out."

Even with "three out"—even three out on the same wing—a B-52 is still airworthy and controllable. However, in this case what the pilot saw from his round dials was three out with a fourth looking very unhealthy, and so he called: "Abort."

The jet had not yet become airborne; it was hurtling down the runway at a hundred and sixty miles an hour. Upon the pilot's command, all flight-deck attention turned to getting the jet stopped as soon as possible. The main hazard of an aborted takeoff is running out of runway before the aircraft slows down sufficiently. A plane which cannot stop within the length of the runway will likely "depart the prepared surface," meaning that it will career off the end of the given runway and out onto surrounding fields, usually of grass or scrub.

The order of activity for the crew was fourfold: place engine throttles to idle; place airbrakes (lift-defeating structures on the wing) to full; apply wheel brakes; and release drag parachute. The B-52 is fitted with a huge rear parachute used to slow the jet in just such takeoff aborts. But it cannot be used above 150 m.p.h. as it is very likely to tear through, becoming nothing more than a useless "streamer."

With his jet roaring down the runway, airbrakes screaming, the pilot held off the chute lever for a few seconds. He was watching closely his speedometer needle, and as it hit 150 m.ph., he deployed. The parachute canopy billowed out and opened behind the plane momentarily before rupturing and sagging down—the parachute had failed.

As the chute deployed, the navigator began to call the "boards"—the clearly marked signboards at the side of every runway that indicate how much runway is left. The navigator's first call was: "three board," or three thousand feet of runway left. Then a second call: "two board," and immediately following it, another command from him: "Hatches! Hatches! Hatches!" It was now obvious to all on the flight deck that they were going to overshoot.

Crew access in and out of a B-52 is via a hatch underneath the jet, and if it is going to go down onto its belly, then an emergency escape hatch above in the roof should be prepared. At his command, the electronic warfare officer—in charge of electromagnetic jamming on the mission—made his way to the roof hatch and pulled the emergency handle, causing a detonating charge to successfully blow the hatch off.

They were slowing as they went, but it was not enough; the smooth "prepared surface" asphalt runway beneath them was almost gone, with the rumbling eight-engine bomber still moving at sixty miles per hour.

Beyond the runway at Andersen there is a large field of rough grass. The jet careered off the runway and into the grass, bumping along for around three hundred feet, until the front landing gear hit a long thin concrete block. The front wheel was sheared off, and the jet crashed down onto its belly and scraped along the ground for a short distance before finally coming to rest.

All seven aboard pulled themselves up through the roof hatch and sprinted. As the pilot—the last of the seven to egress—clambered clear, a post-crash fire took hold and the B-52 was engulfed in flames. The crew watched on helpless from a distance as a fireball burning a hundred tons of jet fuel consumed the aircraft.

The cost of the lost B-52 was estimated to be $112 million.

39 Inadvertent shutoff

Location: El Paso County, Colorado
Date: 2 June 2016
Aircraft type: F-16
Fatalities: none
Cost of damage: $29.5 million

The Air Force Academy is close to the city of Colorado Springs, in the state of Colorado. As an institution it resembles closely a campus-type civilian university, with students agreeing at enrollment to serve in the USAF for a fixed number of years upon graduation. Undergraduates

39 Inadvertent shutoff

The wreckage of the F-16 that crashed following a fly-by and air show event at the Air Force Academy graduation event for the class of 2016.

are known as cadets and study their specialism for four years while living on-campus. The AFA has nine square miles of facilities and grounds.

Freshman cadets (all in the top two to three percent academically at their respective high schools) arrive at AFA on chartered buses, and their first taste of the Academy is being ordered off the bus zealously and officiously by their designated sergeant major ("Get off the bus. Off. Off. Get OFF the Bus...."). Upon descending from the vehicle, the new cadets line up for the first time parade-ground-style on the grass verge, still in their T-shirts and jeans, to be taught how to stand to attention.

As this transition from civilian life to service life is occurring each year, many cadets begin to suffer from a range of symptoms including headache, nausea, vomiting, dizziness, shortness of breath, fatigue, dry throat and loss of appetite. These are not induced by the rude awakening of the barked commands of their sergeant major, but rather by the high-altitude of the Air Force Academy, which is six thousand feet above mean sea level. (The U.S. Olympic high-altitude training camp is also based in Colorado Springs.)

At the end of their four years of study and learning (about 70 percent of initial recruits complete), graduating cadets are passed out with great pomp and ceremonials at a formal graduation held in the on-campus 47,000-seat Falcon Stadium. The stadium is easily filled to capacity with friends and family of those graduating.

The AFA graduation ceremony is a significant event for the Air Force too: the graduates represent year-by-year the mainstay of USAF personnel, and therefore a basic and indispensable component of U.S. military force.

For the Class of 2016, the graduation ceremony—set for 2 June—was even more anticipated than usual, because President Barack Obama was to address the cadets at around eleven o'clock. The ceremony began just before ten o'clock with the national anthem, followed by a series of addresses to the massed Class of 2016 and the capacity crowd.

Obama's focus that morning was "the place of America in the world today." His coda stressed the Air Force ethos: "Take care of each other. Take care of those under your command … stay true to the values you've learned here—integrity, service before self, excellence. Do this and I'm confident that we will always remain one nation, under God, indivisible, with liberty and justice for all."

The proceedings of the graduation ceremony each year are brought to a close with a much-loved and eagerly awaited visual spectacle. The end of the formalities is pronounced with the dean of AFA announcing dramatically, exaggeratedly: "Class.... Dismissed!" At this news, the assembled now-ex-cadets standing to attention in rows in front of the lectern histrionically "fall out" from the parade, tossing their large white-and-blue peaked Cadet Service Dress White Caps high into the air with abandon (they will not be needing these ever again). They then proceed to dance about in delight, hugging all around them, as the gathered family members crowded around the stadium cheer and clap wildly.

And at this moment, as the dean calls the dismissal, the drama and release of the moment is underlined by a low-altitude fly-by—a group of F-16 fighter jets screaming overhead, then swooping away in unison. The initial exciting fly-by is followed by the group of F-16s performing a series of air-show maneuvers.

Any such fly-by and air show is arranged with the same high level of planning and coordination as any USAF sortie. The "six ship" sortie for the 2 June fly-by began with the pilots getting an on-base briefing at Peterson Air Force Base, the nearest air base to the Academy, about twelve miles away—located to the east of Colorado Springs.

The pilots were all members of the Thunderbirds, a USAF display team whose primary role is really marketing and public relations for the USAF—the goal being to maintain and increase recruitment levels. The

39 Inadvertent shutoff

Thunderbirds fly many sorties to air shows with the ambition to wow and impress the public as to the excellence in aviation and actually the glamor of being a USAF pilot.

On that day the jets were delayed on the ground for around a half-hour due to a longer-than-expected graduation ceremony. The six eventually departed Peterson round twelve o'clock, making their timed fly-by as requested—on cue to coincide with the "class dismissed" sign-off.

The fly-by and following air-show profiles were completed absolutely uneventfully and with excellence. (Thunderbirds pilots are all experienced F-16 pilots with hundreds of flying hours logged.) Upon regrouping, the six began their descent back towards the Peterson runway. The jets entered a designated air traffic control tower pattern for landing shortly before one o'clock.

As the six aircraft were lining up in their holding pattern in readiness to land—at around 2,000 feet and 250 m.p.h.—the pilot of one of the F-16s, Major Alex Turner, inadvertently and bizarrely turned his jet-engine throttle control to the "cutoff" position, an action which instantly shut down his F100 engine—his only means of propulsion. This accidental turning-off of the single engine main thrust source occurred at twelve fifty-nine and thirty-eight seconds.

Turner was perplexed and baffled as to the status of his engine: he could not believe what he had just done—or not done. He was in confusion about whether or not he had truly pulled and twisted the throttle to the cutoff position. ("[In his testimony] the pilot states multiple times that he was initially confused about whether or not he had truly pulled the throttle to the cutoff position.")

At almost any other time during a flight—apart from immediately after takeoff—such an error can very easily be rectified. Midair engine restarts ("flame-out" restarts) are much practiced and trained for; the engine system needs around twenty seconds to cycle back up, so the pilot is safer the higher up he is when such an event occurs.

The other option for the pilot who is "engine out" is to glide in to land (the jet has an automatic backup electricity supply, enough to feed the cockpit controls and displays) in a maneuver known as a "deadstick landing." These too are also much practiced—but usually commence from at least 10,000 feet, with plenty of time to declare forced landing to the nearest runway tower and gain permission for an emergency landing. In this particular instance, Turner had flicked off his engine at only 2,000 feet up: he had only seconds to consider his options and put his emergency recovery plan into operation.

Turner determined that with his jet flying at only 250 m.p.h., it just did not have enough forward momentum for a "deadstick" to be a realistic option. He didn't have an airfield in sight and, as per the flight manual, at 2,000 feet the jet should be not more than two miles from its intended touchdown point.

The only possibility was airstart. It would cost him around 1,200 feet of his 2,000 feet, but he did not hesitate.

In order to restart an F-16 in midair, the pilot begins by moving his throttle to shutoff, then to a mid-setting, and turns on the Jet Fuel Starter switch. From there, the restart sequence is automatic. At twelve fifty-nine and forty-four seconds, Turner moved his throttle—this time intentionally—to shutoff, and then to a mid-position, commencing his engine-out restart. Then, a few seconds later, he flicked his Jet Fuel Starter switch on. Unfortunately, the restart effort was not successful—his round-dial thrust and r.p.m. gauges were still "rolling back," or declining.

At twelve fifty-nine and fifty-three seconds, the pilot communicated his loss of power to the Peterson tower, making it clear that he was pointing his jet away from houses and "getting out"—he would be ejecting imminently. In effect, Turner was hedging, as seconds later, with his intention to ditch relayed to air traffic, at one o'clock and three seconds, for a third time he turned his throttle to shutoff, and began air-restart or flame-out restart effort.

This time he was immediately successful, and the engine burst into life rapidly building thrust. But it was too late: with the ground only three hundred feet below, the jet did not have the altitude for the pilot to be confident of pulling up and climbing away from danger.

At one o'clock and twenty-eight seconds—exactly fifty seconds after the original inadvertent action—Turner made a final steering towards what he hoped was open land below and yanked his yellow ejection lever. His ejection was successful, with his parachute opening fully within two seconds.

Eight seconds after pilot ejection, the pilotless and condemned F-16 crashed into a field two miles south of Peterson, in El Paso County—a forlorn, unsalvageable wreck resting on its belly in scrubland.

The value of the lost jet was later estimated at $29.5 million.

40 Eject, dude

Location: Sutter Buttes lava domes, Northern California
Date: 20 September 2016
Aircraft type: U-2
Fatalities: 1
Cost of damage: Classified

The U-2 Dragon Lady "spy plane" is a high-flying jet that cruises in the upper stratosphere, 70,000 feet above Earth, capturing high-resolution aerial images of the land below as it goes. "The U-2S is a single-seat, single-engine, high-altitude near-space reconnaissance and surveillance aircraft providing signals, imagery, and electronic measurements and signature intelligence."

The image-gathering capabilities include "multi-spectral electro-optic, infrared, and synthetic-aperture radar products which can be stored or sent to ground exploitation centers ... it also supports high-resolution broad-area synoptic coverage provided by the optical bar camera

The wreckage of a U-2 plane that crashed near the Sutter Buttes lava domes in Northern California in 2016.

producing traditional film products which are developed and analyzed after landing."

The jet has an unusual form: "Long and narrow wings give the U-2 glider-like characteristics and allow it to quickly lift heavy sensor payloads to unmatched altitudes, keeping them there for extended periods of time."

The U-2 has very long, slender wings much like a glider, and like a glider, it is really not very maneuverable or robust. In addition, due its wing design, the jet is susceptible to aerodynamic stalls: it is a slow-flying aircraft, and even slight reductions in speed can bring the jet into the realm of its aerodynamic stall-speed or its minimum speed. The U-2 pilot is trained to instantly recognize the signs of an impending stall and go into stall recovery procedure (push the control column forward to lower the nose and add full throttle; then bring the nose back to the horizon). In the U-2, stall recovery is not so much a rarity—or an emergency—but an ordinary and actually unavoidable aspect of flying the jet.

Pilots seeking to move to flying U-2s (there are only thirty in service) must already be rated experienced and exceptional aviators. The first step for a prospective pilot hoping to transition to U-2s is an invitation to attend a series of three training-interview sessions organized by the 1st Reconnaissance Squadron at Beale Air Force Base in Yuba County, California. At Beale there are a number of U-2s converted for use as two-seat trainers.

Stall recovery is such a basic component of U-2 aviation that the recovery procedure practice takes up much of the three appraisal-interview flights that pilot candidates participate in. On 20 September 2016, a certain prospective U-2 pilot was on his first-of-three training-evaluation missions in a U-2.

That morning the pilot was accompanied by his instructor, who was at the controls for takeoff with the jet departing Beale at 8:55 a.m. and heading out into a designated training airspace twenty miles west of the base. The flight was the trainee's first-ever flight in a U-2. The instructor was sitting up in the front seat with the trainee behind him in the second seat. Soon after climb-out, the instructor leveled off at 9,000 feet and transferred control of the aircraft to the trainee.

The first exercise was to be a stall recovery: intentionally slowing airspeed—reducing the throttle to idle—and waiting for the telltale signs of aerodynamic stall to occur: a general shuddering of the jet together with in-cockpit warnings and alerts both visual and aural.

As the aerodynamic stall was occurring, the U-2 began to rapidly lose altitude—around five hundred feet. Within five seconds the trainee

40 Eject, dude

dipped the nose and brought in throttle power for a successful recovery. Not bad, but could have been smoother and less aggressive, the instructor told him. The instructor then took it upon himself to offer a demonstration, which the trainee was to follow by "shadowing" (holding loosely his control stick and concentrating on the instructor's movements of it). The demonstration enabled the instructor to show how the recovery inputs could be smoother than his first effort had been.

Then once again the trainee took the controls. This time the trainee had the aim that his inputs would be more free-flowing and continuous. At 9:07 a.m.—twelve minutes after takeoff—flying at 9,200 feet, the trainee commenced his second stall-approach effort. He intentionally let his airspeed decay to a critical level, and as the jet began to enter its aerodynamic stall, he began his recovery procedure.

As he was mid-maneuver, with his attention on smoothing the controls as directed, suddenly his left wing dropped uncommanded and the jet rolled left, dramatically nose-low 40 degrees and 80 degrees of bank. The jet had entered a "secondary stall" and was descending alarmingly and out of control.

As the plane was diving, there seemed to be in those moments something of a time-slip or temporal distortion experienced by the candidate: for four to five seconds, with the jet descending out of control, the instructor gave no specific instructions, nor did he take back the controls and attempt to pull up.

The instructor finally gave his direction to the trainee: "Eject, dude."

The trainee was stunned. He was expecting that he or the instructor would pull up out of the dive. It had not crossed his mind that this was a midair emergency requiring immediate emergency egress.

Equally surprising, the language that the instructor had used was just so laconic. Direction to eject should usually come as a definitive and unmistakable call three times repeated: "Bail out! Bail out! Bail out!"

"Eject, dude," was unconventional. For the trainee the words just hung there almost surreal until a second later he was blinded by searing red and black flashes in front of his face: the instructor sitting up ahead of him had ejected, and he was getting the blast from the under-chair catapult charge in his face.

At this the trainee reached down for his own ejection ring and pulled.

As the two ejected, the plane was not wings-level, but was still left-wing low, rolling in its uncommanded dive.

As the instructor was blasted from the jet he was thrown up and into the right wing. His impact with wing was with such force that his collision with it caused a five-foot section of the wingtip to break away. The instructor pilot was killed in the collision with the jet's wing.

The trainee ejected successfully and landed his parachute safely. He had suffered minor burns to his face caused by the front ejection seat explosive charge detonating, but was otherwise unharmed.

The U-2 crashed into scrubland in the Sutter Buttes Mountains.

As the aircraft impacted terrain, it burst into a post-crash fireball, setting off a forest fire that burned across two hundred acres of land before it was brought under control.

Conclusions

In terms of the *reasons* for a mishap or blunder, the U.S. Department of Defense uses a system known as Human Factors Analysis and Classification System—or HFACS—as their principal "mishap investigation and data analysis tool." The system is essentially a list of explanations with a short text giving an overview of each causal factor. These tend to be specialized psychology and psychiatry-oriented categories and include: inattention; channelized attention; task oversaturation; negative transfer; distraction; geographic misorientation; checklist interference; pre-existing personality disorder; pre-existing psychological disorder; pre-existing psychosocial problem; emotional state; personality style; overconfidence; pressing; complacency; inadequate motivation; misplaced motivation; overaggressive; excessive motivation to succeed; motivational exhaustion.

The USAF general tasked with delivering an accident report will often state the HFACS factors which the board deemed to have been causal to the accident, and some of these I have introduced in specific articles.

Here, however, rather than discuss the official taxonomy, in keeping with my effort to work towards a plain-English-based text comprehensible to any lay reader, I shall eschew all such rarified language and coding of psychiatry and/or military jargon and offer instead six key categories by which to group the above described accidents, and these are: "For want of a nail"; "Too cocky!"; "It only takes a second"; "Birds!"; "An absolute mystery"; and "Shit happens."

For each of these categories I shall introduce the rationale and content and then offer a number of examples from the Accident Report material.

For want of a nail

This grouping may be understood by reference to the ancient proverb *For Want of a Nail*: "For want of a nail a shoe was lost; for want of a shoe a horse was lost; for want of horse a rider was lost; for want of a rider a battle was lost; for want of a battle a kingdom was lost … and all for the want of a nail." The well-known proverb describes a causal narrative which begins with some trivial—silly or easily avoidable—action that sets in motion a chain of events that eventually leads to a significant defeat or disaster.

The basic cause in these accidents is, above all, human error, and one of the striking aspects of these so categorized Reports is the extent to which no matter how super-high-tech the warplane (and its on-board facilities) becomes, there will always remain the risk of human operator faultiness or fallibility. The Romans of antiquity noted well: *errare humanum est*, or *to err is to be human*, and so it remains. A human may be left in charge of a $200 lawn-mower or a $100 million jet, but an essential reality remains constant: all humans (it seems) even the brightest, smartest humans, make dumb-ass mistakes.

For the reason of human neuro-susceptibility, some military experts have argued that such factors are justification for a coming age of automated drone warfare. Perhaps, but thus far all non-secret USAF unmanned aircraft types do still require an *imperfect* remote on-the-ground operator.

In case 1, "Pitch up," a ground-crew team member *failed to turn on the pitot heaters* for certain of the air-pressure sensors (and so burn off excess moisture) before calibrating them, thus setting in motion the chain of events that soon led to a B-2 Spirit pitching up violently at takeoff. The onboard computers and autopilot (the B-2 uses an autopilot system for takeoff, as its unusual aerodynamic form make it very hard to fly) were receiving conflicting information, causing the jet to become completely uncontrollable and crash seconds after leaving the ground.

In case 2, "Number 3 engine idle," a pilot's mistake of *shutting down a perfectly functioning engine* in midair (of four in total) instead of a known-to-be-malfunctioning one (and none of the other crew noticing this error) caused his aircraft to be underpowered as it came in to land, and so crash short of the runway.

In case 6, "Zero-G parabolas," a pilot's hand-held pressure gauge fell out of his reach in the cockpit while he was airborne. His *elaborate technique* for retrieving it (flying an over-the-top zero-G maneuver) was

Conclusions

not well executed and quickly led to the aircraft entering an unrecoverable nose dive.

In case 10, "Flameout Volk," the apparent cause of the accident (and the loss of an F-16) was an undiscovered foreign object lodged in the engine (apparently a roll of Teflon wire), which and been inadvertently left *inside the engine* by a careless mechanic during an engine overhaul.

In case 15, "Paddy field," an F-16 pilot lost his engine over South Korea. Analysis indicated that at least one year before the accident, some no-longer-necessary painted ground-markings in the F-16 hangars at Osan Air Force Base had been removed using shot-blasting equipment. After the job was complete, some of the shot material (tiny, intensely abrasive particles) was left behind as a near-invisible residue. This abrasive residue was later sucked into the engine of one F-16, causing some of its internal rotor-blades to suffer abrasive damage as the shot residue made its way through the jet engine under significantly higher compression than the original equipment.

In case 18, "Belly flop," the pilot of a valuable F-22 had just taken off from Tyndall AFB and had retracted his wheels (he was "gear up"), but in those moments he forgot to turn his engine thrust via the throttle from idle to main power (from IDLE to MIL setting), causing his jet to "settle" back down onto the runway on its belly and career along the ground for several thousand feet.

In case 20, "Fuel-line shutoff," the main fuel supply was cut off from the engine in mid-flight. This may well have been caused by an other-than-conscientious mechanic who likely—during routine maintenance—treated the jet's main fuel shutoff valve using Electron 22 (a solvent-degreaser), rather than the required Con-Tac Corrosion Preventative Compound (a lubricant and corrosion prevention spray for metal surfaces).

In case 21, "Flaps gone," a wayward and careless mechanic (and those supervising and checking his work) failed to notice that the retainer end-caps had not been refitted to the main flap assembly after maintenance, causing two of the two-ton objects to fall off the back of the wings in mid-flight.

In case 35, "Fire by the microwave," poor workmanship during the maintenance of an RC-135V left a number of pipework joints only finger-tight rather than fully-tightened ("torqued"), causing easily ignited pure oxygen to pour from the pipes minutes after the engines started.

In case 36, "Unseen traffic," an F-16 pilot was informed by a civilian air traffic control tower operative of an unknown civilian plane close by at around *two miles away*. The F-16 pilot assumed or heard "twenty miles away," but could not be sure and asked for clarification. The F-16 was closing on the civilian Cessna at around two hundred miles an hour. The F-16 pilot had just seconds to understand *two miles* rather than twenty, and before he could comprehend the urgency to act to avoid an impending collision, he crashed into the civilian aircraft in midair.

In case 37, "Goggles case," pilot Jordan Pierson, while loading and flying at night, inadvertently left an empty hard-shell night-vision goggles case wedged in the cockpit immediately in front of the main control stick. The case blocked the stick's nose-down movements, causing the aircraft to pitch up unrecoverably soon after takeoff.

In case 39, "Inadvertent shutoff," the pilot of an F-16 inexplicably turned his main (and only) jet engine to *shutoff* position for no known reason at low altitude, making restart recovery impossible.

Beyond having not eaten all day and general fatigue, there are few excuses offered in mitigation on the reports. To those in civilian society, this may bring some small comfort: these often foolish errors were made by some of the most quick-witted and sharp minds in the USA. In light of this observation, it might be postulated that error-proneness is in fact a basic human quality rather than one that tends to afflict those of only average intelligence. The evidence above points to error-making as a quality that is in a sense an inalienable and absolute quality of our species.

In reviewing the content of the category *For want of a nail*, it seems also worth noting that in the Accident Report into each of the above, the presumption is always of some kind of *honest mistake*. No ill will is ever presumed or even mentioned as a possibility. Although not discussed, real possibilities remain that at least some of the above were actually acts of *deliberate sabotage* by hostile operatives posing as mechanics, etc. One picture that emerges through the reports is of little attention paid to screening and vetting the lowliest mechanics employed on certain air bases. In addition, when jet engines leave USAF hands, as they often do for super-specialist maintenance, and are returned to the manufacturer, the chain of oversight and cross-checking of work carried out inevitably breaks down.

Too cocky!

Several of the accidents in the forty that I have covered are the result of a pilot flying *recklessly with excessive confidence*. In each of the below examples, the pilot flew with a macho attitude—"ostentatiously or notably

Conclusions

manly and virile; an assertively vigorous man." The fact is that some USAF pilots do become bullish and overconfident and perceive their skill at controlling their jet to be near absolute. They perhaps feel themselves to be invincible, superhuman, with a prowess which is beyond any requirement to respond to, say, in-cockpit audible crash warnings, for example.

In case 4, "Caught a tailwind," the pilot at the controls of a HH-60G helicopter took off and climbed away from a landing pad with a stiff tailwind by rising a few feet and flying away in a wide dramatic arc, and so crashing. He could have risen from his landing spot vertically and "pedal turned"—a much lower risk maneuver without the catastrophic end result.

In case 7, "Arctic Thunder," the pilot of a valuable C-17 Globemaster ($180 million) made the decision to fly an airshow display practice as an unusual self-innovated maximum performance effort, flying the display practice using only full throttle and his tail rudder control. Then, when hearing stall warnings, during a very tight turn, he *ignored them*, causing his aircraft to enter an unrecoverable aerodynamic stall at low altitude and crash to Earth.

In case 22, "Roll off the top," the pilot of an F-16 flew a series of Immelmann turns or roll-off-the-top maneuvers during which his jet slowed to stall speed with many audible warnings. The pilot ignored these warnings until, on one of the occasions that he performed the maneuver, he entered an unrecoverable aerodynamic stall.

In case 25, "Stockton impromptu," the pilot of an A-10 flew in slow-and-low over a public-civilian pleasure lake—at around 150 feet up—in order to carry out a pre-arranged or absolutely spontaneous (it was not conclusively established which one it was) impromptu low-altitude fly-by over a civilian boat on the water. His low altitude and fascination with the prohibited fly-by caused him to crash into a fixed object in the ground terrain.

In case 28, "Lights-out intercept," an F-16 pilot flew a practice lights-out intercept with his sole reference being only the simulated hostile's tailpipe vapor trail, causing him to close in on the target jet at hundreds of miles an hour and crash into the back of the target. This had been proposed to a trainee as an exemplary intercept flown as a demonstration to a student-cadet.

These accidents were all caused by some or other incautious act by an airman who would have known well enough that what he was doing was at the least ill-considered.

The psychological tension in this category is fascinating. Of course the pilot of a warplane must be at least somewhat confident, fearless and bold; after all, "Fortuna Favet Fortibus" (Fortune favors the brave) is the official motto of several classes of the United States Naval Academy Classes.

The question remains: at what precise point do confidence and prowess cross over into overconfidence and foolishness? Those who manage and teach airmen must be continuously aware of the vexed territory demarcating the limits of each behavior. (On this topic, speaking in favor of professional caution, the experienced deep-sea diver Commander Jacques Cousteau famously asserted: "There are old divers and there are bold divers but there are no old, bold divers.")

One possible explanation for the above *aberrations* is to understand them in the context of the culture of rules and regulations or constraint and control that is so dominant in the USAF. For some airmen, it may be surmised, the daily privation apparently becomes simply too constricting and they rebel against control by carrying on unauthorized actions. Interpreted this way, the above actions are not principally reckless (as per thrill-seeking or overconfident), but rather primarily actions intended to demonstrate some measure of freedom and autonomy away from the tyranny of the pilot's innumerable procedural checklists.

It only takes a second

No matter how experienced, a pilot remains subject to getting into trouble due to entering a mental state of confusion or even panic. This is true regardless of whether the individual is a recent recruit or an extremely experienced airman with no history whatsoever of any such episode through more than ten or fifteen years of service. Such psychological episodes are often known as attacks of "spatial disorientation"—a total disorientation which can strike at any moment, out of the blue.

In case 9, "Ground-rush in Germany," an experienced A-10 Thunderbolt pilot lost his bearings and became bewildered while flying over southern Germany. The pilot was able to eject—only one second before his jet crashed and was destroyed.

In case 16, "Communications mast," an F-15 Strike Eagle pilot became disoriented while flying at night over unlit desert terrain. During the moments of disorientation, the F-15 was flying low altitude and crashed into a fixed object in the ground terrain.

In case 23, "Spatial D," an F-16 pilot lost his bearings (it seems) as he flew fast and low over the Adriatic Sea at night off the coast of Italy. The pilot ejected, but with his jet flying at a speed of at least five hundred miles per hour, he was killed in the initial windrush of the ejection sequence. His jet was destroyed as it disintegrated on impact with the sea.

In case 29, "Racetrack gun pattern," an HH-60 Pave Hawk helicopter pilot seemingly perceived a second helicopter on the same training sortie (his "wingman") to be alarmingly near to his aircraft, causing him to take dramatic (and seemingly unnecessary) evasive action to avoid it. His "deconflicting" action ironically brought his own aircraft into an unstable state as it lost "lift" and crashed.

With these examples, as with those cases mentioned in *For want of a nail*, it seems credible to propose that some aspects of the human psyche remain somewhat mysterious, uncheckable, and so unvetted. One supposition here might be of a pre-existing psychological "trigger"—a set of factors or a thought process, or a mental image perhaps, that can activate panic, disorientation or sudden onset of loss of concentration. This "Achilles heel" is perhaps present in all humans, each with a perfectly unique weakness. In some humans, such a trigger becomes known and well identified; in others it remains a hidden malignancy: present but unrecognized and undiagnosed until, in some astonishing moment, it is revealed.

Birds!

The horrifying reality of the hazard that flying birds pose to a USAF warplane is surprising, but apparently not easy to overcome or nullify.

The fact is that even a tiny bird as unassuming and seemingly innocuous as a sparrow can cause havoc to a U.S. jet plane. Larger birds pose a more obvious hazard, but these too cannot be definitively eradicated from the skies, or even from the vicinity of an air base.

Each year many USAF jets, worth tens of millions or hundreds of millions of dollars, are regularly compromised and actually caused to crash because of birds being sucked into ("ingested") the front air intake turbines of their jet engines or caught in an unexpected midair collision with an aircraft.

In case 27, "Birdstrike Luke," an F-16 encountered a bird-strike event immediately after takeoff, causing his jet engine to splutter and convulse (a series of compressor stalls). The pilot sought to land urgently (rather than continue to climb), and in his maneuvering entered an *aerodynamic* stall, unrecoverable at low altitude, and crashed.

In case 31, "Cley goose strike," the crew of an HH-60 helicopter were hit midair by a group of startled geese that impacted the front windshield of the helicopter at around a hundred and fifty miles per hour. The birds smashed through the windshield as missiles, knocking the pilot and other crew members unconscious, and so causing the helicopter to crash.

In case 38, "Three-out takeoff," a B-52 encountered a bird strike during takeoff, causing the pilot to abort his takeoff at the very last moment. Due to the fast speed of the jet on the runway, the plane careered off the far end of the tarmac surface and crashed.

These accidents occur even with much effort made by the USAF to mitigate via the Air Force Bird Aircraft Strike Hazard (BASH) reduction program, the Bird Hazard Working Group (BHWG), and the Bird Watch Condition (BWC).

BASH is broken into Phase I and II. Phase I represents normal, baseline wildlife activity. Phase II represents times of significant increases in local wildlife activity—normally associated with migratory movements and other seasonal movements. Bird Watch Conditions is used to increase or decrease awareness for aircrews based on real-time observations: Low, Moderate, and Severe local airfield wildlife activity. If observed bird activity is defined as Moderate or High, "wildlife activity near the active runway or other specific location representing increased potential for strikes/ Wildlife activity on or immediately above the active runway or other specific location representing high potential for strikes." This requires "increased vigilance by all agencies and supervisors along with caution by aircrews. Supervision and aircrews must evaluate mission need before conducting operations in areas under severe conditions." Moderate or severe status "requires action from the installation's wildlife dispersal team to reduce the bird watch condition to Low *as soon as possible* ... however, even the most effective techniques for dispersing wildlife from the aerodrome cannot promise long term results or a wildlife-free airfield." As the Report into case 38 notes well, "Although wildlife strikes can never be eliminated, an aggressive, well-planned program developed on the basis of wildlife habits, the environment, and the base mission may limit the potential for these strikes to occur."

An absolute mystery

The fact is that even with all the modern technology that abounds in and around the modern USAF aircraft (including the crash-survivable digital data recorder, or "black box"), a jet can still crash without any clear-cut explanation—even after considerable effort to salvage and piece together the events of the final moments of the aircraft.

Conclusions

In case 5, "Fly-by," a B-52 departed Andersen AF Base on Guam in the Pacific with a mission to perform a civilian fly-by. A few minutes after takeoff, before carrying out the fly-past, it crashed into open sea about thirty miles from the island with no in-flight emergency called by the crew or any radio contact of any kind on the subject of a malfunction.

In case 8, "C-Bleed hot," the pilot of an F-22 Raptor flying at speed over Alaska lost his air supply to his oxygen mask. For an unknown reason, the pilot did not reach for his emergency air-canister supply or eject from his jet. The F-22 crashed nose-down into the Talkeetna Mountains seconds later without any radio contact from the pilot giving any explanation; the pilot was killed in the crash.

In case 11, "Mist up AirVenture," an F-16 pilot experienced a misting-up in his cockpit as he came in to land: suddenly there was a thick fog in the cockpit and the airman could see nothing at all. Later analysis was not able to determine definitively how the mist-up had happened.

In case 17, "Titanium fire," one of the two jet engines powering an F-15 exploded midair with no warning. Later analysis was inconclusive as to the precise reasons for the catastrophic event.

In case 33, "Down to Louisiana," an F-15 began to descend from high altitude at near full power close to supersonic speed directly down towards the ground. The pilot called an in-flight emergency but did nothing to pull out of the nose dive and was killed seconds later as the F-15 crashed to earth.

"Shit happens"

All the other cases would come under this broad category. In case 3, the actual terrain at a desert landing-zone was softer soil-and-sand than the flight crew predicted it would be, causing their helicopter's front wheel (and support-strut) to collapse into the soft ground. In case 12, an FCF pilot was a little blasé about his unnecessarily slow-speed and unnecessarily high-altitude as he carried out a post-maintenance check-flight. In case 13, a hard landing in very poor weather at an extremely remote uneven landing-strip caused the plane to become uncontrollable. In case 14, the pilot's approach speed was slightly incorrect as there was confusion in the control tower as to whether his runway had been de-iced and cleared of snow. In case 19, one helicopter got unexpectedly and unpredictably caught-up in the backwash of another's. In case 24, the usually minor annoyance of a Dutch Roll effect on an aircraft in flight was not brought under control and eventually set-in-motion a catastrophic mid-air structural fail. In case 26, a well maintained jet became uncontrollable during a high-speed spin maneuver. In case 30, a pivoting wing cut into a jet's main fuel-line. In case 32, a jet engine failed catastrophically, very unexpectedly, during an ordinary training mission. In case 34, a test-pilot team temporarily lost control of the jet while intentionally flying at the boundaries of its flight envelope. In case 40, a training aircraft's left wing dropped suddenly uncommanded.

Here—with the prospect of intentional sabotage in several of the cases reviewed under *For want of a nail*—it is worth noting that the remote but definitely existing possibility that the crash was an *intentional suicidal act* is not introduced or proposed in any of the Accident Reports. Here once again it is interesting to note that in a culture so defined by its orderliness and rational decision-making (the USAF), there remains in a sense a blind spot for aspects of human thought and decision-making that inverts or *perverts* the foundational beliefs and values of the airman in service.

Looking more broadly at the material, one conclusion that can be drawn from the details of the Accident Reports above is further confirmation of the much discussed "global network" of U.S. air bases. The reports taken as a whole reveal how a number of interconnected bases allow for and enable the USAF to create and preserve their "continuous strike presence" across the Earth.

For French theorist Paul Virilio, the post–Cold War epoch in the liberal West is defined by an always-fragile doctrine of global security or Total Peace—as opposed to Total War (a war in which the general population is under attack by an enemy force). For Virilio, this era of enforced Total Peace in terms of military history links back not to warfare as such but to the tactic of siege and blockade: the creation of paralysis in an enemy. Hence for Virilio, the era of Total Peace is also the age of "polar inertia" (Virilio, 2005: 8–9).

The USAF's "primary mission" is to "promote stability, dissuade/deter aggression, and swiftly defeat enemies." Its given role is essentially that of a global security service with the Earth's surface divided into several designated "areas of responsibility." These include the United States Air Forces in Europe (USAFE) and the large area overseen by Pacific Air Forces (PACAF)."

From the evidence accrued in the above Accident Reports, perhaps the most fraught of the USAF "forward bases" is Andersen, the vital strategic outpost in the middle of the Pacific on a tiny island (not twenty miles across) at least one thousand miles from any significant landmass in every direction. Andersen has suffered significantly in the twenty-first century as regards non-combat tragedies: the loss of a B-2 Spirit on 23 February 2008; the loss of a B-52 on 21 July 2008; and the loss of a B-52 on 19 May 2016.

The USAF is also divided into a number of MAJCOMs: Air Combat Command; Air Mobility Command; and Air Force Special Operations. As is seen in several of the accidents above, Special Operations units can be "infiltrated" to any point around the globe at short notice or following extensive planning—and accurate usually to 0.2 of a mile to any given map-reference insertion point.

The picture that is revealed through the reports is of a definite splitting off and separation between the USAF and ordinary civilian life. The two exist in parallel or are "parallel universes" as theorized by French intellectual and theorist Jean Baudrillard (2014). The USAF carries on its activities continuously but essentially unseen and unnoticed by the ordinary civilian citizen of Earth.

The Baudrillardian "parallel universe" is any system that seems to function absolutely independently of ordinary daily-life experience. Examples often given by Baudrillard include nuclear weapons (wars are generally fought as if they did not exist) and the global stock-trading markets (in the present era, precipitous stock market crashes seem to have no discernable impact on daily life—as opposed to, say, the Great Crash of 1929). Of course in this context the disparity and disconnection is between ordinary "civilian" life and military activity. Judging from the case histories above, the picture of USAF operations is par excellence an instance of Baudrillard's concept.

Activities at most of the U.S. bases around the world rarely come to the attention of the public. Andersen was in the news briefly in July 2017 after Kim Jong Un threatened to target the island of Guam with a rocket. The more typical picture is of U.S. bases, such as at, say, Camp Lemmonier, being as it were off the radar of the news broadcasters. Djibouti, the host country in Africa of Camp Lemmonier, is rarely in the news.

Journalists and reporters are more or less stymied and often cannot state with any credibility or certainty facts about what is actually happening at any specific base operationally. They may have their "sources," but information from such is questionable and remains uncorroborated.

One example of "parallel universe" in Europe is Ramstein Air Base in the Rhineland of Germany. The base is in near continuous use for missions commencing in the U.S. en route to the Middle East; it is a major staging post for U.S. operations in Iraq, Afghanistan, and beyond (the

SEAL team on their mission to kill Bin Laden stopped off at Ramstein, for example), but few Germans, *if any*, have detailed knowledge of operations arriving or departing Ramstein.

One of the slight disguises in place at many U.S. bases is to allow the host country to retain its national designation. This is the case in the UK, but of course, in reality, the Royal Air Force has scant knowledge of the missions of flights arriving and departing RAF Lakenheath or RAF Mildenhall.

This picture of the USAF as do-as-you-please overlord is perhaps reassuring. If we (in the West) live free, we live free precisely because our safety and security are continuously insisted upon and ensured by a truly astonishing global-reach military force. This force works relentlessly, and in fact rather selflessly, to ensure and preserve the scene of freedom and peace.

In the context of the USAF as a "parallel universe" to the civilian one, it is interesting (and maybe reassuring) to note that judging from the events described above, the two "worlds" *do* share many of the causes and sources of human irritation, annoyance, and aggravation: a stinking broken toilet "out of order" where a fully functioning one would be most welcome; a hot-food cart that is offered but is nowhere to be found; the requirement to be back at work only six hours after arriving home from a particularly exhausting shift; new admin procedures that make life more stressful and not easier; etc.

The authentic picture of day-to-day operations that emerges from the reports is dominated by the principle of readiness through practice: the USAF bomber crew will fly practice bombing missions; the fighter pilot will attack simulated ground targets and nominated hostile aircraft air-to-air. Outside of deployment into an active theater of operations and active combat, USAF pilots and aircrews are generally involved in planning and carrying out practice missions. The fact is that the ordinary life of a USAF pilot is built up around simulation and artificially concocted warlike scenarios—the basic staple of the airman's flying career is the war game.

But this is not to denigrate the significance of the notional target and the nominal hostile. Aleksander Suvarov, a Russian general of the 18th century, exhorted his men: "Train hard, fight easy." This remains a basic and entrenched military doctrine.

Training against fake enemies has actually become—the Reports reveal—a significant ancillary industry with entire squadrons of jets (F-15s in particular) set up and organized in order that they effectively offer "Red Air" simulated hostiles for practice missions.

Conclusions

The somber reality, as seen above in several instances, is that the practice mission is no less hazardous for being a simulation: the aviator heading in at nine hundred miles per hour at three hundred feet altitude over undulating terrain towards a simulated target in a metropolitan suburb in darkness wearing night-vision goggles may be only "practicing," but the hazards and risks are absolutely real. And this being the case, it sometimes happens that pilots and aircrews are killed (and planes lost and destroyed) during *practice* missions. For the airman's surviving family, this may be even more painful than a loss during a heroic, elevated, worthy combat mission.

A second aspect of the ordinary daily life of the airman that emerges with clarity above is the extraordinary *fetishization* of order, regulation, control and dictate that abounds in the USAF. Almost every possible activity on base and at work is regulated by directives and boiled down to a checklist of required actions: the pilot is something like an automaton of best practice. Over decades, the most efficient and safe way of carrying out an action has been scrutinized and eventually schematized.

The airman's life is dominated by the systematic discipline and orderliness—and abstemiousness: tobacco and alcohol are frowned upon and rarely taken. Even taking frequently used meds like hay-fever pills is allowed only with a USAF physician's certificate (even when purchased over the counter off-base).

The overall picture that emerges from the Reports is of a hyper-banalized lifestyle in which even the number of hours an airman spends in quarters asleep is subject to regulation and requirements. In short, the airman's life is so (arguably necessarily) governed by order that his quality of life as per *enjoyment* is always secondary. Hence service is very definitely a form of sacrifice: the airman sacrifices the *quality* of autonomy in much of his ordinary life; he is a *regulated* human.

Sources

Preface

Barnet, Richard. *The Economy of Death*. London: Atheneum Books, 1969.
Baudrillard, Jean. *Fatal Strategies*. New York: Semiotexte, 2008.
____. *Screened Out*. London: Verso, 2014.
Benjamin, Walter. "A Short History of Photography" [1931]. In *One-Way Street and Other Writings*. London: Penguin, 2009.
Burroughs, William. *The Job*. London: Penguin, 1989.
Chomsky, Noam, and Edward Herman. *Manufacturing Consent*. London: Vintage, 1995.
Fulbright, James. *The Pentagon Propaganda Machine*. New York: Liveright, 1970.
Hooks, Gregory. *Forging the Military-Industrial Complex*. Chicago: University of Illinois Press, 1991.
O'Neill, Robert. *The Operator*. London: Simon and Schuster, 2017.
Owen, Mark. *No Easy Day*. New York: Dutton, 2012.
Swofford, Anthony. *Jarhead*. London: Simon and Schuster, 2004.
Virilio, Paul. *The Original Accident*. London: Polity Press, 2007.
____. *Politics of the Very Worst*. New York: Semiotexte, 1999.
____. *Pure War*. New York: Semiotexte, 2008.

1 Pitch up

"B-2 Spirit Stealth Bomber." Airforce-technology.com, undated.
Carpenter, Brig. Gen. Floyd. "USAF Accident Investigation Board Report." Accident of 23 February 2008.
"The Known Unknown." *NASA: System Failure Case Studies* 3, No. 1 (January 2009).
Kwiatkowski, Mark. "Global Strike Deployment 2014." Aeroresource.co.uk, 18 June 2014.
Letman, Jon. "Proposed US military buildup on Guam angers locals who liken it to colonization." *The Guardian*, 1 August 2016.
Pappalardo, Joe. "We Fly a B-2 Stealth Bomber." Popular Mechanics.com, 7 January 2013.

2 Number 3 engine idle

Lockheed-Martin C-5M Super Galaxy sales brochure, Fort Worth, Texas, 2017.
"Snapped USAF C-5 Galaxy Report Blames Aircrew." Flightglobal.com, 14 June 2006.

Torres, Raymond. "Aircraft Accident Investigation Executive Summary." Accident of 3 April 2006.
USAF Fact Sheet: C-5 A/B/C Galaxy and C-5M Super Galaxy. www.af.mil, undated.

3 Landing strut

Dillow, Clay. "The Helicopter That Crashed in the Bin Laden Raid Was a Secret Stealth Helicopter." Popularscience.com, 3 May 2011.
Pike, John. "Udairi Training Range." Globalsecurity.org, 7 May 2011.
Reay, Colonel Roderick. "United States Air Force Aircraft Investigation Report." Accident of 13 February 2003.
USAF Fact Sheet: Sikorsky MH-53M Pave Low IV. www.af.mil, undated.

4 Caught a tailwind

"Helicopter pedal turns, LTE and the Critical Wind Azimuth." Helicopterflight.net, undated.
Shaffer, Col. Jim. "United States Air Force Command Directed Investigation Board Report." Accident of 3 July 2005.

5 Fly-by

Barrett, Brigadier General Mark. "United States Air Force Aircraft Accident Investigation Board Report." Accident of 21 July 2008.
Letman, Jon, "Guam: Where the US Military is Revered and Reviled." Thediplomat.com, 29 August 2016.
_____. "Proposed US military buildup on Guam angers locals who liken it to colonization." *The Guardian*, 1 August 2016.
USAF Fact Sheet: B-52 Stratofortress. www.af.mil, undated.

6 Zero-G parabolas

Bedke, Maj. Gen. Curtis. "United States Air Force Aircraft Accident Investigation Board Report." Accident of 21 May 2009.
"Edwards AFB T-38 Crash Claimed the Life of TPS Pilot." Aero-news.net, 24 May 2009.

7 Arctic Thunder

Everhart, Brig. Gen, Carlton. "United States Air Force Aircraft Accident Investigation Board Report." Accident of 28 July 2010.
Shedlock, Jerzy. "Judge tosses suit tied to widow of Alaska airman who died in C-17 crash." *Anchorage Daily News*, 5 May 2015.
Trimble, Stephen. "C-17 crash report exposes cracks in USAF safety culture." Flightglobal.com, 17 December 2010.

8 C-Bleed hot

Browne, Brig. Gen James. "United States Air Force Aircraft Accident Investigation Board Report." Accident of 16 November 2010.

Ellis, Tim. "JBER F-22s Scramble to Intercept Russian Jets Near Alaska Air Space." *Alaska Public Media*, 25 September 2014.
Lilley, Steve. "Breathe." *NASA Safety Center System Failure Case Study* 7, No. 2 (March 2013).

9 Ground-rush Germany

Davey, Col. Peter. "United States Air Force Aircraft Accident Investigation Board Report." Accident of 1 April 2011.
"Pilot Identified in Spangdahlem A-10 Crash." Usafe.af.mil, 2 April 2011.
Svan, Jennifer. "Investigators: Pilot Error, Weather Contributed to A-10 Crash Near Spangdahlem." Stripes.com, 6 March 2012.

10 Flameout Volk

Adams, Barry. "'I'm glad it was my empty house,' homeowner says of F-16 crash." *Wisconsin State Journal*, 11 June 2011.
Air Combat Command. "F-16 Combat Aircraft Fundamentals." USAF publications, 1996.
"Engine Failure Cause of F16 Fighter Crash." WRJCRadio.com, 21 October 2011.
Faulk, Lt. Col. David. "[ANG] Aircraft Accident Investigation Board Report." Accident of 7 June 2011.
Kliese, Jennifer. "Owner of Home Hit by F-16 Fighter Reacts." WSAW.com, 9 June 2011.

11 Mist-up AirVenture

Carter, Jimmy. "Alabama Air Guard F16 loses brakes at Oshkosh Airshow…Whoops." Askjimmycarter.co.uk, 29 July 2011.
Kelley, Col. Michael. "United States Air Force Aircraft Accident Investigation Board Report." Accident of 28 July 2011.
Phillips, Rick. "Runway runs short on an F-16 (25 HQ Photos)." Thechive.com, 21 January 2015.

12 Warthog seizure

Haag, Sgt. Jason. "Wounded Warthog." *The Combat Edge*, April 2014, pp. 12–15.
Rodock, David. "Moody AFB plane crashes in Cook County." *The Moultrie Observer*, 26 September 2011.
Standifer, Col. Douglas. "United States Air Force Aircraft Accident Investigation Board Report." Accident of 26 September 2011.

13 Walan Rabat

"Crash of a PZL Mielec C145A Skytruck in Walan Rabat 18 December, 2011." Bureau of Aircraft Accidents Archives, Geneva ("B3A").
"First Airstrip in Zabul Province." U.S. Agency for International Development, 1 September 2006.
Jordan, Col. Lewis. "United States Air Force Aircraft Accident Investigation Board Report." Accident of 18 December 2011.

"Why Lockheed Martin will keep on truckin'," African Aerospace Online News Service, 13 December 2016.

14 Overshoot Shank

"FOB Shank C-17 Accident Report Released." Military.com, 2017.
Oliver, Col. Kevin. "United States Air Force Aircraft Accident Investigation Board Report." Accident of 22 January 2012.

15 Paddy field

Browne, Ryan. "Top General: Cheaper to Keep Troops in South Korea than U.S." CNN.com, 21 April 2016.
Jones, Lt. Col. William. "United States Air Force Aircraft Accident Investigation Board Report." Accident of 21 March 2012.
Shamin, Asif. "F-16 from 36 FS Crashes Near Kunsan," F-16.net, 21 March 2012.
"'We are grateful he's safe': U.S. Air Force pilot successfully bails out of doomed F-16 before crash during training mission." Daily Mail Online, 21 March 2012.

16 Communications mast

Moore, Brig. Gen. Charles. "United States Air Force Aircraft Accident Investigation Board Report." Accident of 28 March 2012.
Thompson, Mark. "Death in 11 Seconds: When Headlights Become Stars." *Time*, 24 August 2012.
Whitlock, Craig. "Remote US Base at Core of Secret Operations." *The Washington Post*, 26 October 2012.

17 Titanium fire

Cenciotti, David. "Some Interesting Details About the F-15 Strike Eagle Crashed in UAE While En Route to Afghanistan." *The Aviationist*, 3 May 2012.
Cyr, Col. Henry. "United States Air Force Aircraft Accident Investigation Report." Accident of 3 May 2012.

18 Belly flop

Axe, David, "Another Day, Another $678 Million Stealth Jet Wrecked." Wired.com, 16 November 2012.
Murphy, Col. Richard. "United States Air Force Aircraft Accident Investigation Report." Accident of 31 May 2012.

19 Cut-up wake

"Air Force squadron commander removed after Osprey crash." CNN.com, 22 June 2012.
Axe, David. "General: 'My Career Was Done' When I Criticized Flawed Warplane." Wired.com, 4 October 2012.
Cenciotti, David. "U.S. Air Force CV-22 Osprey tilt rotor aircraft crashes on Eglin range." Theaviationist.com, 14 June 2012.

Kaspar, Col. Hans. "United States Air Force Aircraft Accident Investigation Report." Accident of 13 June 2012.
Pick, Airman Joseph. "Air Commandos receive Distinguished Flying Cross." Hurlburt.af.mil, 21 April 2017.
Whittle, Richard. "AFSOC Osprey Pilot's Crash Was His Second In CV-22s." Breakingdefense.com, 22 June 2012.

20 Fuel-line shutoff

Gorenburg, Dmitry. "The Southern Kuril Islands Dispute." PONARS Eurasia Policy Memo No. 226, September 2012.
Scott, Col. Terry. "United States Air Force Aircraft Accident Investigation Report." Accident of 22 July 2012.
"US F-16 crashes in Pacific; pilot rescued." Stripes.com, 22 July 2012.
"U.S. fighter pilot rescued after plane crash off Japan coast." *Daily Mail*, 22 July 2012.

21 Flaps gone

Wright, Lt. Col. David. "United States Air Force Aircraft Accident Investigation Report." Accident of 1 November 2012.

22 Roll off the top

Alholinna, Col. Nathan. "United States Air Force Aircraft Accident Investigation Report." Accident of 27 December 2012.
"Fresno-based F-16 Crashes Near Owens Valley." ABC7.com, 27 December 2012.
Kessler, Benett. "Military plane crashes at Owens Dry Lake." Sierrawave.net, 27 December 2012.
"Military plane crash reported at Owens Lake in Eastern Sierra," Pete Thomas Outdoors, 17 December 2012.

23 Spatial D

Air Combat Command. "F-16 Operations Procedures." Revised July 1999.
Rydholm, Brig. Gen. Derek. "United States Air Force Aircraft Accident Investigation Report." Accident of 28 January 2013.
Svan, Jennifer. "Report into F-16 crash cites spatial disorientation by pilot." Stripes.com, 30 October 2013.
Wynbrandt, James. "Spatial Disorientation: Confusion that Kills." AOPA Air Safety Foundation, undated.

24 Dutch roll

Arquette, Brig. Gen. Steven "United States Air Force Aircraft Accident Investigation Report." Accident of 3 May 2013.
"Capt. Victoria Ann Pinckney: Obituary." *Winona Daily News*, 2 June 2013.
Cenciotti, David. "US KC-135 Refueling Plane Crashed in Kyrgyzstan. Air Force Got Rid of Parachutes on These Tankers in 2008." Theaviationist.com, 3 May 2013.
Thompson, Mark. "Disaster in the Sky: Old Planes, Inexperienced Pilots—and No More Parachutes." *Time*, 14 April 2014.

Villacorte, Christina. "Air Force Capt. Victoria Pinckney remembered fondly." *Los Angeles Daily News*, 6 May 2013.

25 Stockton impromptu

"A-10C Accident Investigation Report Released." Air Force Reserve Command, 13 August 2013.
Doughtery, Justin. "Low-Flying Fighter Jet Knocks Down Power Lines at Stockton Lake." OzarksFirst.com, undated.
Lyons, Col. William. "United States Air Force Aircraft Accident Investigation Report." Accident of 22 May 2013.
"What Caused A-10C Thunderbolt II to Crash into Power Line Cables?" *Torch Magazine* (Torch.af.mil), 26 August 2014.

26 Okinawa corkscrew

Mitchell, Jon. "What Awaits Okinawa Forty Years After Reversion?" *The Japan Times*, 13 May 2012.
Scott, Col. Terry. "United States Air Force Aircraft Accident Investigation Report." Accident of 28 May 2013.

27 Birdstrike Luke

Menozzi, Col. John. "United States Air Force Aircraft Investigation Report." Accident of 26 June 2013.

28 Lights-out intercept

"Aerospace Control Alert Mission." Colorado National Guard (CONG) public affairs document, 2015.
Deveans, Maj. Tom, and Dr. Robert Kewley. "Overcoming Information Overload in the Cockpit." Department of Systems Engineering, USMA, Operations Research Center of Excellence, West Point, 2009.
LaGrone, Sam. "Updated: Coast Guard Rescues F-16 Pilot After Late Thursday Crash." USNI News, 2 August 2013.
Purcell, Col. Howard. "United States Air Force Aircraft Investigation Report." Accident of 1 August 2013.

29 Racetrack gun pattern

Basham, Brig. Gen. Steven. "United States Air Force Aircraft Investigation Report." Accident of 5 August 2013.
Beech, Hannah, "The Tense Relationship Between Japan and the U.S. Military." Time.com, 8 June 2016.
Callaghan, Staff Sgt. Ryan. "41st HMU supports 'spin-up.'" *Moody Air Force Base News*, 19 December 2016.
"Ginoza residents protest against U.S. helicopter crash." *Ryukyu Shimpo*, 23 August 2013.
Harlan, Chico. "U.S. Military Helicopter Crashes in Okinawa." *The Washington Post*, 5 August 2013.

Mie, Ayako. "U.S. return of Okinawa training area faces harsh criticism from local residents." *The Japan Times*, 21 December 2016.

"U.S. grounds HH-60 helicopters in Japan after accident." *The Japan Times*, 6 August 2013.

"U.S. military helicopter crashes in Okinawa." Reuters, 5 August 2013.

Wakatsuki, Yoko. "Body found at site of U.S. chopper crash in Japan." CNN.com, 6 August 2013.

30 Fuel-line leak

Humphrey, Col. Brian. "United States Air Force Aircraft Investigation Report." Accident of 19 August 2013.

Jones, Brian. "Crash Site Images Of Yesterday's B-1 Bomber Crash In Montana Are Startling." BusinessInsider.com, 20 August 2013.

Simmons-Ritchie, Daniel. "Stranded in cattle country, bomber crew aided by ranchers." *Rapid City Journal*, 25 August 2013.

Thompson, Mark. "The 21st Century's 'For Want of a Nail': B1 bomber doomed when wayward part sliced open a fuel line during wing sweep." Time.com, 6 January 2014.

31 Cley goose strike

"Geese caused fatal USAF helicopter crash in Cley, report says." BBC.co.uk, 9 July 2014.

Halliday, Josh. "Geese 'caused fatal US air force helicopter crash' in Norfolk." *The Guardian*, 9 July 2014.

Norman, Brig. Gen. Jon. "United States Air Force Aircraft Investigation Report." Accident of 7 January 2014.

"Welcome To RAF Lakenheath," Internal Airman welcome pack, undated.

32 Domestic object

Ciralsky, Adam "Will the F-35, the U.S. Military's Flaw-Filled, Years-Overdue Joint Strike Fighter, Ever Actually Fly?" *Vanity Fair*, 16 September 2013.

Keeton, Col. Gregory. "United States Air Force Aircraft Investigation Report." Accident of 23 June 2014.

33 Down to Louisiana

Hudson, Brig. Gen. Michael. "United States Air Force Aircraft Investigation Report." Accident of 27 August 2014.

LaGrone, Sam. "Updated: Air Force Identifies F15C Pilot Killed in Wednesday Crash." USNI News, 29 August 2014.

Saulmon, Greg. "Air Force releases report on crash that killed 104th Fighter Wing pilot Morris Fontenot." *Hampshire Daily Gazette*, 21 July 2015.

Wolff, Scott. "A Toast to Moose: A Husband, Father, Fighter Pilot ... and Friend." Fightersweep.com, undated.

34 Ghostrider

Davis, Lt. Col. Michael. "United States Air Force Aircraft Investigation Report." Accident of 21 April 2015.

35 Fire by the microwave
"Combat Sent RC-135U," GlobalSecurity.org, undated.
Evans, Lt. Col. William. "United States Air Force Aircraft Investigation Report." Accident of 30 April 2015.
Liewer, Steve. "Disaster narrowly averted at Offutt with plane fire, but major questions remain." *Omaha World Herald*, 25 August 2015.

36 Unseen traffic
Kindsvater, Brig. Gen. Scott. "United States Air Force Aircraft Investigation Report." Accident of 7 July 2015.
Pager, Tyler. "2 killed when F-16, Cessna collide in midair over S.C." *USA Today*, 7 July 2015.
Robinson, Willis, and Sophie Evans. "Air Force pilot who collided with small plane carrying father and son was warned of 'traffic' ahead just moments before deadly crash." Mail Online, 20 July 2015.

37 Goggles case
Drew, James. "How a pilot's NVG case brought down a USAF C-130J in Afghanistan." FlightGlobal.com, 19 April 2016.
Lekic, Slobodan. "Victims of C-130 crash in Afghanistan identified." Stripes.com, 3 October 2015.
Mordente, Brig. Gen. Patrick. "United States Air Force Aircraft Investigation Report." Accident of 2 October 2015.
Swarts, Phillip. "C-130J co-pilot's unauthorized maneuver didn't cause crash in Afghanistan." AirForceTimes.com, 11 May 2016.

38 Three-out takeoff
Martignetti, Col. Edward. "United States Air Force Aircraft Investigation Report." Accident of 19 May 2016.

39 Inadvertent shutoff
Gorman, Michele. "Full Transcript: President Obama's U.S. Air Force Academy Commencement Speech." *Newsweek*, 3 June 2016.
Kamp, Col. Brian. "United States Air Force Aircraft Investigation Report." Accident of 2 June 2016.
Panzino, Charlsy. "Report: Malfunction caused Thunderbird crash after academy flyover." AirForceTimes.com, 14 December 2014.

40 Eject, dude
Nahom, Brig. Gen. David. "United States Air Force Aircraft Investigation Report." Accident of 20 September 2016.

Conclusions
Baudrillard, Jean. *Screened Out*. London: Verso, 2014.
Virilio, Paul. *Desert Screen*. London: Continuum, 2005.

Index

Numbers in *bold italics* indicate pages with illustrations

A-10 Thunderbolt 41–44, 52–56, *53*, 104–108, *105*
AC-130J Ghostrider 139–143, *140*
acronyms (copious use of in USAF) 5
Aerospace Control Alert 116–118
afterburner 37, 39, 46, 71, 74, 79, 94, 98, 111, 126–128, 134
Ahmed al Jaber Air Base 19
Air Force Academy 160–164
Air Force One (VC-25) 118
Air Logistics Complex (Oklahoma) 88–91
Air National Guard 45
air-to-air refuel 85, 106
airbrakes 50
AirVenture 48–52
Al Dhafra Air Base 69, 73–76
Al Udeid Air Base 61
Ali al salem Air Base 18
Ambien 15
amphetamines 15, 56
Andersen Air Force Base 9, 10, 11, 13, 26, 156–160
anomaly 52
Arabian Desert 70
Arctic Thunder 34–36
Aviano Air Base 96–100
audible warnings 16, 35, 54–55, 72, 75, 94–65, 99, 106–107, 119, 134, 141, 155

B-2 *9*, 9–13, 105
B-52 25–29, 87–91, 156–160, *157*
Baghdad international Airport 22, 23
Bagram Airfield 151–154
Balad Air Base 21, 22
Barksdale Air Force Base 27, 90
Barnes Air national Guard Base 136–137

Basic Fighter Maneuvers (BFM) 38, 42, 45–46, 92–93, 110–111
Baudrillard, Jean 1, 2, 179
Beale Air Force Base 166–168
Benjamin, Walter 2
Bering Strait 34, 84
bird strike 131–132, 114–116, 153, 158–160
black-box 28
Blakeney Point Nature Reserve 129–130
bleed air 39–41
borescope inspection 68
Brecht, Bertold 2
brown-out (wake) 20, 24
"burn-down" (jet fuel) 90
"buzzing" (hostile action) 38

C-5 Galaxy 13–17, *14*
C-17 Globemaster *33*–36, 61–65, *62*
C-130 Hercules 151–156, *152*
California Highway Patrol 95
Camp Lemonnier 69
CBP (continuous bomber presence) 156–157
Cervia Air Base 99
Cessna 149–150
channelized attention 25, 41
Charleston Airport 148–149
Cherry Point Naval Air Depot 21
combat entry 63
compensation (paid) 69
compressor stall 6, 24, 25, 55, 159, 175
Con-Tac corrosion preventative compound 87
concussion 31
consciousness (loss of) 31
control-stick pressure-gage 30

192　INDEX

crash-site 21, *22*, *37*, 40, 47, *53*, 72, *74*, *80*, 83, 86, *101*, 104, *125*, 128, 130–131, *137*–138, 148, 151
cross-country 49
CV-22 Osprey 80–83

damaged airfoils 68
Dannelly Field 49
DEFOG 50
demonstration profile 34–36, 37
dichotic audio 146
dirt strip 59
distinguished visitor support 23
"dogfight" *see* Basic Fighter Maneuvers
Dover Air Force Base 13, 14
Dutch roll 102–103

EADI (Electronic Attitude Director-Indicator) 72–73
Edwards Air Base 29
Edwards Test Pilot School 29–32
Eglin Air Force Base 80–83, 132–136, 139–143
Eilson Air Base 84
ejection 13, 32, 41, 44, 46–47, 56, 67, 72, 75–76, 86, 95, 99, 103–104, 111–112, 116, 120, 128, 150, 164, 167–168, 175
Ellsworth Air Force Base 126–128
emergency oxygen supply 40
environmental control system 51, 138
Exelis contractors 63–64
exhaust plume 119

F-15 32, 38, 69–76, 108–112, 136–139
F-16 27, 45–48, 48–52, *49*, 65–69, 83–87, 92–95, *96*–100, 112–120, *113*, 147–151, *148*, 160–164, *161*
F-22 Raptor 36–41, *37*, 76–79, *77*
F-35 Lightning II 132–136
fire-extinguisher system 75–76, 127, 142–143
flame out 24, 45–48, 52–56, 66–67, 83–87, 163–164
flying wing 10
Foal Eagle (Operation) 66
FOI request 4
Forward Operating Base Shank 61–65
Fresno Air National Guard Base 93–95
Freud, Sigmund 3
full-performance takeoff 34–35
functional check flight (FCF) 54–55, 88, 147–151

General Electric F110 67–69
General Electric GAU-8 Avenger 41
General Electric TF-34 53
General Electric TF-39 15
George Washington National Forest 138
Geum River 67
glide ratios 46, 66
ground rush 43–44
Guam (US territory) 9–10, 26, 44
Guam Liberation Day 26
gun patrol 122–123

heptafluoropropane 127
HH-60G Pave Hawk 21–25, *22*, 60, 67, 81, 120–124, 128–132, 173
Hokko Maru 86
Human Factors Analysis and Classification System (HFACS) 169
Hurlburt Field 18, 81
Hwachon-ri, Hwa-yang-myeon, Seocheon- gun (Region of Korea) 67

icy surface 64–65
Immelmann turn 93–94
independent legal advice 108
interception 38–39, 90, 118–119

Jalalabad Airfield 151–156
Japanese Air Self-Defense Force 112
jargon (copious use of in USAF) 5–6
Jim Crow 48
Joint Base Andrews 118
Joint Base Charleston 61
Joint Base Elmendorf-Richardson 34, 38, 84

Kadena Air Base 110–112
KC-135 30, 86, 100–104, 106
"knock it off" (cease training mission) 46, 66, 98, 108, 111
Korean War 65
Kunsan Air Base 66–67
Kuwait City International Airport 14, 19, 61
Kyrgyzstan Army 104

"last ditch" maneuver 98
Laufeld, Germany 44
live-fire 19, 81–82
lockout (rotor) 24
lost wingman 43
Luke Air Force Base 112–116

M-28 Skytruck *57*–60
Manukai 86
Maverick (missile) 106
"maxing" 35–36
MH-53 Pave Low 18–21

Index

military-industrial Complex 1
Misawa Air Base 83–87
Moody Air Force Base 21, 52–56
Mount Whitney 93
Museum of the Accident 3
Myrtle Beach Airport 148–149

NATO 42
Naval Air station Joint Reserve Base New Orleans 137
negative box 60
New Chester, Adams County 47
night-vision goggles (NVGs) 19, 39, 70, 97, 130
9/11 58
North Korea 65
North Norfolk 128–132

OBOGS 39
Offutt Air Force Base 143–147
Okinawa (Island) 108–112, 120–124
Oklahoma Air Logistics Complex 48
"one out" (loss of power in a jet engine) 15, 45–46, 66, 75, 85, 150, 163, 164
Osan Air Base 65–69

Pearl Harbor (attack on) 26
pedal turn 23
Peterson Air Force Base 162–164
pitot heat 11
Powder River Training Complex 126–128
power transmission line (electric supply) 107–108
Pratt and Whitney F100 45, 51, 75, 137, 163
prepared surface (loss of) 50–51, 62, 65, 158–159, 160
protest march 124

R2508 93
RAF Lakenheath 128–132
RAM cladding 37
Ramstein Air Base 15
Ravens 144–147
RC-125V 143–147, *144*
RCR (runway conditions reading) 64
"red air" *see* simulated hostile aircraft
rescue plan 122
Robbins Air Force Base 17
Rockwell B-1 Lancer 124–128
"roll-off-the-top" *see* Immelmann turn
rudder hunting 100–104
Ryukyu Islands 109

scramble 122
Shaw Air Force Base 147–151
shot-blasting 67–68
sideslip 141–143
SIGINT 144
simulated hostile aircraft 38, 70, 73, 74, 97–98, 118–119, 173, 180
Spangdahlem Air Base 42
spatial disorientation 43, 71–73, 98
special operations 15, 18, 20, 21, 33, 57–60, 81
stall 6–7, 12, 16–17, 24, 35–36, 38, 54–55, 36, 94–95, 116, 134, 136, 141, 155, 159, 166–167, 173, 175
stator rings 68
Stockton Lake 105–108
surgeon representative 100

T-38 29–32, 90, 114
Taliban 58
Teflon 47–48
test pilot 29–32, 133, 139–143
Thunderbirds 162–163
tilt-rotor 80–83
time on target 71
Tinker Air Force Base 87–91
touch-and-go 63, 78, 114
Transit Center at Manas 100–104
transnational ethos 62
Truax Field 45
Tuskegee Airmen 48–49
Tyndall Air Force Base 76–79

U-2 Dragon Lady **165**–168
Udairi Training Range 19
uncommanded (aircraft movement) 21, 31, 74, 82–83, 87, 89, 131, 167, 178
underqualified 68
U.S. Navy 28
unmarked plane 58
unusual attitude 40, 41, 43

Virilio, Paul 1, 3, 4, 178, 179
vortex-ring 82

W-173 (restricted military airspace) 110
Walan Rabat Landing Zone 57–60
Whiteman Air Force Base 10–11, 105–108
wild geese 129, 131
Wittman Airport 48–52
Work Control Document (WCD) 90
WSO (Weapons System Officer) 69–76

Zabul, Afghanistan 57–60

www.ingramcontent.com/pod-product-compliance
Lightning Source LLC
Chambersburg PA
CBHW032101300426
44116CB00007B/845